Object Orie Programming with Angular

Build and Deploy Your Web Application
Using Angular with Ease

Balram Morsing Chavan

www.bpbonline.com

FIRST EDITION 2020

Copyright © BPB Publications, India

ISBN: 978-93-89328-363

Distributors:

BPB PUBLICATIONS
20, Ansari Road, Darya Ganj
New Delhi-110002
Ph: 23254990/23254991

DECCAN AGENCIES
4-3-329, Bank Street,
Hyderabad-500195
Ph: 24756967/24756400

MICRO MEDIA
Shop No. 5, Mahendra Chambers,
150 DN Rd. Next to Capital Cinema,
V.T. (C.S.T.) Station, MUMBAI-400 001
Ph: 22078296/22078297

BPB BOOK CENTRE
376 Old Lajpat Rai Market,
Delhi-110006
Ph: 23861747

Published by Manish Jain for BPB Publications, 20 Ansari Road, Darya Ganj, New Delhi-110002 and Printed by him at Repro India Ltd, Mumbai

www.bpbonline.com

Dedicated to

My mother
She made me what I am today…

About the Author

 **Balram Morsing Chavan** is a software professional having 11+ years of relevant experience working with various companies like Siemens, Wolters Kluwer Financial Services, Morgen Stanley Financial Services, Barclays, Boehringer Ingelheim. He has cross domain experience spanning across Building Automation technologies, GIS solutions, Image processing, Financial services, E-Commerce, Automobile Engineering, Human Pharmatheutical innovative digital solutions. Balram has expertise in various technology stack including Microsoft .Net stack, MEAN stack, MERN stack, Hybrid mobile application development using Ionic, React Native, Python, AWS cloud solutions, Azure cloud solutions and of course special interest in Angular framework!

Balram loves to contribute to open source projects. He has been awarded with GitHub Developer Program Membership for his contribution to open source world. He also contributes to multiple technology blogs and forums. Balram has also published many npm.js packages (e.g. ng-connection-service package) for Angular framework that are widely used and appreciated.

Balram has been developing web applications in Angular since its alpha version. He is an active contributor to Angular projects GitHub repository and multiple seed projects apart from his own GitHub Angular open source projects. Balram is often sought for technical consulting and delivering corporate training on Angular, Microsoft .Net stack, MEAN stack and other technologies. As a corporate trainer, Balram believes that exploring Angular with Object-Oriented/C#.Net/ Java concepts makes it very easy for learner to understand fundamentals. This book is step towards the same direction!

Beside works, Balram like to spend time with friends and family, gardening, mentoring and watching TV shows.

About the Reviewer

Kushal Lakhotia is over eight years of experience in the Product based IT industry, Kushal Lakhotia is a Senior Engineer and an enthusiast in Blockchain technology and Web development. He has a knack of helping companies convert their monolithic architecture in REST-based microservices and provide generalist solutions to its users. He is seasoned and successful in creating a team from scratch and handling the entire product in and out. He has also been successful in creating a freshers training program from the engineering background and flourished them to excel in the company. He loves to work on JS and solving problems to the scale.

Acknowledgement

Thank you, Lord, for blessing me with a family and friends who have always been with me to love, help and support. Thank you my mother Leela, for shaping my life despite challenges. Love you mom! Thank you, my loving wife, Madhuri and my sweetheart daughter, Hetavi. You have been very supportive and patient with me.

I would like to special thank my friend Sarang Jain for motivating me to write this book. Thank you to brother Krishna Chavan, for taking good care of me since my childhood. Thank you, brother, Ajmal Chavan, for your support and help. Thanks sister, Shalini Chavan, for your love. Thank you mate, Abhishek Kumar, for your friendship.

With all your love, support, and encouragement, I was able to complete this book.

Many thanks to BPB Publications, team, for giving me this opportunity, help and support to write my first book. You guys made it possible!

Thank you!!!

Preface

Web application development has witnessed constant changes over past several years. There are many technology stacks, tools, languages, frameworks and libraries to pick from. Any new technology we pick to build a website, may become obsolete in a few years. How can we adapt to this change? Well, we can do only one thing, keep learning and adapting.

Angular is one of such frameworks for building web application built by Google as open source project. Angular should not be misunderstood as a newer version of AngularJs. It is a complete re-write, re-design, a new framework! Yes, it is framework not a JavaScript library like React.js, Vue.js etc. Angular provides many features out of the box making it bloated and bulky as compared to React.js. So, why Angular? Well, when we want to build enterprise web applications, we would need to use many of these features anyways. With Angular, we don't need to worry about adding various library for Dependency Injection, HTTP communication etc. Angular framework is built with TypeScript language, a superset of JavaScript. This gives us an opportunity to write client-side application in Object Oriented fashion. TypeScript allows writing classes, implement interface, inheritance, generics, strong typing and other features of Object-Oriented Programming languages.

TypeScript's syntax is mix of C#.Net and Java language. Angular framework is modular. Thus, if we have prior experience with C#.Net and/or Java with web application development then we can map many concepts with Angular, learn it fast and that's the idea of writing this book. We want to build Object-Oriented, module Angular web application using C#.Net/Java analogies. We will be referring to C# Windows Form, Windows Presentation Foundation (WPF), Java and other similar technology stack during this book.

Angular framework is vast. In this book we will learn all major features, tips and tricks along with their references and analogies with C#.Net and Java wherever applicable. This book doesn't intend to teach everything as its scope is to develop a right Object-Oriented and module application development mindset with technical features overview. For deep learning of Angular, one should visit official Angular documentation at www.angular.io website. This book is best suited for someone who has basic experience with Object-Oriented concepts and programming hands on, basic experience with web development concepts and hands-on. If this is your first experience with web programming, then you would need to keep visiting official documentation of Web programming, Angular, Object-Oriented programming languages like C#.Net/Java for gaining basic knowledge whenever required.

Google constantly upgrade newer and better version of Angular on frequent basis. Generally, a newer version typically offers bug fixes, compiler optimization, and backend change. There have also been a few disruptive releases in the past. One of the significant advancements was from version 2 to 4 (yes, they skipped Angular 3 version). This book contains code with Angular version 10. Angular team tries to keep minimum breaking changes for major version changes and as we are focusing on core concepts of Angular in this book, thus I believe, the code and concepts elaborated in this book will work seamless with newer Angular versions in future. While building enterprise level web application, we need to make sure the architecture is robust and maintainable. This book contains guidelines and best practices to build such applications.

This book contains lots of code and less theory. The book contains excerpts of complete code that is important for topic in discussion. The complete code can be found in separate digitally downloadable version.

This book contains 11 chapters covering various topics as follow:
Chapter 1 – We will start with TypeScript introduction in Chapter 1. Since we are going to build our Angular applications using TypeScript, it's a good to know how TypeScript code is written and it works under the hood.

Chapter 2 – We will create a new Angular project using Angular CLI and will go through project structure, important files and their significance to the project, VS Code IDE etc.

Chapter 3 – We will create a sign-up form using basic Angular concepts like @ NgModule, @Component, NgFor, NgIf, debugging etc. We will learn quickly how to build and deploy our first Angular application.

Chapter 4 – Data binding is one of the powerful features of Angular. In this chapter, we will learn different types of data binding available and Pipes concepts in Angular.

Chapter 5 – The @NgModule decorator is such a beast that it deserves a chapter to itself. In this chapter we will learn all about @NgModule types, features with hands-on practice.

Chapter 6 – Building enterprise application requires a robust and decoupled system. Angular provides strong Dependency Injection engine and Service classes to achieve this goal using various types of Providers and Decorators.

Chapter 7 – Most of the times, web application needs to collect some data from using Forms. In this chapter we will learn how to build Template and Reactive forms and validation techniques.

Chapter 8 – In decoupled application, communication between components is the key to success. In this chapter we will learn how to pass data between components, services using various way.

Chapter 9 – The Angular application is client side and it needs to talk with server. In this chapter we will learn how to consume HTTP resources and process them using Rx.js effectively.

Chapter 10 – Angular routing allows us to breakdown application into small feature modules. In this chapter we will learn how to implement regular and lazy routed modules.

Chapter 11 – Before going to production, we need to make sure our application is secure, fast, small and robust. In this chapter we will learn how to deploy our application with best industry practices.

Downloading the code bundle and coloured images:

Please follow the link to download the
Code Bundle and the *Coloured Images* of the book:

https://rebrand.ly/ho3oldm

Errata

We take immense pride in our work at BPB Publications and follow best practices to ensure the accuracy of our content to provide with an indulging reading experience to our subscribers. Our readers are our mirrors, and we use their inputs to reflect and improve upon human errors if any, occurred during the publishing processes involved. To let us maintain the quality and help us reach out to any readers who might be having difficulties due to any unforeseen errors, please write to us at :

errata@bpbonline.com

Your support, suggestions and feedbacks are highly appreciated by the BPB Publications' Family.

BPB is searching for authors like you

If you're interested in becoming an author for BPB, please visit **www.bpbonline.com** and apply today. We have worked with thousands of developers and tech professionals, just like you, to help them share their insight with the global tech community. You can make a general application, apply for a specific hot topic that we are recruiting an author for, or submit your own idea.

The code bundle for the book is also hosted on GitHub at **https://github.com/bpbpublications/Object-Oriented-Programming-with-Angular**. In case there's an update to the code, it will be updated on the existing GitHub repository.

We also have other code bundles from our rich catalog of books and videos available at **https://github.com/bpbpublications**. Check them out!

PIRACY

If you come across any illegal copies of our works in any form on the internet, we would be grateful if you would provide us with the location address or website name. Please contact us at **business@bpbonline.com** with a link to the material.

If you are interested in becoming an author

If there is a topic that you have expertise in, and you are interested in either writing or contributing to a book, please visit **www.bpbonline.com**.

REVIEWS

Please leave a review. Once you have read and used this book, why not leave a review on the site that you purchased it from? Potential readers can then see and use your unbiased opinion to make purchase decisions, we at BPB can understand what you think about our products, and our authors can see your feedback on their book. Thank you!

For more information about BPB, please visit **www.bpbonline.com**.

Table of Contents

Learning Angular in Object-Oriented Way

Angular is Google's open-source framework for building a **Single Page Application (SPA)** web applications. The AngularJS framework was first released on October 20, 2010. On April 30, 2015, Angular 2 was announced by the Angular team, and its first stable release was out on September 14, 2016. The Angular team has wholly re-written the Angular framework and not just a version upgrade of AngularJS, which is a common belief. I have been working on AngularJS since 2011 and started working on Angular 2 since 2015 when it was in the alpha version. Believe me; it is a paradigm shift if you are coming from an AngularJS background.

In this book, I have tried to explain Angular concepts in Object-Oriented, C#.NET, ASP.NET, WPF, and so on. The book assumes that you have basic web development experience, understanding of Object-Oriented concepts, and experience with C#.NET or Java, but it's optional.

So, let's get started!!!

CHAPTER 1
Typescript – The Underdog

Introduction

JavaScript is a dynamic, weakly typed, and prototype-based programming language. It is one of the implementations of the **European Computer Manufacturers Association Script (ECMAScript)** or simply ES specifications. All standard browsers must accord to ES specifications but can differ in version. Hence few JavaScript keywords/functions/syntax works with few browsers and not with others. To bridge this gap, polyfills libraries exist, but they are not the silver bullets, though.

In *October 2012*, Microsoft released Typescript – an open-source programming language that is heavily inspired by C#.NET and Java syntax. It is a superset of ECMAScript 5 (that is, JavaScript). Typescript allows a developer to write a web application in an Object-Oriented model, thus allowing constructs like class, inheritance, interfaces, generics, and so on, available to JavaScript developer. All Typescript programs get transpiled into plain JavaScript, which browsers or JavaScript rendering engines (like Google V8) can render. If you have Object Oriented programming background, then you will find Typescript very easy to grab. One of the hurdles with JavaScript is that it is weakly typed language. Without strongly typed language, writing commercial or enterprise-level web applications is not easy. Of course, we can write a well-structured JavaScript application, but it requires expertise and knowledge of subtle rules and features of JavaScript.

Angular has been wholly written in Typescript. In an earlier version of Angular (that is, Angular 2), it was possible to write Angular application using JavaScript as well. You can also write an Angular application using the Dart programming language.

https://webdev.dartlang.org/angular

> **Tip: Since Angular + Dart combination is not that popular with the web community, Google team has launched another framework called "Flutter" for building a hybrid mobile application using Dart and React like syntax.**

Before diving into Angular code, I always strive to have my audience have a clear understanding between Typescript code and Angular framework code. The goal of this chapter is to get you experienced with Typescript constructs and techniques.

Structure

- Basic Data Types
    - Numbers
    - Boolean
    - String
    - Array
    - Tuple
    - Enums
    - Object
    - Void
    - Null and Undefined
    - Never
- Variable Declaration
    - Let
    - Var
    - Const
    - Declare
- Functions
    - Regular functions
    - Anonymous functions
    - Arrow functions
- Classes and Interfaces
- Inheritance
- Interface

- Type Conversion
- Union Types
- Generics
- Decorators
- Modules and Namespaces
- Advance types
  - o Static
  - o Readonly and Const
  - o String and Number literal Types
  - o Type Aliases

Objective

This chapter aims to cover the basics of the TypeScript language. The Angular framework has been built using TypeScript; thus, understanding it is very crucial. We will get into the most commonly used language features and syntax and keep learning more throughout the rest of the book.

Basic Data Types

Every programming language has data types of holding data for the program. Typescript provides basic data types similar to JavaScript and advanced data types like high-rank language like C#.NET or Java.

Number

Like JavaScript, all numeric values are stored in a `number` data type. If we are coming from C# / Java languages, then for numeric data types like int, long, float, double, `decimal`, and so on, we will have to settle down with `number` data type in Typescript. Note that to store hexadecimal number, prefix value with `0x`, for binary number prefix with `0b` and octal number prefix with `0o` (zero and small letter O). Please refer to *Code 1.1* for an example:

```
let intData: number = 100;

let floatData: number = 20.53;

let longData: number = 9873423524523442319;

let hexData: number = 0x1f2d3;

let binaryData: number = 0b1001;

let octalData: number = 0o1373;
```

Code 1.1: number data type usage

Boolean

Like C# and Java, we can store true or false value in the boolean data type. Nevertheless, we cannot store a positive number as true value or 0 for `false`. Note that `null` and undefined are valid values for a `boolean` data type, which is not the case with C#. Please refer to *Code 1.2* for an example:

```
let isTypescriptGreat: boolean = true; // works
let noOldStyleBool: boolean = 0; // compiler error
let nullIsValid: boolean = null; // works - no compiler error
let undefinedIsValid: boolean = undefined; // works - no compiler
error
```

Code 1.2: boolean data type usage

String

Typescript has a `string` data type to hold a `string` value. The `string` value can be provided in a single quote or double quote. A string can also contain variable within template expression format if a `string` is between backquote. A template expression can be any legal Typescript code put inside `${expression}` string. Please refer to *Code 1.3* for an example:

```
let bestLanguage: string = 'Typescript';
let bestFramework: string = "Angular";
let templateExample: string = `I love ${bestLanguage} and
${bestFramework}!!!`;
```

Code 1.3: string data type usage

Array

With the Array data type, we can store a collection of values of other data types. Array in Typescript is similar to C#. Array data types provide some basic built-in functions like sort, reverse, and so on. Unlike C#, Typescript Array is an implementation of Stack data structure. There are `Push()` and `Pop()` stack methods available out of the box. In C#, we get a separate data type called Stack apart from the basic array data type. We can also use the generic implementation of `Array<data_type>` version of Array. Please refer to *Code 1.4* for an example.

```
let oddNumbers: number[] = [1, 3, 5, 7, 9];
oddNumbers.push(11);
const lastValue = oddNumbers.pop();
let evenNumbers: Array<number> = [0, 2, 4, 6, 8];
evenNumbers.push(10);
const lastEvenValue = evenNumbers.pop();
```

Code 1.4: array data type usage

Tuple

In C#, if we want to maintain <key,value> pair collection, then you can use Tuple or KeyValueCollection generics data structure. In Typescript, Tuple is used to keep key-value pairs. Its syntax is not that intuitive, though. Declaring Tuple is like define a custom data type with array syntax. *Code 1.5* shows how to declare Tuple in Typescript:

```
let employeeMap: [number, string] = [10, 'Employee 1'];
console.log(employeeMap[0], employeeMap[1]);
```

Code 1.5: Tuple data type usage in TypeScript

Code 1.6 shows how to declare KeyValuePair in C#:

```
KeyValuePair<int, string> employeeMap = new KeyValuePair<int,
string>(10, "Employee 1");
Console.WriteLine(employeeMap.Key +  employeeMap.Value);
```

Code 1.6: KeyValuePair data type usage in C#

Dictionary data type in C# is a beneficial data structure to keep a list of key-value pairs. Unfortunately, there is no built-in data structure in Typescript like Dictionary, but we can use Array and Tuple to achieve Dictionary like features. Please refer to *Code 1.7* for an example:

```
Dictionary<int, string> employeeDictionary = new Dictionary<int,
string>();
employeeDictionary[1] = "Employee 1";
employeeDictionary[2] = "Employee 2";
employeeDictionary[3] = "Employee 3";
Console.WriteLine(employeeDictionary[2]);
```

Code 1.7: Dictionary data type usage in C#

The *Code 1.8* shows how we can create a Dictionary like data structure in TypeScript:

```
let employeeDictionary: Array<[number, string]> = new
Array<[number, string]>();

    employeeDictionary.push([1, 'Employee 1']);

    employeeDictionary.push([2, 'Employee 2']);

    employeeDictionary.push([3, 'Employee 3']);

    console.log('Second tuple: ', employeeDictionary[1][0],
employeeDictionary[1][1]);
```

Code 1.8: *Dictionary like data type usage in TypeScript*

Enum

Enum allows a programmer to give meaningful names to constant values grouped. The first member of Enum has a value of 0 (zero) and incremented by one for subsequent members. We can override these values by specifying them explicitly. We can have non-sequential values for all members as well if you define values for each of them. Please refer to *Code 1.9* for an example.

```
enum FileTypes {
            Jpeg, // FileTypes.Jpeg = 0
            Png,  // FileTypes.Png = 1
            Bitmap,  // FileTypes.Bitmap = 2
            Svg  // FileTypes.Svg = 3
}


enum FileTypes {
            Jpeg = 10, // FileTypes.Jpeg = 10
            Png,  // FileTypes.Png = 11
            Bitmap,  // FileTypes.Bitmap = 12
            Svg  // FileTypes.Svg = 13
}


enum FileTypes {
            Jpeg = 10, // FileTypes.Jpeg = 10
            Png = 20,  // FileTypes.Png = 20
            Bitmap = 30,  // FileTypes.Bitmap = 30
```

```
     Svg= 40  // FileTypes.Svg = 40
}
```

Code 1.9: Dictionary like data type usage in TypeScript

Any

C# has a **dynamic** data type, which tells the compiler to skip type checking of a declared variable at compile-time and try to execute code at runtime. Typescript has any data type which can hold any data type value. This is very useful while working with a third party library whose type is not known at compile time but might be present at runtime. any data type variable can change different data type value throughout the program. Note that any data type is not the same as the Object data type is type-checked at compile time. Please refer to Code 1.10 for an example.

> **Tip: As per the best coding practices, our code should have a minimum of "any" variables and more of strongly typed variables to avoid runtime error(s).**

```
let fuzzyData: any;

fuzzyData = "some value";

fuzzyData.someMethod();

// no compiler error.

// It will throw runtime exception if someMethod() not found on object
fuzzyData.


let rawData: Object;

rawData = 4;

rawData.unknownMethod(); // compile time error for unknownMethod()
```

Code 1.10: "any" data type usage

Object

The Object data type holds non-primitive values with custom members fields and methods. In C#, we have "anonymous type" to declare object properties without declaring class. *Code 1.11* shows how to declare an anonymous type in C#:

```
var employee = new { ID = 1, Name = "Employee 1" };

Console.WriteLine(employee.ID);
```

Code 1.11: anonymous type usage in C#

In TypeScript, we can declare an object, as shown in *Code 1.12:*

```
let employee = { id: 1, name: 'Employee 1' };
console.log(employee.id);
```

Code 1.12: *Custom object type in TypeScript*

We should not declare a variable of an Object type to hold class level or module level object. We should have a proper class with member fields and methods. A temporary object mapping, a loop variable can be a situation where we would declare such Object type where creating class will be overengineering.

void

the void is a data type that is mostly used as a return type for function if it doesn't return anything. Though we can declare a variable with a void data type, we cannot assign any value to it besides undefined and null. Please refer to Code 1.13 for an example:

```
let nothing: void;
nothing = undefined; // ok
nothing = null; // ok
nothing = 10; // compile time error


function processSomething(): void{
        //do some mundane operation
}
```

Code 1.13: *void data type in TypeScript*

null and undefined

The null and undefined data types do not hold any other values apart from undefined and null. Both of these data types are subtypes of other primitive data types; hence you can assign them to them. Please refer to Code 1.14 for an example:

```
let undefinedValue: undefined = undefined;
let nullValue: null = null;

let password: string = 'neo';
password = undefined;
password = null;
```

```
let salary: number = 10000;
salary = undefined;
salary = null;

let isStatusOn: boolean = true;
isStatusOn = undefined;
isStatusOn = null;
```

Code 1.14: null and undefined data types in TypeScript

never

never is a new data type introduced in Typescript. Like void, never data type is used mostly with a function return type and not suitable for variable declaration. The difference between void and never data type return value function is that void function can have reachable endpoint whereas never function cannot; it must throw an exception. Please refer to *Code 1.15* for an example:

```
function normalFunction(): never {
        // compile time error: A function returning 'never' cannot
have a reachable endpoint

}


function throwException(): never {
        throw new Error('something went wrong!');
        // ok

}
```

Code 1.15: never data types in TypeScript

Variable Declaration

We can declare variables using let, var, const, and declare keywords. Each of them defines different life scope of the variable.

Let

Variable declared using let keyword has local block scope. If we need a variable within the current execution block, for example, for loop variable, then we should use let keyword.

Var

This is a classic var keyword from JavaScript. The variables declared with var keyword has a function-level scope. Do you remember the tricky variable scoping rule of **var** like hoisting in JavaScript? They exist here too.

Const

"const" keyword is similar to let keyword for variable scoping, but it won't allow value to be reassigned. It is best practice to declare a variable as const if it is not going to hold another value again. Please refer to *Code 1.16*, for example, of let, var, and const keywords:

```
function someFunction() {
        var evenNumber = 10;
        let oddNumber = 11;
        const xFactor = 20;
        xFactor = 30; // compiler error: cannot change const


        if (true) {
            evenNumber = 20; // ok. var is function scoped
            oddNumber = 13; // ok. var is function scoped
            let someString = 'local variable'; // available to
if block only
            var trickyValue = 100; // available at function
level
        }


        something = 'out of scope here'; // compile time error.
out of scope variable
        trickyValue = 200; // ok, var is function scoped
}
```

Code 1.16: "let", "var" and "const" keywords usage

Declare

While building a web application, many times, we will need to import some third party libraries into Angular applications. If we are lucky, then the target library will have its type definitions available so that we can write Typescript code. But if the third-party library doesn't have type library and just a global variable exposed in JavaScript file, then how will we use it? That's where declare comes into the picture. It `declares` a variable that might be available at runtime, and of course, it's data type will be most of the time **any** as it is unknown at compile time. Please refer to *Code 1.17* for an example.

```
declare var some3rdPartyLib: any;

some3rdPartyLib.someFunction();
```

Code 1.17: "declare" keyword usage

Functions

In JavaScript, writing global functions is acceptable as it is not Object-Oriented, but when it comes to Typescript, then most of the time, functions will be inside some class or interface. Nevertheless, we can still write some helper/global function in Typescript if required.

We can variously declare functions in Typescript.

Regular Function

It is a vanilla JavaScript style function with a function keyword followed by the name of the function, followed by an optional argument.

Anonymous Function

When function name has no significance, then we can define an anonymous function. It is many times used with inline function computations.

Arrow Function

The arrow function is similar to the `anonymous` function but with one crucial distinction. The `this` object inside the `anonymous` function refers to the current function's `this` object, whereas `this` object inside arrow function refers to the current context `this` object, for example, class. `this` is very important when we work with libraries like `D3.js`, where event handler function has its own `this` keyword. Accessing class members in such an event handler will be possible using arrow functions. Please refer to *Code 1.18* for an example:

```
// regular JavaScript function
function square(value: number): number {
        return value * value;
```

```
}


const answer = square(10);


// anonymous function
var square = function (value: number): number {
    return value * value;
}


const answer = square(10);


// arrow function
var square = (value: number): number => {
    return value * value;
}


const answer = square(10);
```

***Code 1.18**: declaring functions in TypeScript*

There is a lot of details about TypeScript "Functions" but due to the sake of focus, we won't cover it here. It is highly recommended to go through the official documentation of TypeScript for details.

Classes and Interfaces

Feels good to read Class and Interface finally, isn't it? Yes, JavaScript is a prototype-based language. TypeScript is a superset of JavaScript, and still, we can write well maintained Object-Oriented code using Typescript. How? Well, thanks to classes and interfaces of TypeScript. The transpiler of Typescript does lots of work to make sure proper JavaScript code is generated for classes and interface keywords of TypeScript.

Most of the rules of C# and Java classes apply to Typescript classes, but there are few differences. For example, the constructor in C# class has the same name as of class name, whereas in Typescript, it is a `constructor` keyword. We can have overloaded constructors in C#, but in Typescript, there can be the utmost one. For implementing proper Encapsulation, Typescript provides us access specifiers similar to C# wiz `public`, `private`, `protected`, but `internal` and protected internal keywords are not available here.

Like in C# and Java, members are accessible through this keyword, an object is created through a new keyword in TypeScript. Please refer to *Code 1.19* for an example.

```
class Employee {
        public firstName: string;
        private salary: number;
        protected age: number;


        constructor() {
            this.firstName = 'Employee 1';
            this.age = 34;
            this.salary = 5000;
        }


        public getAge(): number {
            return this.age;
        }


        private computeBonus() {
            this.salary = this.salary * 1.5;
        }
}
```

Code 1.19: declaring class in TypeScript

Brain Teaser: How can you implement a Singleton design pattern in Typescript with example?

Inheritance

Typescript's inheritance and interface syntax is inspired by Java, not from C#. We can create a derived class from the base class using the extend keyword. If we want to call the base class's constructor, then we can use the `super()` function like Java. Nevertheless, there are no keywords like `virtual, override`. If we define the same method signature in a derived class, then it is considered method overriding by default. We can call the base call's method from the overridden method through `super.method()` syntax if required.

In Typescript, we can define *abstract* classes as well, which does not allow a new object to be created. To mark an abstract class, we have to prefix it with an `abstract` keyword. Similarly, a method can be marked as an abstract as well. Please refer to *Code 1.20* for an example:

```
class Map {
        latitude: number;
        longitude: number;


        constructor()
        {
                //some initialization
        }


        zoomIn() { }

        zoomOut() { }
}

class GoogleMap extends Map {
        apiKey: string;

        constructor(){
                super();
                //some initialization
        }
        advancedOperation() { }
}
```

Code 1.20: *Inheritance example in TypeScript*

Interface

Interfaces are used to define abstract contracts. If any class implements an interface, then it must implement all methods defined in an interface. Interfaces are a means to implement loosely coupled solutions in OOP. In Typescript, the `implements` keyword is used to implement an interface over a class like Java. A class can implement zero or more interfaces separated by a comma. Please refer to *Code 1.21* for an example.

```typescript
interface Print {

        print(): void;

}

    interface Copy {

        copy(): void;

}

class ColourPrinter implements Print, Copy {

        print(): void {
                // print colour copy
        }

        copy(): void {
                // do a copy
        }

}
```

Code 1.21: Interface example in TypeScript

Note: In C# or Java, if a class implements an interface, then it should implement all of its methods and properties defined. Most of the time, an empty function body is provided for methods that do not serve a purpose in implementing class. Whereas in Typescript, the interface can have optional fields, which means a different class can implement. Optional fields in the interface are suffixed with a question mark (?). Please refer to Code 1.22 for an example:

```typescript
export interface Printer {
        copy(): void;
        serial_number: string;
        price?: number; //Optional field
}
```

Code 1.22: Interface with optional fields

> **Trick: Remember one of the interface caveats in C#? If a class implements two interfaces with the same method signature, how would we implement this method? Solution is explicit implementation that is, "Interface1.method()" and "Interface2.method()". In Typescript, we don't have to mention the interface name nor implement method twice. We just have to implement a method once, and another different method is ignored. Please refer to Code 1.23 for an example.**

```typescript
export interface Printer {


        copy(): void;

        serial_number: string;

        price?: number; //Optional field
}


export interface Scan {
        copy(): void;
}

export class HP implements Printer, Scan {

        serial_number: string;
        price?: number;


        copy(): void {
            console.log('copy called...');
        }
}

var hp = new HP();

hp.copy();
```

Code 1.23: Implementing a duplicate method from different Interfaces

Type Conversion

In Typescript, type conversion works a bit differently than C# and Java. In C# and Java, if a class is implementing the interface, then only the variable of the interface can hold an instance of that class. But in Typescript, if the interface's definition matches with class's definition, then interface variable can hold an instance of that class even if it doesn't implement it. A weirdness goes further when two different classes having the same structure can hold an instance of a similar class. Please refer to *Code 1.24* for an example:

```
export interface IMovable {
        speed: number;
        break(): void;
}

export class Car {
        speed: number;


        break() {
                console.log('car break applied on speed: ', this.
speed);
        }
}

export class Truck {
        speed: number;


        break() {
                console.log('truck break applied on speed: ', this.
speed);
        }
}

let suv: IMovable = new Car();
suv.speed = 150;
suv.break();

let monster: Truck = new Car();
monster.speed = 200;
monster.break();
```

```
// tsc type-conversion.ts && node type-conversion
// Output
// car break applied on speed:   150
// car break applied on speed:   200
```

Code 1.24: Type conversion example

Note that **IMovable** interface and **Truck** class both do not have any relationship like interface implementation or base-derived class. Still, they can hold an instance of **Car** object and can invoke the method and set member variables.

There is an operator in Typescript called **instanceof**, which returns **true** if the object is of a specific type. It is beneficial while working with dynamic/generic types or union types. For the preceding example, if we check the instance of **suv** object against **Truck** and **Car**, we shall get below output, as shown in *Code 1.25*:

```
console.log(suv instanceof Truck); // Output - false
console.log(suv instanceof Car); // Output – true
```

Code 1.25: Type checking example using instanceof

Converting an object to another type is relatively easy, though. We can use a triangular bracket (**<type>**) to specify the target type to covert, or we can use as operator. Please refer to *Code 1.26* for an example:

```
let fakeSUV = <Truck>suv;
let anotherFakeSUV = suv as Truck;
console.log(fakeSUV);
console.log(anotherFakeSUV);


// Output
// Car { speed: 150 }
// Car { speed: 150 }
```

Code 1.26: Type conversion example using "as" keyword and <> syntax

Union Types

In C# and Java, a member field can be defined with only one type, and a function can return at most only one data type value. Whereas in Typescript, we can specify more than one data type for a member field, and function can return multiple data type value. This is called Union Types in Typescript. Please refer to Code 1.27 for an example:

```typescript
export class Bottle {
        capacity: number | string;
        color: string;
}


function getWebResponse(param: string): string | JSON | number {
        return "some web response";
}
```

Code 1.27: Returning multiple data types from function

In the preceding example, the `capacity` field can hold a value of type number or string. But if we try to assign any other type, then we will get a compile-time error. Similarly, `getWebResponse()` function can return either string/JSON/number data type value.

When we work with third-party libraries whose function accepts multiple type data types or returns, in that case, union types are helpful.

Generics

Generics makes programmers life easy if used correctly. Typescript has a Generics feature like C# and Java. Generics allows defining function/class/interface with type agnostics fashion and lets the type be determined when a consumer calls it. We can use any data type for writing generic functionalities, but if we do so, it will be dynamic programming, meaning we won't get type information at compile time. Hence Generics is superior to any. Please refer to *Code 1.28* for an example:

```typescript
export function getResponse<T>(httpUrl: string): T {
        let response: T;
        // call http service and return a response
        return response;
}


let httpClient1 = getResponse<string>('someurl');
let httpClient2 = getResponse<number>('someurl');
```
Code 1.28: Generics example in TypeScript

Note that, at compile-time, `httpClient1` is of type `string`, and `httpClient2` is of type `number` since `getReponse()` has T as a return data type. Angular library heavily uses Generics in its implementation. We shall see many Angular classes and functions with Generics like `EventEmitter<type>`, `HttpClient.get<T>()`, and so on. It is essential to understand how Generics works hence this introduction.

Decorators

Decorators in Typescript is similar to Annotation in Java and Attributes in C#. It is a way of metaprogramming. We can attach decorators to class, function, member field, function parameters. A decorator is a special function that evaluates before the target is evaluated. Target is passed as a function argument to a decorator; hence Decorator can modify its target. A decorator function is prefixed with @ like Java's annotations.

If we explore the Angular library, then we will find tons of decorators. In fact, a typical way to identify what is Angular and what is pure Typescript artifact is to check for Angular decorators. The most common decorators we will encounter in Angular application are `@Component()`, `@NgModule()`, `@Injectable()`, but there are tons of decorators provided by Angular and other NPM packages.

Note that we can apply more than one decorator to its target. If applied, then evaluate of multiple decorators happens from top to bottom, and the result of decorator functions is called in the bottom to the top order. *Code 1.29* shows a simple method decorator which intercept method argument and changes it to 911:

```
function interceptor() {
        return function (target: any, propertyKey: string,
descriptor: PropertyDescriptor) {
                const originalMethod = descriptor.value;
                descriptor.value = () => originalMethod.apply(this,
[911])
                return descriptor;
        }
    }


export class Mobile {

        @interceptor()
        answerCall(caller: number): void {
                console.log('answering call from caller: ', caller);
        }
    }
```

```
    let iPhone = new Mobile();
    iPhone.answerCall(900);


// Output
// answering call from caller:   911
```

Code 1.29: *Method decorator example*

Decorator is a beneficial and intricate concept in Typescript. But to get started with Angular, all we need to know is that it is a function that is executed before its target and has the power to modify its target – meta programming.

Note that decorators are an experimental feature of Typescript. While compiling our Typescript program, we will need to specify a special flag to the **tsc** compiler called **–experimentalDecorator** as shown in *Command 1.1*:

```
    tsc --target ES5 --experimentalDecorators decorators.ts
```

Command 1.1: *"tsc" compiler called with experimental parameters*

Or we can specify them in your **tsconfig.json** file, as shown in *Code 1.30*:

```
{

        "compilerOptions": {
                "target": "ES5",
                "experimentalDecorators": true
        }
}
```

Code 1.30: *Specifying an experimental parameter in the configuration file*

When we create an Angular project through Angular/cli, the tsconfig.json file sets this flag by default.

> **Note: Decorators' function can take an argument(s). @Component, @ NgModule decorators from Angular, takes configuration object to the bootstrap application. We shall revisit decorators when we talk about @ Component and @NgModule.**

Modules and Namespaces

Modules and Namespaces are often get misused in the Typescript world. Especially when the developer is coming from a C# or Java background where Namespaces are logical grouping of classes to avoid name collision and providing wrapper layer. In Typescript, Namespaces are named JavaScript objects in the global namespace. We can wrap our classes or functions inside namespaces, but it will not be maintainable if we are trying to build a big application. Modules in Typescript on other hand structure codes in a good manner. Modules can contain code, declaration, and dependencies on other modules specific to a module. It is ideal for exporting one class/function from one TypeScript file as a Module for code maintainability. Please refer to *Code 1.31* for an example:

```typescript
// employee.ts
export class Employee {

        private _name : string;

        public get name() : string {
                return this._name;
        }

        public set name(name: string) {
                this._name = name;
        }
}


// employee-list.ts
import { Employee } from "./employee";

export class EmployeeList {

        private employeeList: Array<Employee>;

        constructor() {
                this.employeeList = new Array<Employee>();
        }
}
```

Code 1.31: Import class from different file

In the preceding example, the `employee.ts` file exports a class Employee as a module using keyword export. `employee-list.ts` file imports this Module through the `import` keyword. Note that we have put the `Employee` class in curly brackets while importing. It is because we are not exporting this class by "default". The best practice is if the module exports only one class/function/value, then it should be marked as an `export default` to make it easier for the consumer.

`Employee-factory.ts` - returns a new employee object. Please refer to *Code 1.32* for an example:

```
// employee-factory.ts
import { Employee } from "./employee";


export default function addEmployee(employeeName: string):
Employee {
        const newEmployee = new Employee();
        newEmployee.name = employeeName;
        return newEmployee;
}
```

Code 1.32: export function from the Module

Code 1.33 shows how to import function inside the employee-list.ts file

```
// employee-list.ts
import { Employee } from "./employee";
import addEmployee from "./employee-factory";


export class EmployeeList {

        private employeeList: Array<Employee>;


        constructor() {

                this.employeeList = new Array<Employee>();
                const newEmployee = addEmployee('Employee-1');
        }
}
```

Code 1.33: import class and function from different files

Note the difference between two "imports" statements. If a TypeScript file exports multiple artifacts, then we can import them by specifying between curly brackets. If there are "default" exports, then we just need to import it without brackets.

In C#, we use `namespace` keyword for grouping classes and namespaces, and in Java, we have `packages`. Though we have `namespace` keyword in Typescript, we should use `Module` for grouping classes as they provide good encapsulation.

It is recommended to read more about Typescript Modules and Namespaces at the official documentation.

In Angular, `@NgModule` is a decorator and not a Typescript Module. Do not get it confused. Unfortunately, `@NgModule` also has "`imports`," and "`exports`" properties of the configuration object passed as an argument to make it more confusing. We will discuss this difference more when we will get to `@NgModule` in the next chapters.

Advanced Types and Other Keywords

Static

Static members are not bound to a specific object instance, but their scope is per class. In C# / Java, we can mark class, constructor as static, but in Typescript, we can't. Typescript can have only static member fields and methods. Please refer to *Code 1.34* for an example:

```
export class Math {


    static Square(input: number): number {

        return input * input;

    }

}


const answer = Math.Square(5);

console.log(answer);
```

Code 1.34: static function in TypeScript

readonly and const

In C#, we have `readonly` keyword, which allows the developer to set a value at the declaration or in the constructor but no other place in the program. This is different than `const` field, which must be provided value at declaration only. In Typescript, readonly works similar to C#, but const cannot be applied to class members in Typescript. Only function/global variables can be defined as const in Typescript. In Java, we have the final keyword similar to const in Typescript. Please refer to *Code 1.35* for an example:

```
export class WebClient {


        private readonly url: string;


        constructor() {


                this.url = 'someUrl';
        }


        getResponse() {


                this.url = 'anotherUrl'; // Error - Cannot assign to
'url' because it is a read-only


                const serverIp: string = '127.0.0.1';


                serverIp = '0.0.0.1'; // Error - Cannot assign to
'serverIp' because it is a constant.
        }
    }
}
```

Code 1.35: readonly and const example

String and Number Literal Types

This feature is something we might not have seen in C# and Java. In Typescript, we can define any custom data type, including Literal Type. A literal string type specifies possible values a member field can have. It is something similar to the enum. Please refer to *Code 1.36* for an example:

```
export class Rose {
        color: 'red' | 'yellow' | 'white';
        quantity: 10 | 20 | 30;
}
```

```
const rose = new Rose();
rose.color = 'red';
rose.color = 'black'; // Error - Type '"black"' is not assignable
```
to type '"red" | "yellow" | "white"'

```
rose.quantity = 20;
rose.quantity = 50; // Error - Type '50' is not assignable to
```
type '10 | 20 | 30'.

Code 1.36: string and number literal example

Type Aliases

In Typescript, we can give an alias name to existing data types or our custom data types. There is no direct type alias in C# or Java, but it is similar to Golang Type alias. Here is the example, where we will define int, long, float data type alias for a number like in C#. Please refer to *Code 1.37* for an example:

```
type float = number;
type long = number;
type int = number;


function divide(number1: int, number2: long): float {
        return number1 + number2;
}


const result: float = divide(10, 20);
console.log(result);
```

Code 1.37: Type alias example

Summary

Typescript gives an entirely new way of writing plain JavaScript code as an Object-Oriented code. In this chapter, we have seen basic and advanced data types, how to define classes, functions, interface, inheritance, decorators, defining modules, namespaces, and some other concepts. This chapter intended to give us a background where we can write business logic in a proper OOP way. It is essential as it makes code readable, maintainable, and less error-prone. In the next chapter, we shall get started Angular and explore how Angular concepts maps with other OOP languages.

Questions

1. Can we define multiple inheritances in TypeScript?

2. How can we export multiple functions from a TypeScript file?

3. Can we define a readonly variable inside a function?

4. Can we delete an object's properties? If yes, how?

5. Create a class design and empty structure for the Adapter design pattern.

6. Implement a Singleton design pattern.

7. Implement Queue data structure using basic data types of TypeScript.

8. Write an interface and implement it with any real-world use case.

9. Write a decorator for the method and log its incoming parameters.

10. Write a decorator for a class to provide extra functionality.

CHAPTER 2

Hello Angular!

Welcome to the Angular world; an exciting and brave new one!

We have seen in the previous chapter how TypeScript is similar to C# and Java programming language. In this chapter we will learn a short history of Angular, how to setup Angular, creating a new Angular project, understanding important project file structure, and application workflow

Structure

- History of AngularJS to Angular
- Setup
- Project Structure
- Application Workflow
- IDE for Angular

Objective

The objective of this chapter is to get you started with Angular application development. After reading this chapter, you will have an understanding of Angular history, project structure, essential commands, file structure, and so on. You will also get how **ng serve** command starts the application and which modules and components get loaded and how does browser resolve Angular components as compared to standard HTML components. You should be able to create new Angular projects using Angular CLI commands and launch them.

History of AngularJS to Angular

The history of Angular goes back to AngularJS birth and how it became bottleneck where Google had to come with Angular – rewriting it from scratch! For the sake of context of this book, we won't go in that deep history, but just keep in mind that Angular is NOT version upgrade of AngularJS.

The first version of AngularJS was released in the year 2009 for building **Single Page Applications (SPA)** with **Model-View-Whatever (MVW or MV*)** framework. AngularJS got popularity soon, but it got hit by the release of ReactJS in the year *2011*. The drastically increased adoption of ReactJS emerged as compared to AngularJS in the frontend community. It is tough to judge which one is better as both try to solve the same problem and have their pros and cons. The frontend community is still divided on AngularJS versus ReactJS. There have been other frameworks in the market as well, like Vue.js, Knockout.js, Backbone.js, Ember.js; they are being used but not popular as compared to AngularJS or React.js. Nevertheless, Vue.js is catching up with Angular and ReactJS with its hybrid syntax.

AngularJS framework has been used by industry for the long term, and the community kept reporting complex bugs and limitations of framework. AngularJS team always tried to fix the issue, implement new features whenever they can, but they realized it is not going to last long. They started in-house development of the Angular new version entirely from scratch. They used their learning and shortcoming from AngularJS, took the best of ES6, and picked up TypeScript for the new project. In *September 2016*, Angular 2 first version got released by Google. It had lots of bugs and wasn't much feature-rich, but it was a clue that AngularJS is going to retire soon. Angular 2 came with TypeScript and JavaScript support so that the JavaScript community can pick it up.

> **Fun Fact: After AngularJS, Google released Angular 2. What do you think the next version was after Angular 2? Should be Angular 3, right? Well, no, it was Angular 4. It wasn't the case that the Angular team did arithmetic mistake; it was because of their delayed progress over Angular 3, and the Angular 4 planned date overlapped. Hence, they combined 3 and 4 version features and released them as Angular 4.**

The angular team announced that the newer version should be just referred to as an "**Angular**" without a suffixing version number, for example, Angular 2, Angular 4, Angular 10, and so on. But there is still a community out there who refer Angular as AngularJS and Angular 2 for the latest version of Angular. We should stick with only "Angular" through the rest of this book and going forward.

The new Angular framework was designed with a very well structured Object-Oriented design. If we check Angular source code on GitHub, then we will see how well the OOPs code can be written using TypeScript. The angular design includes modularity, dependency injection, services, classes, interfaces, events, metadata, reactive programming, and much more out of the box. We don't need to add any other library for these features, whereas in ReactJS, we need to add different packages for such features. That's one of the beauties about Angular!

Setup

At the time of writing this book, a stable version of Angular is 10.0.1. Setup instruction in this chapter applies to Angular version 10.0.1. The angular official website has a very detailed instruction about prerequisites and how to do the installation.

Node.js

We have used Node.js version 12.x white writing this book. Angular require any current or maintenance version of Node.js. We can install Node.js by downloading it from the official website for any specific target platform, either Windows, Mac. Node.js installation will install the npm package manager as well with **Command Line Interface (CLI).**

Angular CLI

Angular CLI is a great tool for creating and managing an Angular project with ease. It also helps us create Angular Schematics. The Angular CLI version is always kept up to date with the Angular matching version. Hence if we follow official documentation to setup Angular, we don't need to worry about the Angular CLI version. Angular CLI is similar to "dotnet" CLI for .NET Core framework.

Once we have installed Node.js then we can install Angular CLI by running *Command 2.1:*

```
npm install -g @angular/cli
```

Command 2.1: Install Angular CLI globally using the npm package

We should make sure that we have an Administrative right while running this command as it tries to update the global configuration. If we are trying to install it behind a proxy enabled firewall, then there is a different configuration. We will need to create .npmrc file and setup organization proxy information. The detailed information can be found at **https://docs.npmjs.com/misc/config official website**.

Creating a New Project

Alright, once Node.js and Angular CLI have been installed, then we are ready to create a new Angular project. Open command line terminal and run *Command 2.2*. The **ng** command refers to Angular CLI, **new** is the command parameter specifying operation for **ng**, and hello-angular is the name of the new Angular project we want to create.

```
ng new hello-angular
```

Command 2.2: Create new Angular project using Angular CLI

The Angular CLI shall prompt questions about a new project we want to create to add more functionality, like adding Routing and specifying CSS styling. For getting started, we don't want to use Routing; hence we will select **No** to routing question and select **CSS** as default stylesheet format as shown in *Figure 2.1*:

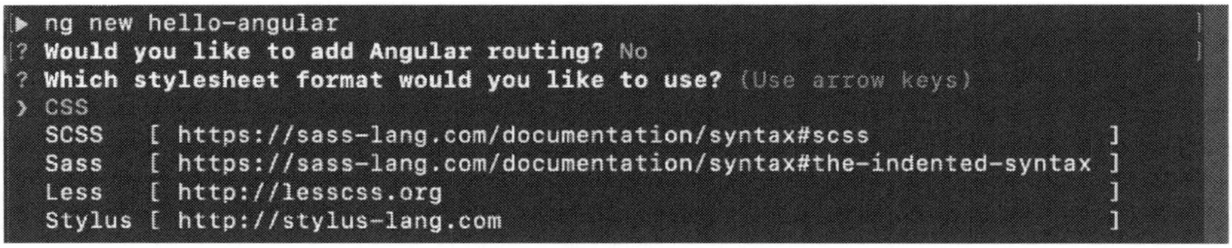

```
▶ ng new hello-angular
? Would you like to add Angular routing? No
? Which stylesheet format would you like to use? (Use arrow keys)
> CSS
  SCSS  [ https://sass-lang.com/documentation/syntax#scss          ]
  Sass  [ https://sass-lang.com/documentation/syntax#the-indented-syntax ]
  Less  [ http://lesscss.org                                       ]
  Stylus [ http://stylus-lang.com                                  ]
```

Figure 2.1: Angular CLI prompt for a new project

We can see all options and parameters for **ng** by running *Command 2.3*:

```
ng help
```

Command 2.3: Create new Angular project using Angular CLI

Figure 2.2 shows the Angular CLI 10.0.1 version help output. For different Angular CLI version, we might get different output.

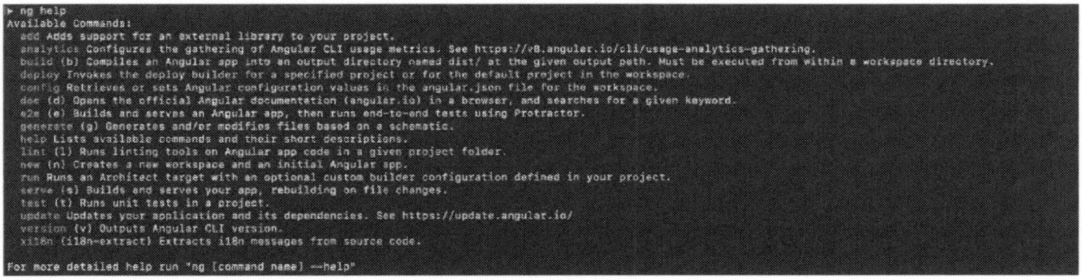

Figure 2.2: Angular CLI help output

The Angular CLI shall create a folder structure for new projects and will download required NPM packages from the internet. If we want to skip the installation of packages, then you can specify the **--skip-install** parameter to **ng new** command. This is useful if we want to use existing node_modules folders instead of downloading them from the internet. node_modules is a folder that contains all the packages required for the project. We will see more about packages when we talk about the package.json file. *Figure 2.3* shows the complete console output of **ng new** command to create a new project.

```
▶ ng new hello-angular
? Would you like to add Angular routing? No
? Which stylesheet format would you like to use? CSS
CREATE hello-angular/README.md (1029 bytes)
CREATE hello-angular/.editorconfig (246 bytes)
CREATE hello-angular/.gitignore (631 bytes)
CREATE hello-angular/angular.json (3623 bytes)
CREATE hello-angular/package.json (1290 bytes)
CREATE hello-angular/tsconfig.json (543 bytes)
CREATE hello-angular/tslint.json (1953 bytes)
CREATE hello-angular/browserslist (429 bytes)
CREATE hello-angular/karma.conf.js (1025 bytes)
CREATE hello-angular/tsconfig.app.json (210 bytes)
CREATE hello-angular/tsconfig.spec.json (270 bytes)
CREATE hello-angular/src/favicon.ico (948 bytes)
CREATE hello-angular/src/index.html (298 bytes)
CREATE hello-angular/src/main.ts (372 bytes)
CREATE hello-angular/src/polyfills.ts (2838 bytes)
CREATE hello-angular/src/styles.css (80 bytes)
CREATE hello-angular/src/test.ts (753 bytes)
CREATE hello-angular/src/assets/.gitkeep (0 bytes)
CREATE hello-angular/src/environments/environment.prod.ts (51 bytes)
CREATE hello-angular/src/environments/environment.ts (662 bytes)
CREATE hello-angular/src/app/app.module.ts (314 bytes)
CREATE hello-angular/src/app/app.component.css (0 bytes)
CREATE hello-angular/src/app/app.component.html (25673 bytes)
CREATE hello-angular/src/app/app.component.spec.ts (963 bytes)
CREATE hello-angular/src/app/app.component.ts (217 bytes)
CREATE hello-angular/e2e/protractor.conf.js (808 bytes)
CREATE hello-angular/e2e/tsconfig.json (214 bytes)
CREATE hello-angular/e2e/src/app.e2e-spec.ts (646 bytes)
CREATE hello-angular/e2e/src/app.po.ts (301 bytes)
✓ Packages installed successfully.
    Directory is already under version control. Skipping initialization of git.
```

Figure 2.3: Angular CLI output of ng new command

Let's change the current working directory in terminal to a new project by running *Command 2.4*:

Cd hello-angular

Command 2.4: Set the working directory to a new project

We can check Angular CLI installed version and current Angular project's version by running *Command 2.5*:

ng version

Command 2.5: Check Angular CLI version in the project directory

The output of *Command 2.5* is shown in *Figure 2.4*. The output includes a version of all dependent packages and libraries because if there is any mismatch in a dependent library, then the Angular project might fail.

Figure 2.4: Angular CLI version output

We can run our very first project by running *Command 2.6*:

```
ng serve --open
```

Command 2.6: Run Angular project

This command will start the development server on address **http://localhost:4200** and open it in a new tab of the default browser. If we do not specify **--open** parameter, then we need to open the browser explicitly and navigate to the URL. Note that we are running the command **ng serve** and not **ng serve** which is a common mistake people do when getting started with Angular. *Figure 2.5* shows the output of *Command 2.6:*

```
▶ ng serve --open
0% compiling
Compiling @angular/core : es2015 as esm2015

Compiling @angular/common : es2015 as esm2015

Compiling @angular/platform-browser : es2015 as esm2015

Compiling @angular/platform-browser-dynamic : es2015 as esm2015

chunk {main} main.js, main.js.map (main) 57.8 kB [initial] [rendered]
chunk {polyfills} polyfills.js, polyfills.js.map (polyfills) 140 kB [initial] [rendered]
chunk {runtime} runtime.js, runtime.js.map (runtime) 6.15 kB [entry] [rendered]
chunk {styles} styles.js, styles.js.map (styles) 9.75 kB [initial] [rendered]
chunk {vendor} vendor.js, vendor.js.map (vendor) 2.68 MB [initial] [rendered]
Date: 2020-02-22T18:18:13.674Z - Hash: 6a71e4f877542a047891 - Time: 10331ms
** Angular Live Development Server is listening on localhost:4200, open your browser on http://localhost:4200/ **
: Compiled successfully.

Date: 2020-02-22T18:18:14.453Z - Hash: 6a71e4f877542a047891
5 unchanged chunks

Time: 317ms
: Compiled successfully.
```

Figure 2.5: *ng serve --open output*

Figure 2.6 shows the default Angular new project output:

Figure 2.6: *The new Angular project output in the browser*

Changing Default Port

The Angular development server starts on port number **4200** by default. We can change this port to any valid port by running *Command 2.7:*

```
ng serve --open --port=9000
```

Command 2.7: *Run Angular project on 9000 port*

The *Command 2.7* shall run the Angular project on **9000** port for a session. If we want to run our project always on another port, then we should update the `package.json` file, as shown in *Code 2.1*. With this change, every time we run **ng serve** command, then the development server will use port 9000:

```json
{
  "name": "hello-angular",
  "version": "0.0.0",
  "scripts": {
    "ng": "ng",
    "start": "ng serve --port=9000",
    "build": "ng build",
    "test": "ng test",
    "lint": "ng lint",
    "e2e": "ng e2e"
  },
 {...}
```

Code 2.1: *package.json — Always open development server on port 9000*

Live Reload

The angular development server starts by default in watch mode. In watch mode, the Angular compiler keeps track of file changes. If there are any changes in the project file, then it recompiles the project and reloads the browser automatically. Let's try it out! We will make sure that **ng serve** command is running, and we will update the app.component.html file, as shown in *Code 2.2*:

```html
<span>{{ title }} app is running! Let's go!!!</span>
```

Code 2.2: *app.component.html —Updated text*

We will save the changes and observe the changes in the browser. We should see out updated text in the browser, as shown in *Figure 2.7*. The live reload is very helpful while development of Angular applications and increase productivity.

Figure 2.7: *Live reloaded changes in a browser*

Project Structure

Figure 2.8 shows the Angular CLI generated folder structure for the `hello-angular` project. Note that we are running the **tree** command, which is an external command package. Based on your Operating System, you can download the **tree** package or use any other library/tool for listing folder structure. We are excluding the `node_modules` folder here as it contains dependent packages.

```
⬚ tree -I node_modules
.
├── README.md
├── angular.json
├── browserslist
├── e2e
│   ├── protractor.conf.js
│   ├── src
│   │   ├── app.e2e-spec.ts
│   │   └── app.po.ts
│   └── tsconfig.json
├── karma.conf.js
├── package-lock.json
├── package.json
├── src
│   ├── app
│   │   ├── app.component.css
│   │   ├── app.component.html
│   │   ├── app.component.spec.ts
│   │   ├── app.component.ts
│   │   └── app.module.ts
│   ├── assets
│   ├── environments
│   │   ├── environment.prod.ts
│   │   └── environment.ts
│   ├── favicon.ico
│   ├── index.html
```

```
|      ├── main.ts
|      ├── polyfills.ts
|      ├── styles.css
|      └── test.ts
├── tsconfig.app.json
├── tsconfig.json
├── tsconfig.spec.json
└── tslint.json


6 directories, 27 files
```

Command 2.8: "tree" command output on the Angular project directory

README.md

As the name suggests, the README markdown file is like documentation about the project. The README file usually contains a short description of the project, instruction to setup and special commands, license, contribution guidelines, known limitations, and so on. Nevertheless, there is no specific format of README, and it varies project to project. We should make sure that our README file contains enough information so that any new developer can get started with our project after going through the README file.

angular.json

The angular.json file contains settings for Angular Ivy workspace. In this file, we can define the configuration for one or more projects. The **projects** key contains all projects in the current workspace. For our example, the **hello-angular** project key contains our current settings. The Angular CLI reads the angular.json file to perform various operations as **ng serve, ng build**, and so on. In this file, we can specify the output folder path, starting the TypeScript file name (default main.ts), use the **Ahead-of-Time (AOT)** compilation method or not, and so on. *Code 1.3* shows the content of angular.json. Note that every time we make any changes to the angular.json file, then we must restart the **ng serve** command to read the new configuration:

```
{
"$schema": "./node_modules/@angular/cli/lib/config/schema.json",
"version": 1,
"newProjectRoot": "projects",
```

```
"projects": {
    "hello-angular": {
    "projectType": "application",
    "schematics": {},
    "root": "",
    "sourceRoot": "src",
    "prefix": "app",
    "architect": {
        "build": {
        "builder": "@angular-devkit/build-angular:browser",
        "options": {
            "outputPath": "dist/hello-angular",
            "index": "src/index.html",
            "main": "src/main.ts",
            "polyfills": "src/polyfills.ts",
            "tsConfig": "tsconfig.app.json",
            "aot": true,
            "assets": [
            "src/favicon.ico",
            "src/assets"
            ],
            "styles": [
            "src/styles.css"
            ],
            "scripts": []
        },
        "configurations": {
            "production": {
            "fileReplacements": [
                {
                "replace": "src/environments/environment.ts",
                "with": "src/environments/environment.prod.ts"
                }
```

```
            ],
            "optimization": true,
            "outputHashing": "all",
            "sourceMap": false,
            "extractCss": true,
            "namedChunks": false,
            "extractLicenses": true,
            "vendorChunk": false,
            "buildOptimizer": true,
            "budgets": [
                {
                "type": "initial",
                "maximumWarning": "2mb",
                "maximumError": "5mb"
                },
                {
                "type": "anyComponentStyle",
                "maximumWarning": "6kb",
                "maximumError": "10kb"
                }
            ]
            }
        }
        },
        "serve": {
        "builder": "@angular-devkit/build-angular:dev-server",
        "options": {
            "browserTarget": "hello-angular:build"
        },
        "configurations": {
            "production": {
            "browserTarget": "hello-angular:build:production"
            }
```

```
        }
      },
      "extract-i18n": {
      "builder": "@angular-devkit/build-angular:extract-i18n",
      "options": {
          "browserTarget": "hello-angular:build"
      }
      },
      "test": {
      "builder": "@angular-devkit/build-angular:karma",
      "options": {
          "main": "src/test.ts",
          "polyfills": "src/polyfills.ts",
          "tsConfig": "tsconfig.spec.json",
          "karmaConfig": "karma.conf.js",
          "assets": [
          "src/favicon.ico",
          "src/assets"
          ],
          "styles": [
          "src/styles.css"
          ],
          "scripts": []
      }
      },
      "lint": {
      "builder": "@angular-devkit/build-angular:tslint",
      "options": {
          "tsConfig": [
          "tsconfig.app.json",
          "tsconfig.spec.json",
          "e2e/tsconfig.json"
          ],
```

```
            "exclude": [
            "**/node_modules/**"
            ]
        }
    },
    "e2e": {
    "builder": "@angular-devkit/build-angular:protractor",
    "options": {
        "protractorConfig": "e2e/protractor.conf.js",
        "devServerTarget": "hello-angular:serve"
    },
    "configurations": {
        "production": {
        "devServerTarget": "hello-angular:serve:production"
        }
    }
    }
    }
    }},
    "defaultProject": "hello-angular"
}
```

Code 2.3: angular.json – Angular configuration file

e2e Folder

The e2e folder contains end to end or integration tests Angular project. By default, e2e tests are generated for the Protractor framework, but you can always change this and use any other framework of your choice, for example, Cypress.

package.json

This file holds the configuration of project dependencies, packages, and scripts to be run by the **npm run** command. This file is similar to app.config in .NET and `appsettings.json` file in .NET Core and gradle file for Spring Boot/Java application. Whenever we change dependencies by adding/removing item(s), we should run **npm install/uninstall/update** commands. The **node_modules** folder contains all the downloaded packages. *Code 2.4* shows the content of `package.json` from our project.

```json
{
"name": "hello-angular",
"version": "0.0.0",
"scripts": {
  "ng": "ng",
  "start": "ng serve",
  "build": "ng build",
  "test": "ng test",
  "lint": "ng lint",
  "e2e": "ng e2e"
},
"private": true,
"dependencies": {
  "@angular/animations": "~10.0.1",
  "@angular/common": "~10.0.1",
  "@angular/compiler": "~10.0.1",
  "@angular/core": "~10.0.1",
  "@angular/forms": "~10.0.1",
  "@angular/platform-browser": "~10.0.1",
  "@angular/platform-browser-dynamic": "~10.0.1",
  "@angular/router": "~10.0.1",
  "rxjs": "~6.5.4",
  "tslib": "^2.0.0",
  "zone.js": "~0.10.2"
},
"devDependencies": {
  "@angular-devkit/build-angular": "~0.1000.0",
  "@angular/cli": "~10.0.0",
  "@angular/compiler-cli": "~10.0.1",
  "@types/node": "^12.11.1",
  "@types/jasmine": "~3.5.0",
```

```
    "@types/jasminewd2": "~2.0.3",
    "codelyzer": "^5.1.2",
    "jasmine-core": "~3.5.0",
    "jasmine-spec-reporter": "~5.0.0",
    "karma": "~5.0.0",
    "karma-chrome-launcher": "~3.1.0",
    "karma-coverage-istanbul-reporter": "~3.0.2",
    "karma-jasmine": "~3.3.0",
    "karma-jasmine-html-reporter": "^1.5.0",
    "protractor": "~7.0.0",
    "ts-node": "~8.3.0",
    "tslint": "~6.1.0",
    "typescript": "~3.9.5"
  }
}
```

Code 2.4: *package.json – NPM package configuration file*

The "**scripts**" section contains the commands for the **npm run**. Remember, how did we start the application? These scripts can be run with syntax **npm run <command name>**. Thus, when we run the **npm run start,** it will launch the **ng serve** command. We can add a custom script in this section as well or edit an existing one.

The "**dependencies**" section holds a list of dependent packages with version information. These packages shall be bundled and deployed when you build your application for production. Make sure to put only packages required for deployment; otherwise, the bundle size will be huge. The Angular AOT compilation method validates the source code for used packages and drops unused packaged in the deployment bundle.

The "**dependencies**" section holds a list of packages that are required at the time of development but not for deployment. For example, typescript is part of "**devDependencies**" as it is not required to run Angular project in the browser as it shall be transpiled to JavaScript code.

package-lock.json

This file holds version information of packages installed for the current project in the node_modules folder. As a best practice, we should add this file into source control for version management. This file is auto-updated whenever we update the package.json file and run **npm install/uninstall** command. We should not manually update this file.

src Folder

This is the source code folder for our Angular project with the following file structure:

- app folder: The app folder contains all Angular modules and components with business logic. We should create a subfolder per our feature inside this folder. This folder should be the root folder of our feature code:

  o **app.component.css**: This file contains CSS stylesheet. The stylesheet format is CSS because we have selected in Angular CLI ng new command.

  o **app.component.html:** This file contains the HTML code for AppComponent.

  o **app.component.spec.ts**: This is a unit test case file for AppComponent.

  o **app.component.ts:** This is a root component class of the Angular project. *Code 1.5* shows the auto-generated code for AppComponent. The AppComponent is a TypeScript class with **@Component** decorator applied to it. The **@Component** decorator is exported by **@angular/ core package**; hence we have imported it. The **@Component** decorator accepts a json object with metadata like:

    ▪ **selector**: unique identifier for AppComponent

    ▪ **templateUrl**: the path to HTML file associated with this component

    ▪ **styleUrls**: An array of the stylesheet file path

```
import { Component } from '@angular/core';


@Component({
selector: 'app-root',
templateUrl: './app.component.html',
styleUrls: ['./app.component.css']
})
export class AppComponent {
   title = 'hello-angular';
}
```

Code 2.5: app.component.ts – AppComponent code

  o **app.module.ts:** This *Code 2.6* shows the content of app.module. ts. The AppModule is a TypeScript class with **@NgModule** decorator. Generally, it is a root module of Angular application.

```
import { BrowserModule } from '@angular/platform-browser';
import { NgModule } from '@angular/core';


import { AppComponent } from './app.component';


@NgModule({
declarations: [
    AppComponent
],
imports: [
    BrowserModule
],
providers: [],
bootstrap: [AppComponent]
})
export class AppModule { }
```

Code 2.6: *app.module.ts – AppModule code*

- **The assets folder**: This folder holds web assets for Angular application, for example, images, videos, audio, and so on. If we want to use any other folder for storing assets, then we should angular.json file. This folder gets deployed along with our build items when ready for production.

- **browserslist**: This file is used to build tools for generating an output of CSS and JavaScript files for different browsers.

- **The environments folder:** This folder contains environment configuration files. By default, we get two files that are environment.ts and environment.prod.ts. While building an Angular application, we would like to maintain different configurations for a different server. For example, we might have the development server, staging server, and production server. During the development phase, we might consume APIs from the development server, and when we are ready to go live, then we can change API to the production server URL. Such configuration can be set in environment files, as shown in *Code 2.7*. When we run **ng serve** command, then environment.ts file is used to read configuration. When we run **ng build --prod** command, then environment.ts file content will get replaced with environment.prod.ts file. Of course, we can always create multiple environment files and specify different deployment configurations.

```
export const environment = {
    production: false
};
```

Code 2.7: environment.ts – The environment configuration

- **favicon.ico**: The **favicon.ico** is an icon which browser shows in the tab for a website. We can use the default Angular icon or use our own by replacing it with another icon file.

- **Index.html**: In the angular.json file, the index key holds the value of for index HTML file to be rendered in the browser. This file generally doesn't contain any Angular specific code apart from root component, that is, **<app-root></app-root> tag,** which represents complete Angular application in a browser. If we need to include any third-party JavaScript libraries or CSS assets, we should not include it in this file but rather mention them in the angular.json file's assets key. *Code 2.8* shows auto-generated index.html file content:

```
<!doctype html>
<html lang="en">
<head>
    <meta charset="utf-8">
    <title>HelloAngular</title>
    <base href="/">
    <meta name="viewport" content="width=device-width,
initial-scale=1">
    <link rel="icon" type="image/x-icon" href="favicon.ico">
</head>
<body>
    <app-root></app-root>
</body>
</html>
```

Code 2.8: index.html – The index.html file content from the src folder

When we build your application for deployment purpose using the **ng build** command, then Angular CLI will create a new folder called dist/<project-name>. This folder contains a bundled package that is deployed on any standard web server like Apache, IIS, Azure, and so on. The **index.html** file in the dist folder will have multiple <script> tags for Angular libraries and polyfills, and so on. *Code 2.9* shows the content of the **index.html** file generated after running **ng build**. Note the highlighted `<script>` tags that are not present in the `index.html` file from `src` folder:

```
<!doctype html>
<html lang="en">


<head>
    <meta charset="utf-8">
    <title>HelloAngular</title>
    <base href="/">
    <meta name="viewport" content="width=device-width, initial-
scale=1">
    <link rel="icon" type="image/x-icon" href="favicon.ico">
</head>


<body>
    <app-root></app-root>
    <script src="runtime-es2015.js" type="module"></script>
    <script src="runtime-es5.js" nomodule defer></script>
    <script src="polyfills-es5.js" nomodule defer></script>
    <script src="polyfills-es2015.js" type="module"></script>
    <script src="styles-es2015.js" type="module"></script>
    <script src="styles-es5.js" nomodule defer></script>
    <script src="vendor-es2015.js" type="module"></script>
    <script src="vendor-es5.js" nomodule defer></script>
    <script src="main-es2015.js" type="module"></script>
    <script src="main-es5.js" nomodule defer></script>
</body>
</html>
```

Code 1.9: index.html – The index.html file content from the dist/hello-angular folder

- **karma.conf.js:** Angular uses the Karma framework for running unit test cases. The `karma.conf.js` file contains the configuration for the Karma framework, as shown in *Code 2.10*. We can change the configuration for your test in this file like code coverage, generating test output, changing browser to test cases from Google Chrome to Safari, for example, and so:

```javascript
// Karma configuration file, see link for more information
// https://karma-runner.github.io/1.0/config/configuration-file.html

module.exports = function (config) {
    config.set({
        basePath: '',
        frameworks: ['jasmine', '@angular-devkit/build-angular'],
        plugins: [
            require('karma-jasmine'),
            require('karma-chrome-launcher'),
            require('karma-jasmine-html-reporter'),
            require('karma-coverage-istanbul-reporter'),
            require('@angular-devkit/build-angular/plugins/karma')
        ],
        client: {
            clearContext: false // leave Jasmine Spec Runner output
visible in browser
        },
        coverageIstanbulReporter: {
            dir: require('path').join(__dirname, './coverage/hello-
angular'),
            reports: ['html', 'lcovonly', 'text-summary'],
            fixWebpackSourcePaths: true
        },
        reporters: ['progress', 'kjhtml'],
        port: 9876,
        colors: true,
        logLevel: config.LOG_INFO,
        autoWatch: true,
        browsers: ['Chrome'],
        singleRun: false,
        restartOnFileChange: true
    });
};
```

Code 2.10: karma.conf.js – unit test configuration for karma framework

- **main.ts:** This is an entry program for Angular application configured in the `angular.json` file. It is similar to the `main()` function in C# and Java programming. The Angular application starts from this file by bootstrapping the root module (AppModule).

- **polyfills.ts:** Polyfills are JavaScript libraries which helps web application to run on different browsers even if there is no native support for specific CSS class or JavaScript functionalities. Angular supports a standard browser, but if we want to target an older version of the browser, then we can setup polyfills in this file.

- **styles.css:** This file contains the global style for the whole application. We can specify themes and/or other third part design libraries like material design, Twitter bootstrap, and so on.

- **test.ts:** This file is the starting point for the unit test framework—Karma. In this file, we can set the configuration for unit test cases like which files to includes, which to excludes, and so on.

- **tsconfig.app.json:** This file contains the TypeScript configuration for the project. Angular CLI invokes the TypeScript compiler and uses this file for setting TypeScript configuration.

- **tsconfig.spec.json:** This file is similar to `tsconfig.app.json`, which specifies more TypeScript compiler options for test case files, that is, `*.spec.ts`.

- **tslint.json:** This file contains TypeScript coding guidelines rules. This file is used by ng lint command, which invokes TSLint internally and passes these configurations.

- **tsconfig.json:** This is a project-wide TypeScript compiler setting file. We can set configurations like output directory, ECMA script supported format, enable source-map or not, and so on.

Application Workflow

When we run Angular application using the **ng serve** command, then Angular CLI does many things in the background. It first compiles Angular application and breaks them into small JavaScript chunk files, create source map file for debugging, starts development server on http://localhost:4200 and keep watching project files for changes. When we browse navigates to **http://localhost:4200** URL, then the `index.html` file is sent to the browser for parsing and rendering. The browser starts parsing all known HTML tags of index.html like `<head></head>`, `<div></div>`, and so on . When browser tries to render non-standard HTML tag like `<app-root></app-root>`, it needs more information how to render it. That's where the Angular framework comes into the picture. Remember how `index.html` file gets extra `<script>` tags for Angular libraries after running **ng build** commands?

One of those libraries is main.js (transpiled from `main.ts`), and it gets loaded in the browser and tells the browser how to parse `<app-root></app-root>`.

We have mentioned that the `main.ts` file is a starting point of the application specified in the `angular.json` file. *Code 2.10* shows the content of the `main.ts` file:

```
import { enableProdMode } from '@angular/core';

import { platformBrowserDynamic } from '@angular/platform-browser-
dynamic';


import { AppModule } from './app/app.module';
import { environment } from './environments/environment';


if (environment.production) {
    enableProdMode();
}


platformBrowserDynamic().bootstrapModule(AppModule)
    .catch(err => console.error(err));
```

Code 2.11: *main.ts – Content of main.ts file*

The Angular application needs to have at least one NgModule as a root module for bootstrapping. That's why we are passing AppModule to function `bootstrapModule()`. The `enableProdMode()` function is used by Angular build tools for optimizing the build process by tree shaking and other mechanisms.

```
import { AppComponent } from './app.component';


@NgModule({
    declarations: [
        AppComponent
    ],
    bootstrap: [AppComponent]
})
export class AppModule { }
```

Code 2.12: *app.module.ts – AppComponent specified as a bootstrap component*

The AppComponent component is passed to the "bootstrap" property of @NgModule decorator marking it as a root component, as shown in *Code 2.12*. In `index.html`, we

have `<app-root></app-root>` tag used, which is the value for the `selector` key of
@Component decorator applied on AppComponent component. The `templateUrl`
property of `@Component` decorator has value `app.component.html`; thus, whenever
the browser tries to render `<app-root></app-root>` tag, it will be redirected to
render `app.component.html` file content. *Figure 2.8* shows the compiled HTML
code of the AppComponent component in browser development tools. Note that
`<app-root>` tag is expanded into `app.component.html` content.

Figure 2.8: <app-root> tag expanded code in the browser

IDE for Angular

The Angular application comprises HTML, JavaScript, TypeScript, and JSON files.
Thus any text editor or IDE can be used for Angular development. I like to use
"Visual Studio Code" IDE, which is an open-source IDE from Microsoft. It is very
lightweight, has firm support for TypeScript language and helpful extensions for
Angular and other languages. But if you want to use different IDE like Visual Studio,
Atom, WebStorm, then feel free to use.

Conclusion

In this chapter, we had a glimpse of Angular history. We have seen how to the
setup development environment and how to create a new Angular project using
Angular CLI. We have gone through an Angular project structure and understood

each and every file and folder purpose. We also did the application workflow step by step and seen in browser how does Angular application starts and how it resolves components. And at the end, we have seen IDE options for developing Angular applications. In the next chapter, we will start building small Angular applications and see how it can be mapped to the OOPs approach.

Questions

1. Create a new Angular application with SAAS stylesheet format and observe the file structure

2. Can we run multiple Angular applications in parallel using **ng serve** command?

3. What will happen if we delete the `angular.json` file and try to run an Angular application?

4. Can we create an Angular application without Angular CLI? If yes, how?

5. If we deleted the `node_module` folder, then how to generate it again?

Building Small and Simple

Introduction

In this chapter, we will build a small Angular application. We will build a simple "Party-Invite" form incrementally. While building applications, we will get familiar with the basic concepts of Angular by their practice usage. We will also see how to debug the application, which is an essential technique to learn as an Angular developer. At the end of this chapter, we will see how to create a distributable package of Angular application which can be hosted on the webserver for production purpose in a nutshell.

Structure

- Project Setup
- Introduction to @NgModule
    - o   What is @NgModule
- Introduction to @Component
    - o   What is @Component
    - o   Inspecting @Component metadata
- Introduction to basic Data Bindings
    - o   Types of data bindings

- Introduction to NgIf, NgFor, and ngForm directives
  - o What is NgIf?
  - o What is NgFor?
  - o What is NgForm
- Building "Party-Invite" Sign-up form
- Production deployment
- Angular Lifecycle events
- Debugging Angular application
- Conclusion
- Questions

Objective

Our goal of this chapter is to learn the essential topics of Angular in practice implementation. The Party-Invite form application will cover how to perform certain tasks at specific lifecycle hook, understand the basic relationship between NgModule and Components, how to process user inputs and event handling, understand which Angular core package(s) to import, how to do debugging and how to deploy applications for production purpose.

Project Setup

Let's create a new project called **party-invite**. Make sure we have installed an angular/cli package globally so that we can run **ng** command in any directory. Open terminal and run *Command 3.1*:

```
ng new party-invite
```

Command 3.1: new project command

If we are running angular/cli version ~10.0.0, then running *Command 1.1* will ask us if a new project should have a routing template. We can select **No** for our example and then select **CSS** for style sheet format. Refer to *Figure 3.1*, for example:

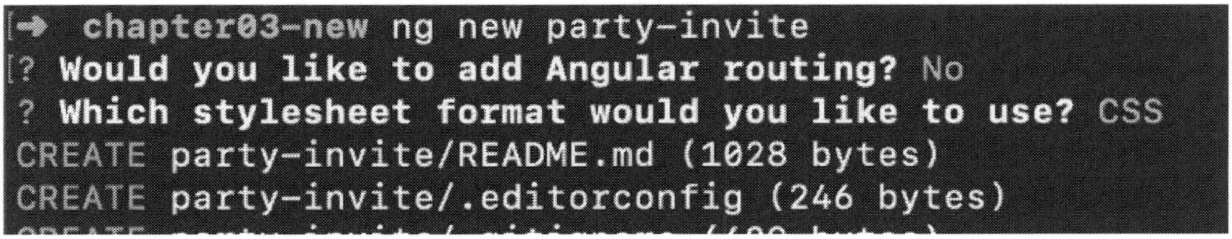

```
[➜  chapter03-new ng new party-invite
[? Would you like to add Angular routing? No
? Which stylesheet format would you like to use? CSS
CREATE party-invite/README.md (1028 bytes)
CREATE party-invite/.editorconfig (246 bytes)
```

Figure 3.1: "ng new party-invite" command output

Once *Command 3.1* ran successfully, it will create a new project directory structure and will install npm packages into the node_modules folder. Now we can run this new project by changing the working directory to our new project and then run the command **ng serve - -open.** We have learned how to run a new project in *Chapter 2.*

Introduction to @NgModule

@NgModule is a basic building block of an Angular application. We have a complete chapter dedicated to understanding NgModule thoroughly; hence here we will just get introduced to it for getting started. Every Angular project has at least one root class with @NgMoodule decorator typically named "AppModule" in file app.module. ts inside the **src/app** directory. *Figure 3.2* shows a snapshot of the auto-generated AppModule snippet:

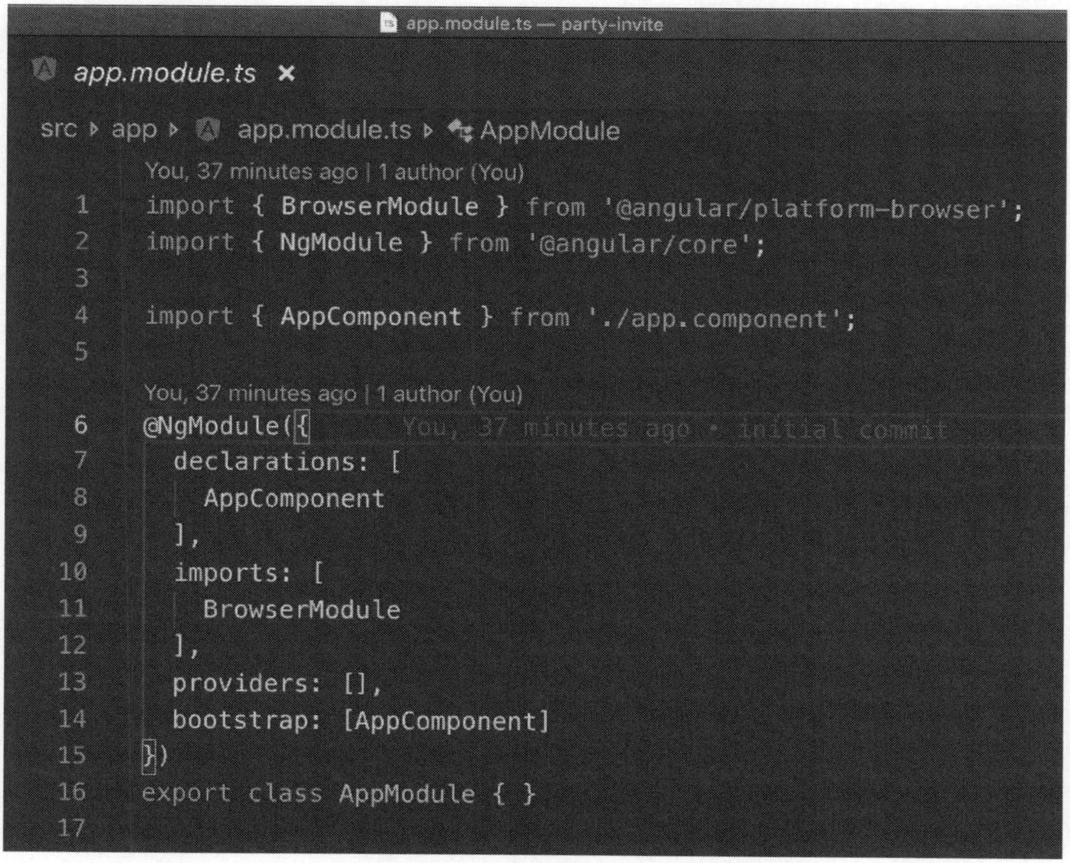

```
app.module.ts — party-invite

 app.module.ts  ✕

src ▶ app ▶  app.module.ts ▶  AppModule
         You, 37 minutes ago | 1 author (You)
  1      import { BrowserModule } from '@angular/platform-browser';
  2      import { NgModule } from '@angular/core';
  3
  4      import { AppComponent } from './app.component';
  5
         You, 37 minutes ago | 1 author (You)
  6      @NgModule({          You, 37 minutes ago • initial commit
  7        declarations: [
  8          AppComponent
  9        ],
 10        imports: [
 11          BrowserModule
 12        ],
 13        providers: [],
 14        bootstrap: [AppComponent]
 15      })
 16      export class AppModule { }
 17
```

Figure 3.2: AppModule generated code

Note: Angular Ivy is a new rendering engine that was available from the Angular 8 version on an opt-in basis. It is a default rendering engine from the Angular 9 version onward.

What is @NgModule?

@NgModule is a decorator applied on simple TypeScript class in this case, "AppModule". Remember that Angular applications are a mix of TypeScript classes and function with Angular decorators and functions. Hence it is essential to understand which part Angular is and which is TypeScript. As for the definition of a decorator, @NgModule is a function that accepts a JSON object as an argument called a metadata object. This metadata object is a crucial part that defines the modularity of Angular application. Ideally, @NgModule class (for example, AppModule) doesn't have any functionality and just metadata, unless we are registering web components or working with AngularJs 1.x in combination with Angular. When we have some special requirements like exporting Angular application as Web Component, then we can override the ngDoBootstrap() lifecycle hook of NgModule.

Inspecting @NgModule metadata object

Let's go through NgModule's metadata properties, shown in *Figure 3.2:*

- **declarations**: This property accepts an array of Components that should be part of this NgModule. Remember, a component can be part of only one NgModule at most, but one NgModule can have multiple components declared inside it. If we try to declare one component in multiple NgModule, then we shall receive a runtime exception. In C# context, a class is part of namespace if defined within that namespace. If we want to use a specific class in other namespaces, we must import declaring namespace first. For Java, the class defined inside the package is part of it. On a similar note, a component is part of NgModule, and if a component from different NgModule wants to use this component, then it must import declaring NgModule in its parent NgModule.

- **imports**: This property accepts an array of NgModules. In C#, we import namespace by "using" keyword, and then we can access classes defined within that namespace and "import" statement for importing packages in Java. If we want to access Component declared with another NgModule, then we can mention the target component's NgModule in source component's NgModule's "imports" property. We will see an example of how to do it shortly.

- **exports**: This property accepts an array of Angular Components. Only Components listed inside exports property can be imported by other NgModules. This property doesn't get auto-generated for NgModule. Since

AppModule is a root module, which is a starting point of application, we will not mark any component for export. For other feature modules, it is quite normal to have this property filled with components. In terms of C#, imagine a class declared inside a namespace with an "internal" access specifier and being used in a different assembly; in this case, the compiler will not find it.

- **providers**: This property accepts a set of injectable objects that are available in the injector of this module, for example, Service class. If we have worked with **Dependency Injection (DI)** framework like Unity or in .NET Web API built-in, DI then try to imagine it as registering class for DI purpose. There are different ways we can specify how to provide an entity, and we will learn more about it in the DI section in upcoming chapters.

- **bootstrap**: This property accepts a set of components that are bootstrapped when this module is bootstrapped. The components listed here are automatically added to the "entryComponents" property of @NgModule.

Introduction to @Component

@Component is a decorator applied to a Typescript class. The Angular application should have at least one root component, typically "AppComponent," and it looks similar to *Figure 3.3*:

```
app.component.ts — party-invite

app.module.ts        app.component.ts  ✕

src ▸ app ▸ app.component.ts ▸ AppComponent ▸ title
        You, 2 hours ago | 1 author (You)
   1    import { Component } from '@angular/core';
   2
        You, 2 hours ago | 1 author (You)
   3    @Component({
   4      selector: 'app-root',
   5      templateUrl: './app.component.html',
   6      styleUrls: ['./app.component.css']
   7    })
   8    export class AppComponent {
   9      title = 'party-invite';
  10    }
  11
```

Figure 3.3: *AppComponent generated code*

What is @Component?

When @Component decorator is applied to a class, then the target class is marked as a Component class. A component is a basic unit of operation in Angular application. It has its own HTML code (which can be specified inline in @Components metadata property or separate HTML file) to render and TypeScript class for data-binding and business operation with one-to-one mapping. We can consider a button, text field, checkbox, and so on as a simple web component. The key to building an Angular application is to break down requirements into the component tree where each component is responsible for a single logical task and aggregate components to solve more significant problems. Imagine Angular application as an inverted tree of components where AppComponent being the root of the tree. A leaf node of this tree will be an independent component.

An Angular component can be viewed as a group of three files as below list:

- **<app>.component.ts:** code-behind file for defining business logic
- **<app>.component.html:** HTML file for specifying the visual appearance of component
- **<app>.component.css (or .scss):** stylesheet for styling component

@Component decorator binds them together to work as one component. For enterprise applications, we can have more associated files like <app>.model.ts for holding application models and <app>.service.ts for handling HTTP requests and computing common business logic, but they will not be part of @Component rather logical grouping.

> **Question: Can there be multiple roots of the Angular application component tree or multiple component trees in one Angular application?**

C# analogy: In the C# Windows Form context, we can imagine Forms as a component that has .designer.cs + form.cs files with one-to-one mapping in WPF, consider the mapping between .xaml file and code behind .cs file.

Inspecting @Component Metadata

- **selector**: This property defines a unique identifier for Component. The selector placed in the HTML file of the Angular component shall render its component's HTML. Open app.component.ts file and observe "selector" property. Now open index.html file of our project and observe <app-root></app-root> tag in <body> section. Now we can understand when we ran our application why did we see app.component.html rendered in the browser instead of <app-root> tag. Note that when building enterprise-level applications, most of the feature components are rendered through routing. In that context, the selector doesn't play any role as the component is rendered by the matching route.

- **templateUrl**: These property maps TypeScript class to associated HTML. templateUrl takes an HTML file name, which should be associated with Component. When the browser finds "selector" for component (for example, <app-root></app-root>), it will try to put all content of templateUrl in place of the selector. If templateUrl HTML contains any data-binding syntax (for example, Welcome to {{ title }}!), then associated TypeScript class (AppComponent) will be evaluated to resolve it.

> **C# analogy:** In the C# Windows Form, we have form.designer.cs and form.cs files. In designer.cs file, we put visual appearance code and in form.cs file, we keep our business logic. Similarly, in template/templateUrl HTML file, we will keep our visual code and <app>.component.ts file, we will keep our business logic code. In C#, we have partial class concepts which glue .designer.cs and .cs file, but in TypeScript, we do not have partial classes; hence we specify the glue between templateUrl <app>.component.html and <app>.component.ts file using @Component decorator's metadata object.

- **template**: This property is similar to templateUrl but takes inline HTML code as a string rather than the file name. If our component has minimal HTML code, then we can choose to provide it template property rather than creating a new HTML file. As per @Component decorator rule, we should either provide templateUrl or template, but not both. What if we define both? Give it a try!

- **styleUrls**: This property accepts an array of strings containing the name of stylesheet files. We can provide .css or .scss stylesheet files. These stylesheets will be applied only to the current Component by default. We can change how styles should be applied by encapsulation property.

- **styles**: This property accepts an array of strings containing inline stylesheets.

There are other properties of NgModule and Component decorator metadata objects, which we will see in upcoming chapters as and when required.

Introduction to Basic Data Bindings

In essence, data binding is passing data between the component's HTML and TypeScript classes. Based on flow data, there are different types of data bindings:

Types of Data Bindings

- **One way data binding:** The one-way data binding can be specified by template syntax of {{expression}}. The expression can be a member variable, function call, or any valid TypeScript expression. Whenever the browser encounters this syntax, it tries to resolve the expression from its associated TypeScript class. In our new project, we have {{title}} expression defined in `app.component.html` file and title member variable defined in `app.component.ts` file, which holds default string "party-invite". Therefore browser is displaying "**Welcome to party-invite!**" as an output for the expression "`Welcome to {{ title }}!`". Note that whenever the value of "`expression`" will be changed by component class, its new value will be rendered in the browser. The direction of data flow in one-way data binding is from TypeScript class to associated HTML.

- **Event binding:** A web application should be responsive. It should react to user action(s) and keep him engaged with the interface. User engagement is specifically handled by event handling. It can be any standard event like button click, mouse move, or custom Angular component's event for a specific task. Event handling is a way of invoking TypeScript class function as a response to user interaction in HTML control(s). For example, if a user presses the **Submit** button on the sign-up form, we would like to initiate the sign-up process in the TypeScript code. The direction of the data flow of in event-binding is from HTML to associated TypeScript class.

- **Two-way data binding:** In two-way data binding, the value can be updated either by the user in HTML or by TypeScript class. `[(ngModel)]` provides a two way data-binding syntax (the syntax `[()]` is also called as **banana-in-the-box).** There is no two-way data binding support in Angular implementation. It was in AngularJs 1.x, which lead to cyclic dependencies and memory leaks. Thus, in newer Angular, they do not have two-way data bindings. Yet, we can get two-way data binding feature using [(ngModel)] directive, which can be imported from "`FormsModule`". It is combination of one-way data binding [ngModel] and event binding (ngModelChange) hence the Banana-in-the-box syntax `[(ngModel)]`. Note that, "`ngModel`" directive is exported by "`FormsModule`" hence one must import this module before using "`ngModel`".

Introduction to NgIf, NgFor, and ngForm directives

While designing an Angular application's HTML layout, it is common to handle some logical conditions to render view. For example, displaying an error message if an invalid email address is provided or duplicate username is given, and so on. For such HTML basic logical operations, Angular provides few directives amongst them; we will learn NgIf and NgFor in this section.

What is NgIf?

In essence, NgIf is an "if" condition in HTML whose true/false value get evaluated by an expression. This expression can refer to either an HTML element or an associated

TypeScript class. If NgIf evaluates to true, then its child HTML element(s) will be part of rendered DOM; otherwise, it will not be. The question we might think is if I have "if" condition, then can I have an "else" block as well? Well, the answer is yes! We can define "else" local references on the HTML section.

What is NgFor?

As its name suggests, NgFor is like a "for" loop rendering HTML elements per iteration. The collection can be defined in TypeScript class, and for each element in that collection, any HTML element can be rendered. NgFor creates some local variables at runtime like "index," which can be used for advanced processing.

> **Note: NgIf and NgFor directives are exported from @CommonModule. Thus one should import this module before using these directives, right? Well, Angular already import @CommonModule for us in @NgModule; hence we do not need to import it again.**

What is ngForm?

We might be familiar with HTML "Form" object, which encapsulates logically related web controls in a single group. It also exposes a few methods and properties for handling web forms. Angular provides "ngForm" directives which enrich native "Form" object with extra methods and properties so that they can be handled in Angular application.

Building Party-Invite Sign-up form

We have got some basic understanding of Angular construct, which we will need to build our "Party-Invite" sign-up form. Our goal is to build a sign-up form with few web controls and a submit button. After the user has entered details and clicks on the **Submit** button, we will log sign-up details in the browser's console and show the user a success message. For the sake of simplicity and focus on core features, we are not going to use any CSS libraries like Google Material Design or Twitter Bootstrap. Our form might not look fancy, but it will work. In the upcoming chapters, we will see how to integrate CSS libraries for building beautiful applications.

- **Clear auto-generated code:** When we create a new Angular project, the Angular CLI generate The auto- default HTML in app.component.html file. Let's remove that code and write our own HTML, as shown in *Figure 3.4:*

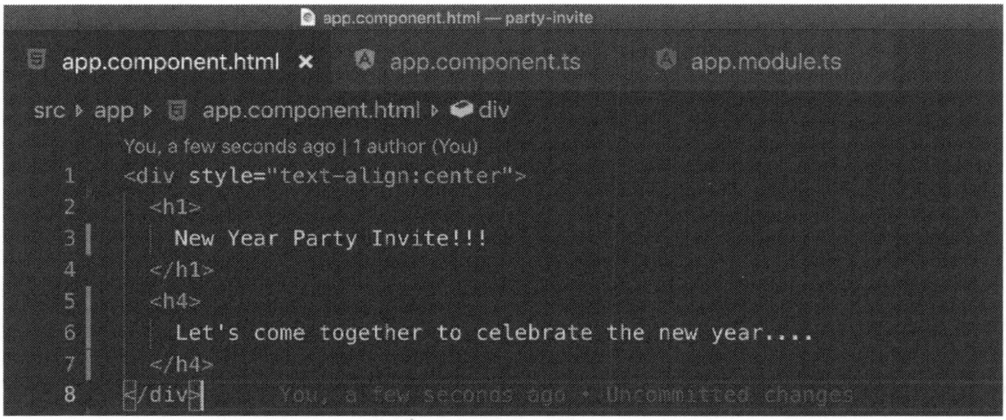

```
app.component.html — party-invite

app.component.html  ✕      app.component.ts        app.module.ts

src ▸ app ▸  app.component.html ▸  div
        You, a few seconds ago | 1 author (You)
    1   <div style="text-align:center">
    2     <h1>
    3       New Year Party Invite!!!
    4     </h1>
    5     <h4>
    6       Let's come together to celebrate the new year....
    7     </h4>
    8   </div>                You, a few seconds ago • Uncommitted changes
```

Figure 3.4: Updated app.component.html file

- **Define Model class:** Let's create a new file called "party-invite.model. ts" inside the "src/app" folder. This will be our "PartInviteModel" class to hold all the fields of sign-up form. *Figure 3.5* shows the member of our model class.

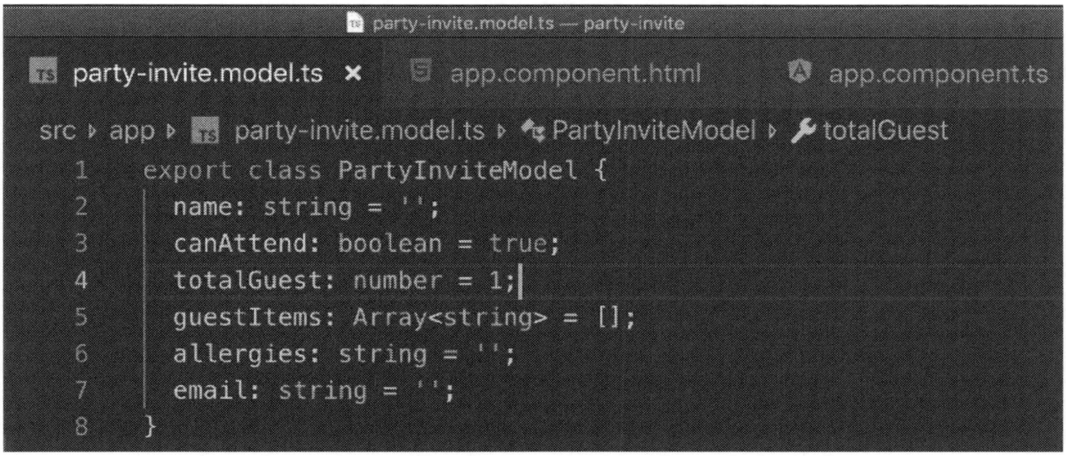

```
party-invite.model.ts — party-invite

party-invite.model.ts  ✕      app.component.html        app.component.ts

src ▸ app ▸  party-invite.model.ts ▸  PartyInviteModel ▸  totalGuest
    1   export class PartyInviteModel {
    2     name: string = '';
    3     canAttend: boolean = true;
    4     totalGuest: number = 1;
    5     guestItems: Array<string> = [];
    6     allergies: string = '';
    7     email: string = '';
    8   }
```

Figure 3.5: PartyInviteModel class definition

- **Declare PartyInviteModel member in AppComponent:** Let's declare a member variable in the AppComponent class of type PartyInviteModel so that we can use data-binding on PartyInviteModel's members in app.component.html file. To declare a member, we need first to import "party-invite.model" file. Observe the line number 2 in *Figure 3.6*. While importing classes from other TypeScript files, we should not mention the ".ts" extension in the "import" statement. This is a common pitfall while learning Angular. Once imported, we can declare a new member variable of type PartyInviteModel, as shown in line number 10 of *Figure 3.6*. Make sure to initialize member variable in the "ngOnInit()" function to avoid any null reference exception at runtime, as shown in line number 15 of *Figure 3.6*. As we have noticed, how "model" member is accessed in "ngOnInit()" because TypeScript class member functions can access member variables using "this" keyword.

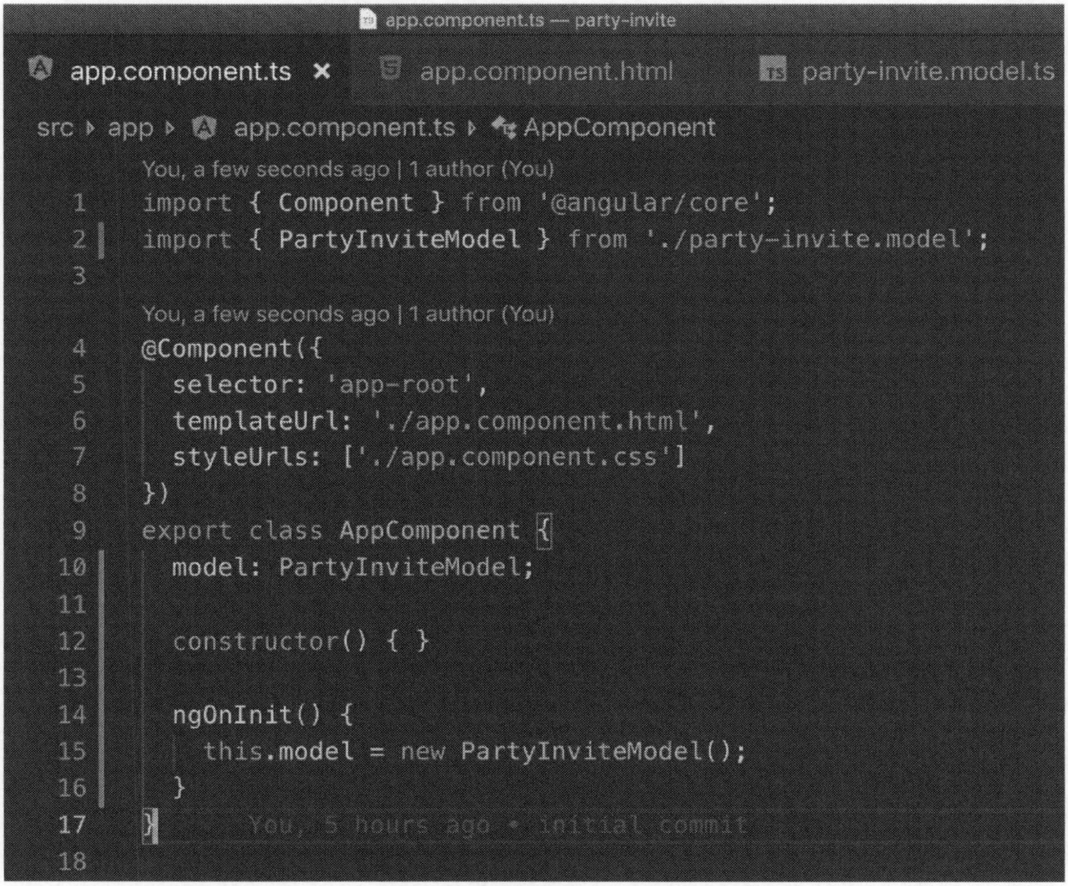

```typescript
app.component.ts — party-invite

 app.component.ts  ×      app.component.html          party-invite.model.ts

src ▸ app ▸  app.component.ts ▸  AppComponent
      You, a few seconds ago | 1 author (You)
  1   import { Component } from '@angular/core';
  2   import { PartyInviteModel } from './party-invite.model';
  3
      You, a few seconds ago | 1 author (You)
  4   @Component({
  5     selector: 'app-root',
  6     templateUrl: './app.component.html',
  7     styleUrls: ['./app.component.css']
  8   })
  9   export class AppComponent {
 10     model: PartyInviteModel;
 11
 12     constructor() { }
 13
 14     ngOnInit() {
 15       this.model = new PartyInviteModel();
 16     }
 17   }          You, 5 hours ago • initial commit
 18
```

Figure 3.6: Declaring PartyInviteModel member variable in AppComponent

- **Ask for the guest's name**: We will ask the user to enter the guest's name in the text field. So let's update app.component.html, as shown in *Figure 3.7*. If we observe line number 15 in *Figure 3.7*, we can find usage of [(ngModel)] - two-way data binding with **PartyInviteModel's** "name" member:

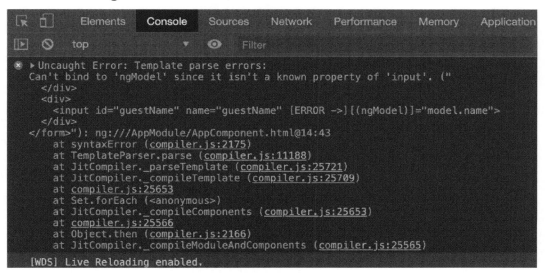

```
app.component.html — party-invite
app.component.html  ✕    app.component.ts    party-invite.model.ts

src ▸ app ▸  app.component.html ▸  form
  9
 10    <form ngForm="signUpForm">              You, a few seconds ago • Uncommitted
 11      <div>
 12        <label for="guestName">What is your name?</label>
 13      </div>
 14      <div>
 15        <input id="guestName" name="guestName" [(ngModel)]="model.name">
 16      </div>
 17    </form>
```

Figure 3.7: *HTML for entering the guest name in app.component.html*

- **Verify Output:** Let's save these changes and run **ng serve - -open** if it is not already running and observe the browser output. If we see a blank page in the browser, then go to the browser's "**Developer Tools → Console**" and observe the error, if any. In *Figure 3.8*, we can see there is an error complaining about "ngModel" not found:

```
⬚  ⬚        Elements   Console   Sources   Network   Performance   Memory   Application
▷  ⊘   top              ▼   ⊙   Filter
⊗ ▸ Uncaught Error: Template parse errors:
   Can't bind to 'ngModel' since it isn't a known property of 'input'. ("
     </div>
     <div>
       <input id="guestName" name="guestName" [ERROR ->][(ngModel)]="model.name">
     </div>
   </form>"): ng:///AppModule/AppComponent.html@14:43
       at syntaxError (compiler.js:2175)
       at TemplateParser.parse (compiler.js:11188)
       at JitCompiler._parseTemplate (compiler.js:25721)
       at JitCompiler._compileTemplate (compiler.js:25709)
       at compiler.js:25653
       at Set.forEach (<anonymous>)
       at JitCompiler._compileComponents (compiler.js:25653)
       at compiler.js:25566
       at Object.then (compiler.js:2166)
       at JitCompiler._compileModuleAndComponents (compiler.js:25565)
[WDS] Live Reloading enabled.
```

Figure 3.8: *Browser's console error for ngModel not found*

- **Fix ngModel error:** As stated in the data binding section, **NgModel** is exported from **FormsModule**. Hence we will import this module into AppModule, as shown in *Figure 3.9*. Make sure to declare "**FormsModule**" inside the "import" property of **@NgModule** decorator and not just import the statement of "FormsModule". In C#, if we just import other namespaces by "using" statement, it resolves the classes, but in Angular, we must specify it "import" property:

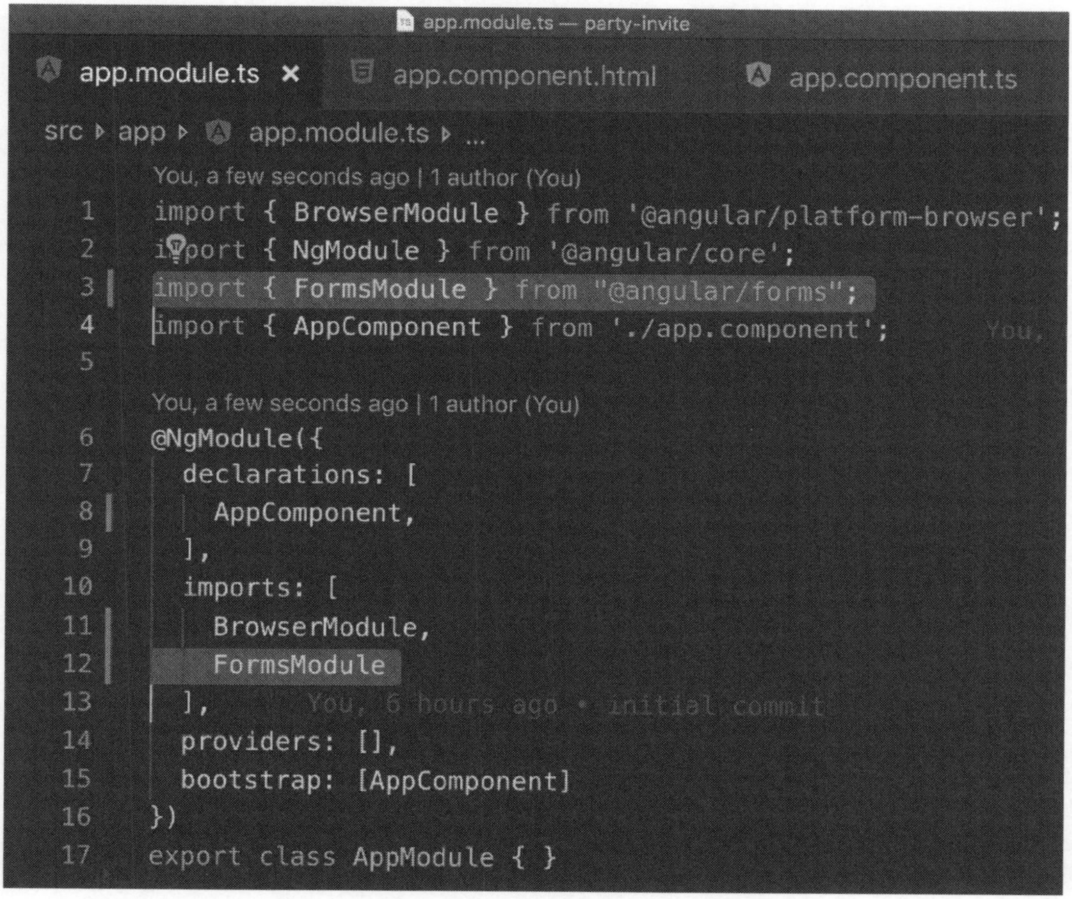

```
app.module.ts — party-invite

app.module.ts ✕       app.component.html       app.component.ts

src ▸ app ▸ app.module.ts ▸ ...
      You, a few seconds ago | 1 author (You)
1     import { BrowserModule } from '@angular/platform-browser';
2     import { NgModule } from '@angular/core';
3     import { FormsModule } from "@angular/forms";
4     import { AppComponent } from './app.component';        You,
5
      You, a few seconds ago | 1 author (You)
6     @NgModule({
7       declarations: [
8         AppComponent,
9       ],
10      imports: [
11        BrowserModule,
12        FormsModule
13      ],        You, 6 hours ago • initial commit
14      providers: [],
15      bootstrap: [AppComponent]
16    })
17    export class AppModule { }
```

Figure 3.9: *Importing FormsModule into AppModule*

- **Verify Output:** Once `FormsModule` is imported, save the changes and verify the output in the browser assuming the "**ng serve**" command is running. We should see the output similar to *Figure 3.10:*

Figure 3.10: Browser output in mobile view mode for asking the guest name

- **Ask if the guest can attend:** Let's ask the user for a presence at the party. We will define two radio boxes to ask the user's presence. We will use two-way data binding to record the user's response. *Figure 3.11* shows the updated HTML of `app.component.ts`. On line number 22 and 26, we are doing data-binding of "`model.canAttend`" with radio input's "`value`". Based on the user's selection, "`model.canAttend`" will contain either "`true`" or "`false`" value:

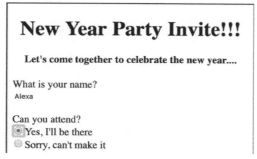

Figure 3.11: Updated app.component.html for recording guest present at the party

- **Verify output:** Save the changes done in `app.component.html` and verify output in the browser. Enter the guest's name again as it will get lost whenever page refreshes. Select one of the radio boxes. The output should look similar to *Figure 3.12*.

New Year Party Invite!!!

Let's come together to celebrate the new year....

What is your name?
Alexa

Can you attend?
◉ Yes, I'll be there
◯ Sorry, can't make it

Figure 3.12: Output of user selection ab]out presence at the party

- **Ask guests about accompanying guests:** The next step is to ask the user if there are any other accompanying guests we can expect. Let's update our `app.component.html` for taking user input in the "number" text field and have two-way data binding in the "`model.totalGuest`" field, as shown in *Figure 3.13*. To keep the focus on current changes, *Figure 3.13* captures only relevant code snippets from `app.component.html`:

```
31      <br>          You, a few seconds ago • Uncommitted changes
32      <div>
33        <label for="">How many of you are attending?</label>
34      </div>
35      <div>
36        <input type="number" [(ngModel)]="model.totalGuest">
37      </div>
```

Figure 3.13: Updated app.component.html to get a total number of accompanying guests

- **Verify output:** Save the changes and verify output in a browser. Enter guest name, select presence, and enter accompanying guest as shown in *Figure 3.14:*

Figure 3.14: Capture total number of accompanying guests

- **Ask the user about what can be expected at the party—HTML changes**: Our guests are generous enough and said they would bring some items at the party. Let's ask the guests what we can expect from them. Let's update `app.component.html` for rendering checkboxes for each dish guest can bring. *Figure 3.15* displays updated `app.component.html`. On line number 44, we are using "ngFor" loop for rendering <input> tags in HTML. Based on a total number of elements in the collection "menuDishes", the number of checkboxes will be rendered in the browser. <input> tag on line number 45 has interesting data binding. First [value]= "dish" expression binds the "value" field of <input> with loop variable "dish" which will iterate through all values of "menuDishes". Then (change) = "updateBasket($event, dish)" is event binding. Whenever user check/uncheck <input>, updateBasket() function will be called with two parameters. The first parameter we are passing is "$event" which is available at runtime by DOM object, which represents target control; in this case, <input>. The second parameter is "dish" which is a loop variable holding the selected value of <input>. Finally, on line number 46, we are using interpolation {{dish}} syntax to render the "dish" name in the browser:

```
39    <br>
40    <div>
41      <label for="">What will you be bringing?</label>
42    </div>
43    <div>
44      <div *ngFor="let dish of menuDishes">
45        <input type="checkbox" [value]="dish" (change)="updateBasket($event, dish)">
46        {{dish}}
47      </div>
48    </div>
```

Figure 3.15: *Updated app.component.html for displaying a list of dishes guest can bring at party*

- **Ask the user about what can be expected at the party—TypeScript changes:** In *Figure 3.15*, we are using the "**menuDishes**" collection for rendering **<input>** fields. We need to create this collection in our TypeScript class and set some values. Then we need to define the "**updateBasket()**" function, which will be invoked whenever **<input>** control fires (change) event. *Figure 3.16* shows the updated **app.component.ts** file. Observe code on line number 26 in *Figure 3.16*, how we are making use of **$event** to check if **<input>** field is checked/unchecked. Based on the result, we are adding/ removing the item to/from "**model.guestItems**" list:

```
app.component.ts ×        app.component.html        app.module.ts

src ▸ app ▸ app.component.ts ▸ AppComponent ▸ updateBasket
4    @Component({
5      selector: 'app-root',
6      templateUrl: './app.component.html',
7      styleUrls: ['./app.component.css']
8    })
9    export class AppComponent {
10     model: PartyInviteModel;
11     menuDishes: Array<string> = [];
12
13     constructor() { }
14
15     ngOnInit() {
16       this.model = new PartyInviteModel();
17
18       this.menuDishes.push('Mains');
19       this.menuDishes.push('Salad');
20       this.menuDishes.push('Dessert');
21       this.menuDishes.push('Drinks');
22       this.menuDishes.push('Sides/Appetizers');
23     }
24
25     updateBasket($event: any, dish: string) {
26       if ($event.target.checked) {
27         this.model.guestItems.push(dish);
28       }
29       else {
30         const index = this.model.guestItems.indexOf(dish);
31         this.model.guestItems.splice(index, 1);
32       }
33     }
34   }
```

Figure 3.16: *Updated app.component.ts for displaying a list of dishes guest can bring at party*

- **Verify output:** Save the changes in both app.component.ts and app. component.html files and observe the output in the browser. It should be similar to Figure 3.17:

Figure 3.17: *Updated party-invite form asking guest what they would like to bring*

- **Submit the form—HTML:** We have got a basic response from our guests, and now it is time to submit a response to our system. For the sake of simplicity, we will not send the response to any web server but just print in the browser's console window. Let's update `app.component.html` for adding the submit button, as shown in *Figure 3.18*. Observe the line number 10 of *Figure 3.18* which declares event binding - `(ngSubmit)= "submitForm()"`. `ngSubmit` event gets fired when the form is `submitted` by a button of type "submit" which we have declared on line number 52. Marking a button of type "submit" also allow the user to submit the form by pressing the "*Enter*" key.

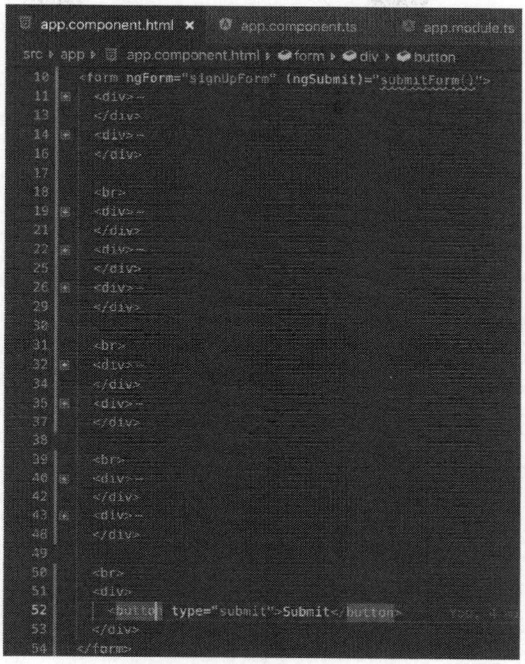

Figure 3.18: *Adding the Submit button and ngSubmit event in app.component.html*

- **Submit the form—TypeScript:** Let's write the "**submitForm()**" method, which just prints the "**model**" object into the browser console, as shown in *Figure 3.19:*

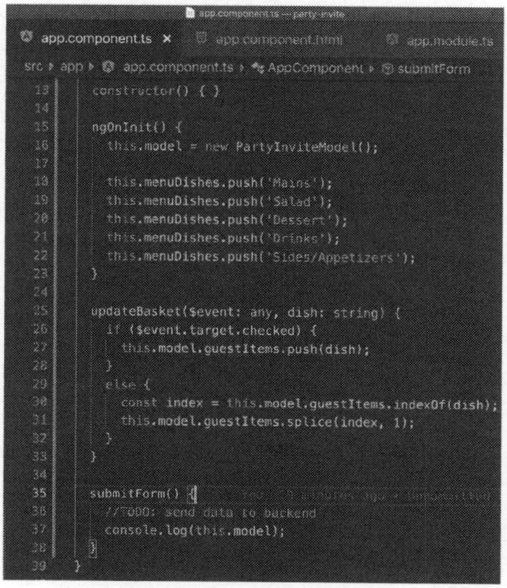

Figure 3.19: *Adding a Submit button and ngSubmit event in app.component.html*

- **Show success message—HTML:** Once the guest has submitted the form, let's display a message to the user and hide the sign-up form. We will keep the message in a label which will be shown only when the user submits the form. Line number 10 in *Figure 3.20* shows the use of "ngIf," which adds <h4> element in DOM only if "isFormSubmitted" is set to "true". Line number 14 in *Figure 3.20* does reverse, which shows form only if "isFormsSubmitted" is false:

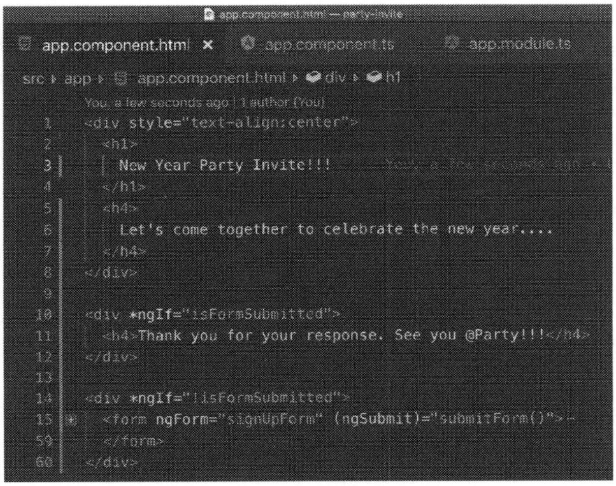

Figure 3.20: *app.component.html changes for showing success message and hiding form once the form is submitted*

- **Show success message—TypeScript:** Let's declare a member field "isFormSubmitted" with default value false in app.component.ts file. When the user submits the form, the "submitForm()" function gets called. Hence let's set "isFormsubmitted" to true in this function as shown in line number 37 in *Figure 3.21:*

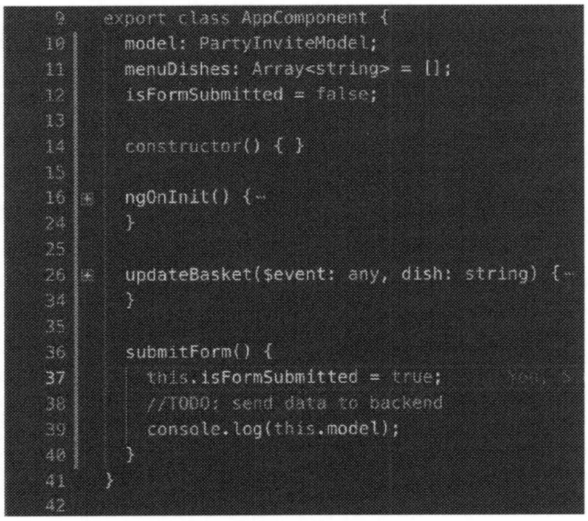

Figure 3.21: *app.component.ts changes for setting "isFormSubmitted" value*

- **Verify output:** Save the changes and observe the browser. Fill in the sign-up form and then click on the **Submit** button or press *Enter* key. The browser should show a success message, and the form should get hidden. Also, the browser's console shall print `PartyInviteModel` in JSON format, as shown in *Figure 3.22*:

Figure 3.22: *Success message shown in the browser after the "Submit" button is pressed*

Production Deployment

Our basic party invite sign-up form is ready to be deployed. Though we are not consuming any web services or real business logic, we will briefly learn how to create a production-ready distribution package.

1. Stop running **"ng serve"** command, if any.

2. Run **"ng build - -prod"** command in the project directory.

3. Step 2 will create a **"dist/party-invite"** project inside the project directory.

This is plain HTML website output, which has no dependency on the angular package(s) or `node_modules`. All required packages and dependencies are compiled into respective JavaScript files and placed inside the build project by the **"ng build"** command. *Figure 3.23* shows the content of the "dist/party-invite" folder.

4. Copy the "dist/party-invite" folder and put into our web server or follow standard web site deployment procedure:

Figure 3.23: Production build folder generated by "ng build - -prod" command

Angular Lifecycle Events

Every Angular application has a lifecycle for each Component and NgModule. A lifecycle event is an event fired during a specific stage of Angular application execution. These lifecycle events are exported by angular core module interfaces, which should be implemented by the respective Component/Module. But few lifecycle events can be implemented without the explicit implementation of the interface(s), and for some, we have to. For a typical Angular Component, lifecycle hooks are as the following list:

- **Constructor**: A `Constructor` function TypeScript concept and not explicit Angular lifecycle hook. The `Constructor` is the first function that gets executed when a Component gets created. It is a similar concept to C# and Java, where `Constructor`.

- **ngOnChanges:** This lifecycle event is executed immediately after `Constructor`. This function gets executed when Angular data-bindings get sets or reset input properties defined by `@Input decorator.`

- **ngOnInit:** This lifecycle event is fired after `Constructor` is called. This is an ideal place to initialize our data-bound members, fetching data from HTTP resources, setting default values, and so on. In the C# Windows Form, we have a `Form_Load` event similar to `ngOnInit()`.

- **ngDoCheck**: This lifecycle event gets called every time change detection cycle runs. For example, if we start typing in the textbox, then for each keydown event, the `ngDoCheck` event will be executed. Be very careful about handling this lifecycle function. If misused, it will drastically affect application performance as for every change detection, there will be code block executed, and sometimes application may get hang or crash. In the C# Windows Form, we have Form_Paint function, which gets executed every time Control gets repainted, similar to the **ngDoCheck()** event.

- **ngAfterContentInit**: This lifecycle event is called only once when Angular projects external content into Component's view. This event handler is generally used for loading and initializing the third-party JavaScript libraries and data sets, for example, Chart.js for displaying charts in application.

- **ngAfterContentChecked**: This lifecycle event is called when Angular checks the content of projected into Component. This is called every time the ngDoCheck() event handler is called. This can be used to put some validation or business logic for validating external content.

- **ngAfterViewInit**: Once Component's view is initialized, this event handler gets called once after ngAfterContentChecked() event.

- **ngAfterViewChecked**: This event handler is called every time **ngAfterContentChecked()** is called and when Angular checks Component's view.

- **ngOnDestroy**: This event handler is like a destructor in C# and Java. It is called by Angular before destroying Component. This is the right place to clean-up components and avoids memory leaks, for example, unsubscribing from events and observables, and so on.

> **Note: Most of the time we will use ngOnInit(), ngAfterViewInit() and ngOnDestroy() lifecycle events.**

Debugging Angular Application

As a web developer debugging is an essential task, one performs regularly. In Angular, we can do debugging in various ways. Here is the list of few options:

- **debugger**: If we are using Visual Studio Code IDE, then we can configure to put a breakpoint at design time and debug it whenever the application execution context reaches to debug point. But it is a bit tedious and complex process. A simple way is to put the "**debugger;**" statement in our TypeScript code, and whenever this statement gets executed, the browser will show the **Sources** tab in "**Developer tools**" and debug session gets initialized from "debugger" statement. Then we can Step in, Step Out, Resume debugging. We can also add a watch, check local variables, and so on. We can see how debugging looks like in the browser, as shown in *Figure 3.24:*

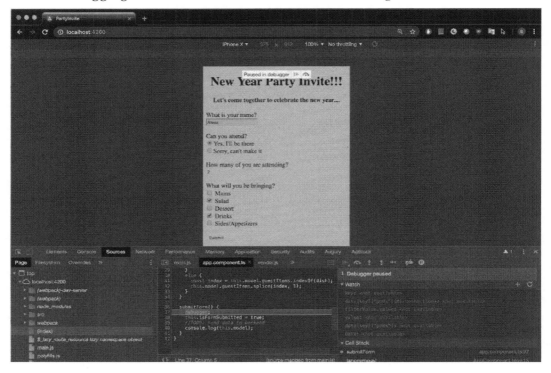

Figure 3.24: Debugging Angular application in the browser

- **console.log:** This is one of the simplest ways of debugging to see the value of the variable during runtime if we do not want to do debugging. But make sure we remove all our debug related **console.log()** message before building application for the Production environment.

- **Evaluate the expression in browser's console during debugging:** During debugging, we can evaluate expressions and check/update values of variables.

Conclusion

In this chapter, we got introduced with NgModule and Component decorators along with their basic metadata properties. We also learned about basic data bindings like one-way binding, event binding, and two-way data binding with the help of [(ngModel)]. Then we learned about conditional **NgIf** construct for HTML DOM manipulation, **NgFor** for repeating HTML element based on the collection, and how to use **NgForm** for enriching native **<form> tag**. With basic knowledge of Angular, we started building the **"Party-Invite"** sign-up form and created its deployment-ready distribution. Understanding the Angular lifecycle event is very important as it gives us exceptional control over application flow. We learned about various ways of how to do debugging of Angular application.

In the next chapter, we shall dive deep into Data bindings.

Questions

1. Can more than one NgModule decorator have "bootstrap" property?

2. Can Component have multiple HTML files associated with it?

3. What will happen if there are multiple Components with the same "selector" value?

4. Can we define Component with empty HTML?

5. Can we do data binding to HTML attribute value? If yes, how?

6. What will happen if the data-bound property is null/undefined at runtime?

7. If there is a need for nested `NgIf` in HTML, which other directives we can use for simplicity?

8. How to get the current "index" of `NgFor` iteration?

9. Extend our Party-Invite sign-up form for below requirements

   a. Guest name is mandatory

   b. Total accompanying guest should not be in negative

   c. Show error message if there is any validation error

   d. Disable the **Submit** button if there is any validation error on the form

10. Build a simple "TODO" list application in Angular.

CHAPTER 4
Data Binding and Pipes

In this chapter, we will cover data binding concepts, various types of data binding syntax, different template expressions, binding targets, how to do data binding for HTML attribute, CSS class, and CSS style fields. After that, we will learn about Angular Pipes, a beneficial data transformation technique for the presentation layer, various types of Pipes, and how to write custom Pipe based on project requirements.

Structure

- Introduction to Data Binding
- One-way Data Binding – Interpolation – Data Source to View
- One-way Data Binding – Event Binding – View to Data Source
- HTML Element Data Binding – Local Reference
- Two-way Data Binding
- HTML Element's Property Binding
- Attribute Data Binding
- CSS Class Data Binding
- Style Binding
- NgClass Binding
- Introduction to Pipes

- Generating Custom Pipe
- Passing Parameters to Pipe
- Pure and Impure Pipes
- List of Built-in Pipes
- Conclusion

Objective

The objective of this chapter is to cover data binding concepts and see how it reassemble with different data binding concepts from Windows Forms, WPF, ASP. NET Web page bindings. Also, Angular pipes concepts will be covered and how they match with IValueConverters and IMultiValueConverter concepts from WPF. After reading this chapter, the reader should be able to build a data-rich web application with data binding and pipe techniques.

Introduction to Data Binding

The **Model-View-Controller (MVC)** and **Model-View-ViewModel (MVVM)** design principles suggest us to segregate View from its Controller/ViewModel. View's responsibility is to just display data without manipulating any business logic, and Controller's responsibility is to fetch data from some source(s) like APIs/Database and provide it to View for display. Data bindings provide a means to bridge data passing between View and Controller. In data binding, an object is bound between View and Controller and based on the type of data binding, the flow of data value is determined. If it is One-way data-binding from Controller to View, then whenever there is a change in object value, View will be updated for a new value. If it is two-way data binding, then if the user changes the value of the object in View, the object's value be updated in Controller. Based on business requirements, we can choose which type of data binding we want to implement. In a nutshell, data binding is passing data back and forth between View and Model, that is, in Angular terms HTML to TypeScript class.

In terms of .NET, data binding is available in Windows Forms, WPF, ASP.NET MVC. In Windows Forms, we get BindingSource class where we can specify DataSource property and DataBindings property for UI component to specify which object to bound with. It is not that sophisticated as in WPF; WPF implements data binding very well and with ease of use. Hence, we will be using WPF references whenever required for data binding.

One-way Data Binding – Interpolation – Data Source to View

Let's consider we are building shopping cart data entry form using Angular. One of the requirements is to show total count of items in cart on **Checkout** page. That means we want to keep updating value of totalItems variable from @Component in our template. This is One-way data binding use case. The simplest implementation of one-way data binding is Interpolation. *Code 4.1* shows declaration of totalItem variable:

```
@Component({
          selector: 'app-root',
          templateUrl: './app.component.html',
          styleUrls: ['./app.component.css']
})
export class AppComponent {
          title = 'Shopping Cart';
          totalItems: number;

}
```

Code 4.1: app.component.ts – declaration of totalItems variable

Code 4.2 shows syntax of interpolation in HTML file:

```
    <div>
          Total items: {{totalItems}}
    </div>
```

Code 4.2: app.component.html – interpolation/One-way data binding of totalItems

WPF Concepts: In WPF, Binding Source has a binding property that is bound to Binding Target with Dependency Property through Binding Object, as shown in *Figure 4.1*. We can map the Component class as a Binding Source and member variable as Binding Source. Then Component's associated HTML page will be Binding Target, and interpolation syntax will be Binding Dependency property (well not precisely dependency property though).

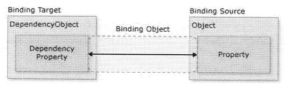

Figure 4.1: WPF data binding model.
Source: *https://docs.microsoft.com/en-us/dotnet/framework/wpf/data/data-binding-overview*

> **Note that double curly braces are called a template expression and we can put any valid expression there to display its result. For example we can put <div> Sum: {{ 10 + 20 }} </div> and in output we will see result as 30. Function call is also a valid expression hence we can call member function which will return value to be displayed for example, <div> Function result: {{ someFunction() }}.**

One-way Data Binding – Event Binding – View to Data Source

In WPF, we can have one-way data-binding from View Target to Data Source using `OneWayToSource` property. In Angular, we can have similar kinds of data binding for event listeners but not actual property to data source binding. We can bind View component's events to Component's method as an event handler; hence whenever the user raises an event on View, respective Component's method will be invoked, as shown in *Code 4.3*. If we run this program and click on the **"Add to Cart"** button, then an alert box will be shown. As we have not used the `selectedItem` variable yet, we will see **undefined is added to the cart!** Message. We can access the default event argument object by passing the $event object in HTML and handle in the component class. We will extend the application as we go further and will use the `selectedItem` variable.

```
<div style="text-align:center">
        <h1>
                Welcome to {{ title }}!
        </h1>
</div>


    <div>
        Total items: {{totalItems}}
    </div>


    <div>
        <button (click)="addToCart()">Add to Cart</button>
    </div>
```

Code 4.3: app.component.html – button click event binding with the component's method

In TypeScript class, we need to define a function for responding to the event as shown in *Code 4.4:*

```
@Component({
          selector: 'app-root',
          templateUrl: './app.component.html',
          styleUrls: ['./app.component.css']
})
export class AppComponent {

          title = 'Shopping Cart';
          totalItems: number;

          selectedItem: string;

          addToCart() {
                alert(`${this.selectedItem} is added to cart!`);
          }

}
```

Code 4.4: app.component.ts – button click event handler method

> **Note: There is one-to-one binding between <app>.component.ts and <app>. component.html. Hence, we can only bind method(s) as an event handler in HTML, which is present in our component class. If we try to bind some global functions, then we will get an error.**

HTML Element Data Binding – Local Reference

Sometimes we would like to refer local HTML tags and use its properties in the same HTML page. In such a use case, we can use the Local HTML reference variable declared with symbol `#variableName`. *Code 4.5* shows an example of how we can get initial value of `<input>` HTML element and show in `<span>` element. The # character used for the prefix of local reference in HTML. But we cannot use local references in TypeScript class. We need to use a special decorator called `@ViewChild()` if we want directly access the HTML component in TypeScript. In JavaScript or jQuery, we used to define name or id field to HTML component, and inside JavaScript function, we used to get reference using CSS selector. Since Angular uses Shadow DOM, we shouldn't use direct access to HTML reference but should use `@ViewChild()` like decorators:

```
<div>
        <input #quantity [value]="1">
        <span>Quantity: {{quantity.value}}</span>
</div>
```

Code 4.5: app.component.html – local HTML reference

In WPF, we do not have to create a separate local reference to control. We can use Binding with ElementName, which is the Name of target control and Path, which is the name of the property we want to bind.

Two-way Data Binding

In two-way data binding, updates propagate from both directions—View to Component and Component to View. If the bounded value gets updated by some calculation or new data fetched from the server, then View will refresh itself and display the new value. If the user update value in View, then the component will update the bounded value in the member variable. This is the most common type of data binding used while building an Angular application. *Code 4.6* shows how two-way data binding is implemented. Note the `[(ngModel)]` attribute added to `<input>` tag. It is not a standard HTML attribute. If we run the application just by adding this code snippet, we will get an error as the browser doesn't know how to process `[(ngModel)]` attribute. Hence we will have to import an Angular module called FormsModule from `@angular/forms` package in `app.module.ts` file:

```
<div>
        <div>
                Customer Name: <input type="text"
[(ngModel)]="customerName">
        </div>
</div>
```

Code 4.6: app.component.ts – two-way data binding implemented using [(ngModel)] syntax

Code 4.7 shows how to import `FormsModule` into `AppModule` module:

```
import { BrowserModule } from '@angular/platform-browser';
import { NgModule } from '@angular/core';
import { FormsModule } from "@angular/forms";
```

```
import { AppComponent } from './app.component';


@NgModule({
        declarations: [AppComponent],
        imports: [
                BrowserModule,
                FormsModule
        ],
        bootstrap: [AppComponent]
})
export class AppModule { }
```

Code 4.7: app.module.ts – importing FormsModule from @angular/forms package

Angular doesn't implement two-way data binding underneath, unlike AngularJs, which has causes memory leaks. The [()] syntax is called a "**banana in a box**," and it's a combination of two bindings as follows:

- **One-way data-binding from component to view–[ngModel]:**

  This data binding updates value from the bounded variable of a component in HTML whenever it is updated in component

- **One-way data-binding from view to component–(ngModelChange):**

  This data binding updates value from view to component whenever a value is changed by raising an event.

This concept can be further extended when we want to implement our own custom two-way binding properties for the component. We will cover it during @Input() and @Output() decorators in upcoming chapters.

HTML Element's Property Binding

We can bind a typical HTML element's property to the component's member variable. For example, we can control the **"disabled"** property of an HTML button control to enable and disable button state based on bound variable value. In our case, we will disable the **Add to Cart** button unless the user selects one of the radio buttons options. *Code 4.8* shows how to set a disabled property of a button with the component member. The "! selectedItem" expression returns true as nothing is selected, and when the user selects one of the radio buttons, then selectedItem gets value, and the expression returns false, making button enabled.

```
<div>
  <h4>List of mobiles: </h4>
</div>
<ul *ngFor="let item of allItems">
  <input type="radio" name="mobileItem" [value]="selectedItem"
(click)="updateSelection(item)">
  {{item}}
</ul>
<div>
  Selected mobile: {{selectedItem}}
</div>
<div>
  Total items: {{cart.length}}
</div>
<div>
  <button (click)="addToCart()" [disabled]="!selectedItem">Add to Cart</
button>
</div>
```

Code 4.8: *app.component.html – binding disabled property to selectedItem member variable*

Figure 4.2 shows how the output looks like when the application loads the first time in the browser:

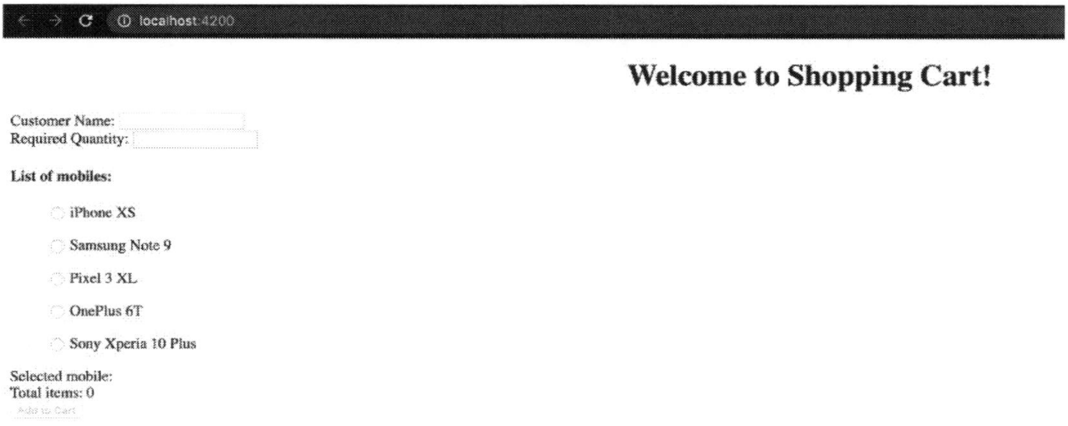

Figure 4.2: *Add to Cart button disabled as none of the radio boxes are selected*

And *Figure 4.3* shows the output of the shopping cart with the **Samsung Note 9** radio button selected:

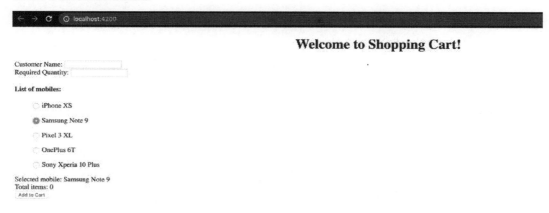

Figure 4.3: *Add to Cart button enabled as Samsung Note 9 is selected*

> **Note: We can bind any standard HTML element's property with [property-name] syntax. In the upcoming chapter, we will have nested components, and they will expose their properties. We can bind them using the same syntax in parent component for passing data.**

Attribute Data Binding

There is a very subtle difference between Attributes and Properties of the HTML element. In simplest terms, attributes are defined by HTML, and properties are defined by DOM. Few HTML attributes have one to one corresponding property defined, but not all of them. For example, the colspan attribute doesn't have a corresponding DOM property. In those cases, we can use Attribute data binding. Its syntax is [attr.<attribute-name>] as shown in *Code 4.9*, where we are binding attribute lang of <input> to hardcoded value en-us, which can be a member variable as well:

```
<ul *ngFor="let item of allItems">

  <input [attr.lang]="'en-us'" [id]="item"
type="radio" name="mobileItem" [value]="selectedItem"
(click)="updateSelection(item)">

  {{item}}

</ul>
```

Code 4.9: *app.component.html – binding lang attribute to a hardcoded string*

CSS Class Data Binding

Using class data binding, we can add or remove the CSS class from the target HTML element based on truthy conditions. It's syntax is [class.<css-class>] = "<expression>".

Let's extend our application. We will highlight the selected radio button in blue color if the user selects it. As soon as the user changes the selection, we will remove a class from the previous item and add it to new items. *Code 4.10* shows the CSS class highlight:

```css
.highlight {
        font-size: bold;
        color: blue;
}
```

Code 4.10: app.component.css highlight class for highlighted selected radio button

And *Code 4.11* shows HTML snippet how to add/remove class based on selectedItem == item condition:

```html
<ul *ngFor="let item of allItems">


        <input [attr.lang]="'en-us'" [id]="item"
type="radio" name="mobileItem" [value]="selectedItem"
(click)="updateSelection(item)">


        <span [class.highlight]="selectedItem == item">


            {{item}}


        </span>
</ul>
```

Code 4.11: app.component.html: class binding for highlight CSS class

Style Binding

Like CSS class binding, we can bind specific CSS style property with expression. For style binding, we need to specify value and expression. Code 4.12 shows how to change the background color of the selected radio button and reset when another radio button is selected. The output of changes will look like *Figure 4.3*:

```
<ul *ngFor="let item of allItems">


            <input [attr.lang]="'en-us'" [id]="item"
type="radio" name="mobileItem" [value]="selectedItem"
(click)="updateSelection(item)">


            <span [class.highlight]="selectedItem == item"
        [style.background-color]="selectedItem == item ? 'yellow' :
'transparent'">


                    {{item}}


            </span>

</ul>
```

Code 4.12: *app.component.html: style binding for backgroundColor CSS property*

The Figure 4.4 shows how background style is applied whenever radio button is selected.

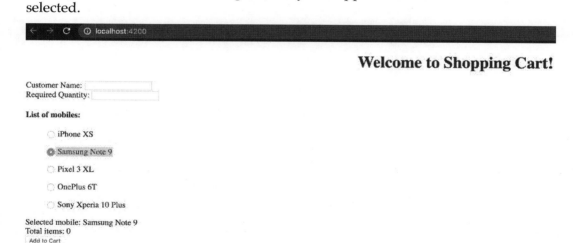

Figure 4.4: *Class and style binding changes the color and background color of the selected option*

Note: Ideally, we should use style binding for a single CSS property. If we have multiple properties to bind, then consider creating a new CSS class or use NgStyle binding.

NgClass Binding

We have seen that we can use [class.<class-name>] for adding/removing CSS class to HTML element. There is another way to do the same using NgClass binding. *Code 4.13* shows how to use NgClass based on condition:

```
<span [ngClass]="selectedItem == item ? 'highlight': ''"
        [style.background-color]="selectedItem == item ? 'yellow' :
'transparent'">


                {{item}}


</span>
```

Code 4.13: app.component.html: NgClass binding example

Code 4.14 shows a complete HTML code with binding:

```
<div style="text-align:center">
        <h1>
                Welcome to {{ title }}!
        </h1>
</div>


<div>
        Customer Name: <input type="text"
[(ngModel)]="customerName">
    </div>


<div>
        Required Quantity: <input type="number"
[(ngModel)]="quantity">
</div>


<div>
        <h4>List of mobiles: </h4>
</div>
```

```html
<ul *ngFor="let item of allItems">


            <input [attr.lang]="'en-us'" [id]="item"
type="radio" name="mobileItem" [value]="selectedItem"
(click)="updateSelection(item)">


  <!-- <span [class.highlight]="selectedItem == item"

      [style.background-color]="selectedItem == item ? 'yellow' :
'transparent'">
    {{item}}
  </span> -->


            <span [ngClass]="selectedItem == item ? 'highlight': ''"

      [style.background-color]="selectedItem == item ? 'yellow' :
'transparent'">


                {{item}}
            </span>


</ul>


<div>
            Selected mobile: {{selectedItem}}
</div>


<div>
            Total items: {{cart.length}}
</div>


<div>
            <button (click)="addToCart()"
[disabled]="!selectedItem">Add to Cart</button>
</div>
```

Code 4.14: *app.component.html*

Code 4.15 shows the complete TypeScript code of the component class:

```typescript
Import { Component } from '@angular/core';

@Component({
        selector: 'app-root',
        templateUrl: './app.component.html',
        styleUrls: ['./app.component.css']
})
export class AppComponent {
        title = 'Shopping Cart';
        totalItems: number;
        customerName: string;
        quantity: number;

        allItems = [
                'iPhone XS',
                'Samsung Note 9',
                'Pixel 3 XL',
                'OnePlus 6T',
                'Sony Xperia 10 Plus'
        ];

        selectedItem: string;
        cart: string[] = [];

        addToCart(item: string) {
                this.cart.push(item);
                alert(`${this.selectedItem} is added to cart!`);
        }

        updateSelection(value: string) {
                this.selectedItem = value;
        }
}

function gobalFunction() {
```

```
        alert('I am global function');
}
```

Code 4.15: app.component.ts

Introduction to Pipes

So far, we have seen that HTML code is responsible for representing data that is fetched and processed by component class. But usually, there is a requirement to change the appearance of data only for UI purposes but not to change underlying value. That's where Pipes comes into pictures. Pipes provides an opportunity to process bounded value for UI. This term is borrowed from shell script where one command's output is fed to the next command's input. For example, Code cat <filename> | less command will pass cat command output as an input to less command.

Pipes in Angular follow a similar purpose. They give us a chance to render bounded value by applying some transformation. Let's take a use case where we want to show text in all upper case. *Code 4.16* shows how to apply a built-in uppercase pipe on selectedItem value:

```
<div>
  Selected mobile: {{selectedItem | uppercase}}
</div>
```

Code 4.16: app.component.html – applying uppercase pipe on the expression

Figure 4.5 shows the output after applying the uppercase pipe:

Figure 4.5: output after applying the uppercase pipe on the selected item

> **Note: In the WPF world, we get IValueConverter and IMultiValueConverter for similar purposes. It gives a separate layer of the transformation of UI logic from underlying value.**

Generating Custom Pipe

Angular provides lots of built-in pipes that we can use in our application. We can also write our custom pipe based on our application requirements. Let's create a custom pipe that will prefix some text to the target value. Let's run command ng generate pipe prefix in the command terminal. Make sure we are in the Angular project directory. This will generate new pipe and output of the above command might look like *Figure 4.6:*

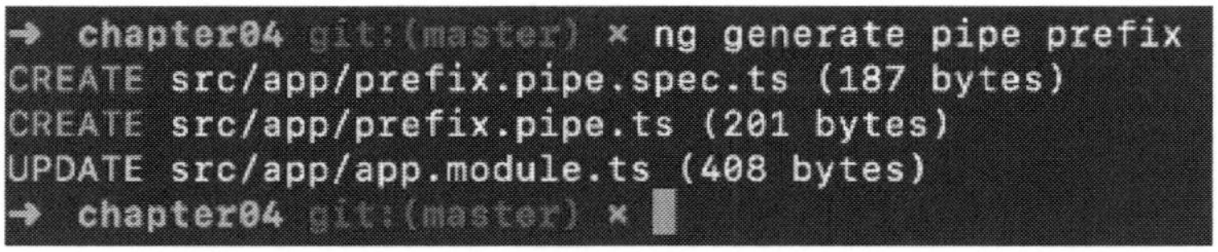

Figure 4.6: generating new pipe using the ng-cli command

This command will generate the `PrefixPipe` class, which we will have to provide in the providers' property of the AppModule class, as shown in *Code 4.17:*

```
import { AppComponent } from './app.component';

import { PrefixPipe } from './prefix.pipe';


@NgModule({
        declarations: [AppComponent, PrefixPipe],
        imports: [
            BrowserModule,
            FormsModule
        ],
        providers: [PrefixPipe],
        bootstrap: [AppComponent]
})
export class AppModule { }
```

Code 4.17: app.module.ts – provide PrefixPipe into AppModule

Every Pipe class should implement the `PipeTransform` interface. This interface has only one method called `transform()`, which must be implemented in custom pipe class. Unlike the C#.NET coding standard, Angular's interface doesn't start with 'I' character. But if we want to write our interface, we are free to implement the .NET coding standard for the interface. *Code 4.18* shows the definition of the `PipeTransform` interface from the Angular core library:

```
export interface PipeTransform {
        transform(value: any, ...args: any[]): any;
}
```

Code 4.18: pipe_transform.d.ts definition

The `transform()` method has two arguments, as follows:

- **Value: any:** this is the value of the target object on which pipe is applied
- **Args: any[]:** this is an optional array of pipe arguments

Note: The return value from the transform() method will be rendered in HTML. That means if we send an empty string from transform function, then no matter what target value has, HTML will output will be empty.

Let's extend our `PrefixPipe` by adding logic to prefix `Mobile:` in front of the target value. *Code 4.19* shows logic put in `PrefixPipe`:

```
import { Pipe, PipeTransform } from '@angular/core';
@Pipe({
        name: 'prefix'
})
export class PrefixPipe implements PipeTransform {

        transform(value: any, args?: any): any {
            if (value) {
                    return 'Mobile: ' + value;
            }
            return '';
        }

}
```

Code 4.19: prefix.pipe.ts – prefixing target value with "Mobile:"

As our prefix pipe is ready, let's apply it to our shopping cart. We will apply it on `selectedItem` expression so that whenever the user selects any of the radio buttons from the list, its value gets prefixed with "`Mobile:`" text, as shown in *Code 4.20:*

```
<div>
        Selected mobile: {{selectedItem | uppercase | prefix}}
</div>
```

Code 4.20: *app.component.html – prefixing selectedItem expression*

As we can see, we have applied the uppercase pipe first and then prefix. This is called pipe chaining. We can apply as many pipes as we want on a single expression. *Figure 4.7* shows output in the browser after applying these pipes on selectedItem expression:

Figure 4.7: *Output of applying uppercase and prefix pipe on selectedItem*

Passing Parameters to Pipe

We can pass multiple optional parameters to the pipe. This gives us the feasibility to transform target object conditionally based on passed parameters. For example, we can pass arguments to our PrefixPipe whether to show text Mobile or Handy based on Boolean argument. We can pass a parameter to the pipe by colons (:) after the pipe name. *Code 4.21* shows how to pass parameter `false` to our `PrefixPipe`:

```
<div>
        Selected mobile: {{selectedItem | uppercase | prefix: false}}
</div>
```

Code 4.21: *app.component.html – passing parameter PrefixPipe*

And Code 4.22 shows modified PrefixPipe code:

```
import { Pipe, PipeTransform } from '@angular/core';


@Pipe({
```

```
            name: 'prefix'
})
export class PrefixPipe implements PipeTransform {
        transform(value: any, args?: any): any {
            if (value) {
                    return args? 'Mobile: ' + value :   'Handy: '
+ value;;
            }
            return '';
        }
}
```

Code 4.22: prefix.pipe.ts – returning different prefix based on parameter

Pure and Impure Pipes

Angular differentiates between pipes in two ways—Pure and Impure pipe. It differs the way change detection works to evaluate expression and call being made for executing the pipe's transform function. Pure pipe gets executed for pure change detection as string value changed, object reference changed, and so on. But it doesn't detect internal changes like adding value to an array. That's where the impure pipe comes into the picture. They do get executed in such an impure change detection cycle.

Let's extend our application. We would add another pipe called AndroidPhonesPipe by running the command, as shown in *Figure 4.8:*

```
→ chapter04 git:(master) × ng generate pipe android-phones
CREATE src/app/android-phones.pipe.spec.ts (216 bytes)
CREATE src/app/android-phones.pipe.ts (215 bytes)
UPDATE src/app/app.module.ts (513 bytes)
→ chapter04 git:(master) ×
```

Figure 4.8: generating android-phones pipe using the ng-cli command

This pipe will accept an array of string as an input and will return a list of string except those which start with the iPhone string. Let's update our HTML page by adding another ***ngFor** for listing only android phones from our cart, as shown in *Code 4.23:*

```
<div>
        <h4>Cart items:</h4>
```

```
      <li *ngFor="let cartItem of (cart | androidPhones)">
            {{cartItem}}
      </li>


      <br>


      Total items: {{cart.length}}
</div>
```

Code 4.23: app.component.html – listing only android phones from our cart

Note the syntax of *ngFor and how we have applied pipe on an array. The parenthesis is very important in this syntax. It gives precedence to pipe execution first, which receives raw array as an input to transform method, and return value is used as a collection for *ngFor loop.

The next step is, we need to provide a new pipe in AppModule providers array as we did for `PrefixPipe`. *Code 4.24* shows how to add it:

```
@NgModule({
      declarations: [AppComponent, PrefixPipe, AndroidPhonesPipe],
      imports: [
            BrowserModule,
            FormsModule
      ],
      providers: [
            PrefixPipe,
            AndroidPhonesPipe
      ],
      bootstrap: [AppComponent]
})
export class AppModule { }
```

Code 4.24: app.module.ts – providing AndroidPhonesPipe in AppModule

As the setup is done, let's write logic to filter iPhones from the input list in our AndroidPhonesPipe's transform method, as shown in *Code 4.25*:

```
import { Pipe, PipeTransform } from '@angular/core';
@Pipe({
```

```
            name: 'androidPhones',

            pure: false

})

export class AndroidPhonesPipe implements PipeTransform {


    transform(mobiles: string[], args?: any): any {


        return mobiles.filter(x => !x.startsWith('iPhone'));


    }

}
```

Code 4.25: *android-phones.pipe.ts – filtering iPhones from cart list*

Did you notice anything different in this pipe definition as compared to PrefixPipe? Check @Pipe() decorator parameter list. We have added another property as pure:false. This property marks pipe as an impure pipe. This pipe will be executed for impure changes, like adding items into our cart array.

Figure 4.9 shows a list of cart items with impure pipe applied. Note that total items are three but the cart items list is displaying only two options because the third item is **iPhone XS,** which is filtered out by our AndroidPhonesPipe:

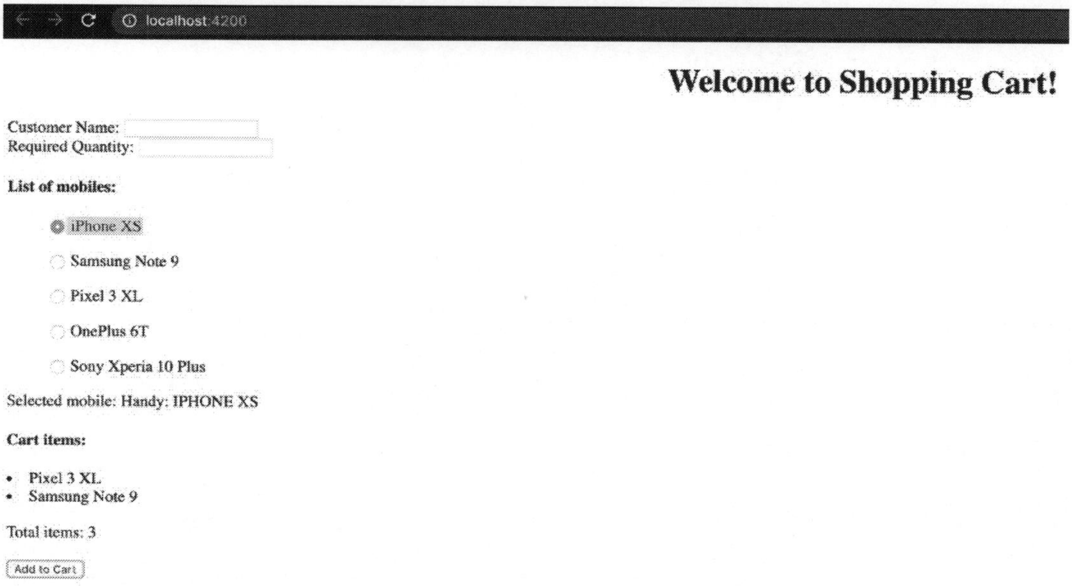

Figure 4.9: *Output of impure pipe AndroidPhonesPipe filtering iPhones*

Warning: As impure pipes get executed for impure change detection cycle, they are performance intensive. This means if we have multiple or complex logic inside our impure pipe, then the application will be slowed down, and user experience might get affected. So be sure when to use impure pipe and keep minimal logic in it.

List of Built-in Pipes

In this section, we will list down few of built-in pipes in Angular:

- **AsyncPipe**: This is a very useful pipe when we are working with an Observable data stream. If applied on an observable object, this pipe will subscribe to the source and will execute whenever there is a next value to consume. When a component is destroyed, this pipe unsubscribes itself from observable.
- **DatePipe:** This is a very common pipe while dealing with formatting date and time on an HTML page. It accepts date object and provides a way to display it in various timezone, format.
- **JsonPipe:** If we apply JsonPipe on the json object, it will render formatted JSON of object structure in the browser.
- **UpperCasePipe:** As we have used this pipe, it transforms input text into upper case.
- **LowerCasePipe:** Transforms input text into lower case.
- **TitleCasePipe:** Transforms input text into title case, making the first letter of every word in upper case.
- **DecimalPipe**: Used when rendering decimal values and formatting numbers.
- **CurrencyPipe**: This pipe transforms the input number into currency notation.
- **SlicePipe**: This pipe is like substr() JavaScript function. It trims the input string with the start and end position number.
- **PercentPipe**: This pipe also accepts a number and transform into percentage string
- **KeyValuePipe**: This pipe works on Object or Map input. It transforms the input object into key-value pairs

Conclusion

In this chapter, we have learned about different ways of data bindings. We understood a different kind of data binding like one-way, two-way, one-way-to-source. We have seen how [(ngModel)] provides us two-way data binding via property binding and event binding combination though internally, there is no support for two-way data binding. After that, we looked into how to bind HTML attribute, DOM property binding, creating a local reference to the HTML element. We also learned how to apply binding for CSS class, NgStyle, NgClass with bounded value and expression. Then we got into Pipes, which provides us a way to transform input value for rendering purposes. We have used a built-in uppercase pipe and created a custom Prefix pipe as well. Then we saw how to create impure pipe for impure change detection. After that, we have listed useful built-in Angular pipes.

In the next chapter, we will explore NgModule in depth.

Questions

1. Which package is required to use [(ngModel)] for two-way data binding?

2. What is the syntax for binding HTML element attributes?

3. How to bind multiple CSS classes to an <div> element based on expression?

4. What is difference between [style.<property-name>] and [NgStyle]?

5. Can we pass multiple arguments to the event bound method from the HTML page?

6. Can we apply pipe on <input>? Why?

7. Can we pass Pipe into component's Providers array instead of module's providers?

8. Is it possible to function overloading of transform into Pipe definition?

9. Why shouldn't we use an impure pipe with complex logic?

10. If our application has a large number of pipes (for example, 50+), then will we provide them into each consumer's Module and Component, or we will devise some other way? If yes, how?

@NgModule()

In this chapter, we will dive deep into @NgModules(). We will learn more about @NgModule() decorator, different types of Angular modules, how do they provide modularity in Angular Application, how components scopes are defined and shared across NgModules. We will also see the lazy loading of @NgModules() for dynamic routing, and then we will see Ivy render engine, which defines a new Angular application paradigm without @NgModules().

Structure

- @NgModule() versus C# Namespace
- Angular Application with @NgModule()
- Mapping Namespace of C# with NgModules of Angular
- @NgModule decorator
- TypeScript Modules versus @NgModule()
- Types of @NgModules()
- Eagerly loaded @NgModule()
- Lazy loaded @NgModule()
- Commonly used @NgModule()
- Hands-on

- Identifying different types of modules
- Introduction to Angular Ivy

Objective

This chapter aims to understand the NgModules feature of Angular in detail. While building enterprise and Angular, complex applications, it is very important to organize Angular code in a modular structure, and NgModules is the best tool to do so.

Hence, we will look into its decorator properties, how to import/export components, how to share information between NgModules, on which NgModule level should you provide Injectable services and lazy loading of NgModules.

Angular Ivy is a new render engine which strives to get rid of tree shaking problem caused by NgModules sometimes. We will get an introduction to Ivy.

@NgModule() versus C# Namespace

The C# has a "namespace" feature for containership, and in Java, we have "packages". By using "namespace" or "packages", we can create a modular solution where related classes are grouped within one unit. The "namespace" and "packages" also provide a solution to the "name collision" problem, that is, there can be multiple classes with the same name but in different "namespace" or "package". We can import specific namespaces or package for accessing class from that package. Let's try to understand modularity with C# namespace analogy. *Code 5.1* shows the Account class defined inside Finance namespace in C#:

```
namespace Finance
{
        public class Account
        {
                public string GetUserName()
                {
                        return "User A";
                }
        }
}
```

Code 5.1: finance.cs –Account class defined inside Finance namespace in C#

Next, we will define `Order` class inside Inventory namespace, as shown in *Code 5.2*. Note that to access `Account` class inside Order.cs file, we have imported `Finance` namespace with **"using"** statement:

```
using Finance;

namespace Inventory

{

        public class Order

        {

                public void placeOrder()

                {

                        var userAccount = new Account();

                }

        }

}
```

Code 5.2: Order.cs – C# Order class defined inside Inventory namespace

And inside `Program.cs` file, at `Main()` function, we will create an object of **"Order"** class, and again we need to import **"Inventory"** namespace as shown in *Code 5.3*:

```
using System;

using Inventory;


public class Program

{

        public static void Main()

        {

                Console.WriteLine("Hello World");

                var order = new Order();

        }

}
```

Code 5.3: Program.cs – Main() function creating object of "Order" class

This example gives us an idea about how to create modularity within C# application by creating classes within namespaces and importing as and when needed. For Java application, we would use **"package"** instead of **"namespace"**. The modularity is very important for building large scale applications. We can split tasks based on modules, and different teams can work on different modules at the same time. With proper modularity, the Application becomes robust, scalable, and maintainable.

Angular Application with @NgModule()

The Angular Application can be built with great modularity with the right combination of TypeScript modularity and Angular framework's decorators. There is a very subtle difference between how we keep modularity in Angular Application by creating classes with `@NgModule()` decorator and exporting class from TypeScript file and importing into another TypeScript file. The Angular framework provides a decorator called "`@NgModule()`" from the "`@angular/core`" package. The `@NgModule()` decorator can be applied to a class. This decorator accepts the JSON object as a parameter. The passed JSON object contains metadata Angular uses while bootstrapping Application. We will see details of the parameter of the JSON object soon.

FinanceModule Example

Let's create a new Angular application with feature modules and components and see how to modularize it. Let's create a finance module by running *Command 5.1:*

ng generate module finance

Command 5.1: *Create a finance module*

Next, we will create an account component by running *Command 5.2*. Note that we have passed component name with the module name as a prefix, that is, "finance/account," which tells Angular CLI to create the "Account" component and place it inside the "Finance" module:

ng generate component finance/account

Command 5.2: *Create Account component inside the finance module*

The *Code 5.4* shows `AccountComponent` boilerplate code:

```
import { Component, OnInit } from '@angular/core';
@Component({
        selector: 'app-account',
        templateUrl: './account.component.html',
        styleUrls: ['./account.component.css']
})
export class AccountComponent implements OnInit {
        constructor() { }
```

```
ngOnInit() {  }
}
```

Code 5.4: account.component.ts - auto generated code for Account component

Code 5.5 shows the `FinanceModule` module boilerplate code. In *Command 5.2*, we have asked Angular CLI to create an `Account` component inside the `Finance` module; that's why the "exports" and "declarations" array parameter of @ `NgModule()` decorator has "`AccountComponent`" as an element:

```
import { NgModule } from '@angular/core';

import { CommonModule } from '@angular/common';

import { AccountComponent } from './account/account.component';


@NgModule({
        declarations: [AccountComponent],

        exports: [AccountComponent],

        imports: [ CommonModule]
})
export class FinanceModule { }
```

Code 5.5: finance.module.ts - export AccountComponent to other NgModules

InventoryModule and Order Component: We will create another module called Inventory by running *Command 5.3*. Please note that we do not specify the "module" as a prefix with the new module name. Angular CLI automatically creates a new item with a specific type name as a suffix. Thus we have `FinanceModule`, `AccountComponent` classes created even though we haven't specified:

ng generate module inventory

Command 5.3: Create Inventory module

Once the Inventory module has been created, we will create an "`Order`" component inside it by running *Command 5.4:*

ng generate component inventory/order

Command 5.4: Create Order component inside the Inventory module

Command 5.4 will not only create Order component, but it will update the Inventory module's `@NgModule()` decorator's "declarations" and "exports" array elements with `OrderComponent` similar to `Finance` module and `Account` component example.

Okay, so we have created two separate modules with components. Now let's try to create a communication link between them. The easiest example is to display the

`Account` component inside the `Order component`. The `AppComponent` shall render `OrderComponent`, and inside OrderComponet, we shall render `AccountComponent`. Let's try to create this component hierarchy. We will use AccountComponent's "`selector`" value, that is, "`app-account`" inside `OrderComponent's` HTML file, as shown in *Code 5.6:*

```
<p>order works!</p>


<app-account></app-account>
```

Code 5.6: *order.component.html - display Account component content*

In Angular, the `Component` class cannot be directly accessed in other modules. A component should be part of at least one NgModule's "declarations" property, which binds component to the module. Now, whenever we want to use a component outside the bounded module, then we must import a bounded module. The module can have multiple components declared inside "declarations" property but can export only selected out of them. That's why `@NgModule()` decorator has "exports" property, which defines which all components should be exported for another module. `AccountComponent` is part of `FinanceModule's` "declarations" property and been exported using "exports" property. Another rule of Angular modules is `Component` class cannot directly import another module. The bounded module should import the required module so that all the components part of "declarations" property can access components exported by the module. In *Code 5.6*, the `OrderComponent` is trying to access `AccountComponent`. The `OrderComponent` is part of the Inventory module, and `AccountComponent` is part of the `Finance` module. Thus Inventory module should import the `Finance module` inside the "**imports**" property of `@NgModule()` decorator, as shown in *Code 5.7*. Note that the top import statement for importing `FinanceModule` is TypeScript module resolution syntax. This import statement allows us to import the `FinanceModule` type and avoid compilation errors of unknown FinanceModule type. Whereas the "imports" property of `@NgModule()` decorator creates the links between Angular modules. It is a common mistake. Angular developers end up making when starting to learn `@NgModules`.

```
import { NgModule } from '@angular/core';
import { CommonModule } from '@angular/common';
import { OrderComponent } from './order/order.component';
import { FinanceModule } from '../finance/finance.module';


@NgModule({
        declarations: [OrderComponent],
```

```
        exports: [OrderComponent],
        imports: [
                CommonModule,
                FinanceModule
        ]
})
export class InventoryModule { }
```

Code 5.7: *inventory.module.ts - import Finance module*

So far, we have completed the links between the Inventory module and `Finance` module. Now we will render the `Order` component inside `AppComponent` HTML. We will use the "app-order" selector property of `OrderComponet` inside the `AppComponent` HTML file, as shown in *Code 5.8*:

```
<div style="text-align:center">
        <h1>
                Welcome to {{ title }}!
        </h1>
</div>


<app-order></app-order>
```

Code 5.8: *app.component.html - display OrderComponent inside AppComponent*

The `OrderComponent` is part of the `Inventory` module. Thus `AppComponent` cannot directly access it. We need to resolve the module path between `AppComponent` and `OrderComponent`. `AppComponent` is part of AppModule; thus, we have to import `InventoryModule` inside AppModule. *Code 5.9* shows how `InventoryModule` is imported inside AppModule's "imports" property of *@NgModule()* decorator. Note that we don't have to import `FinanceModule` inside AppModule. The Angular recursively resolves module dependencies. Angular compiler shall first import `InventoryModule` by parsing the "imports" property of AppModule, and then it will import "FinanceModule" from InventoryModule's "imports" property.

```
import { AppRoutingModule } from './app-routing.module';

import { AppComponent } from './app.component';

import { InventoryModule } from './inventory/inventory.module';


@NgModule({
        declarations: [
```

```
            AppComponent
      ],
      imports: [
            BrowserModule,
            AppRoutingModule,
            InventoryModule
      ],
      providers: [],
      bootstrap: [AppComponent]
})
export class AppModule { }
```

Code 5.9: app.module.ts - import InventoryModule into AppModule

Once we have done all the changes, we will save all the changes and run the Application by running *Command 5.5*:

```
ng serve --open
```

Command 5.5: Start the development server

The *Command 5.5* shall start the development server in watch mode and launch browser and load application. The output should look like *Figure 5.1*:

Figure 5.1: Output and HTML structure showing component nesting

Let's open the developer console of browser for further analysis. Inside developer console, select HTML `Elements` tab to see application HTML code generated for Angular application. *Figure 5.1* shows how HTML structure is nested for `AppComponent` → `OrderComponent` → `AccountComponent`. The `<app-root>` is `AppComponent` selector which contains `<app-order>` HTML tag which is `OrderComponent` selector. Inside `<app-order>` tag, we have `<app-account>` tag which is `AccountComponent` selector.

This is a very simple example of how we can create modular Angular Application. The `AccountComponet` does not know `OrderComponent`, which follows standard software design principle—Single Responsibility Principle. There can be two teams working on the `Account` and `Order` component at the same time without being dependent on each other. The `@NgModule()` decorator contains properties that allow us to import/export components to other modules. In the next section, we will try to understand `@NgModule()` in detail.

Mapping Namespace of C# with @ NgModule() of Angular

We have seen how we can create modular Applications using "`namespace`" in C# and how to create modular Applications in Angular using `@NgModule()`. Now we will try to map these concepts to each other in the following section:

- The namespace provides grouping and encapsulation of classes in C#, whereas `@NgModules()` provides grouping and encapsulation of components in Angular.

- If a class is declared inside a namespace, then it is considered to be part of that namespace. Similarly, if a component is declared inside "`declarations`" metadata property of `@NgModule()` decorator, then it is part of that class with `@NgModule()` decorator. For example, refer *Code 5.5* again, `@NgModule()`'s "declarations" property contains "AccountComponent" and applied to the `FinanceModule` class. This syntax binds a component to its module.

- As a class can be part of only one namespace, the Angular component can be declared inside only one NgModule. If declared more than once, a runtime exception will be thrown by the Angular compiler. If we create a component but don't link it to any module, then the Angular build process will simply drop that component from output build, and this process is called "**Tree Shaking**".

- If we refer to *Code 5.2*, the "`Order`" class can create an object of "`Account`" class only by importing "`Finance`" namespace with "`using Finance;`" a statement otherwise a compile-time error will be encountered as Account class is not known. Similarly, in *Code 5.7*, we are importing "`FinanceModule`" inside InventoryModule using the "`imports`" property of `@NgModule()`

decorator. Note that "import { FinanceModule } from '../finance/ finance.module';" is a TypeScript/JavaScript import statement for importing TypeScript/JavaScript modules for resolving class name at compile time. For Angular, it is not just enough to import the module using import statements but should provide details inside @NgModule() decorator metadata.

- In C#, a class can have access specifier like public, internal, which defines the scope of the class. If a class is public, then it can be used inside other namespaces after importing its parent namespace. There is no such access specifier for NgModule in Angular. By default, all components declared inside NgModules are private. If other NgModules want to use component, then components should be listed in the "exports" metadata property of @NgModule() decorator. Please refer to *Code 5.5*; FinanceModule has "declarations" property, which marks AccountComponent as part of FinanceModule and "exports" property makes AccountComponent available for other NgModules to be imported and used. If it is not exported, then runtime exception will be thrown by the Angular compiler.

The C# and Java have very comprehensive modularity syntax. We define namespace/ package and declare classes within a namespace. When we want to use a class from different namespace/package, then we import that namespace/package. But in Angular, things are a bit tricky. We need to understand how to include components inside @NgModule's "declarations" property and how to export it using "exports" property. Then to access components from a different module, we must import the parent module using the "imports" property of @NgModule. We will see @ NgModule() decorator's properties in detail in the next section.

@NgModule() Decorator

The @NgModule() decorator is exported from the "@angular/core" package. The @NgModule() decorator function accepts a JSON object as a parameter. The @ NgModule() decorator can be applied to a TypeScript class. *Code 5.10* shows the NgModule decorator definition from Angular's official documentation:

```
@NgModule({
  // Static, that is compiler configuration
  declarations: [], // Configure the selectors
  entryComponents: [], // Generate the host factory

  // Runtime, or injector configuration
  providers: [], // Runtime injector configuration
  // Composability / Grouping
```

```
imports: [], // composing NgModules together
exports: [] // making NgModules available to other parts of the app
})
```

Code 5.10: *NgModule decorator official website (https://angular.io/guide/ngmodule-api)*

Let's go through each property of NgModule decorator as below:

- **declarations**: The "declarations" property accepts an array of components, directives, and pipes classes to be part of the @NgModule() module. The classes declared inside "declarations" property cannot be declared inside any other @NgModule()'s "declarations" property. A component should be part of atmost one module with the @NgModule() module. If a component is not part of any module, then during the build process, all those components shall be dropped out of the build output.

- **exports**: The "exports" property accepts an array of components, directive, and pipe classes to be exported from the module. If "exports" property is empty, then no other modules can access component, directive, and pipe from this @NgModule() module. The exception comes when Angular Application uses lazy loading of modules using routing. In that case, we do not need to export anything.

- **providers**: The "providers" property accepts an array of Angular service classes. The Angular service should be provided in one of the "providers" property of @NgModule() decorator. The @Injectable() decorator can also be used to specify in which module to provide service, and it is the preferred way to specify service. The "providers" property sometime doesn't mention whether the provided service has been used by any other component or not, and the tree shaking cannot drop the unused service from output build. Once service is provided into "providers" array, then service can be injected into child components and other imported @NgModule() modules.

- **imports:** The "imports" property accepts an array of modules, that is, TypeScript class with @NgModule() decorator. The "imports" property allows Angular modules to create communication links between modules. We have seen one example in the previous section for OrderComponent and AccountComponent.

- **bootstrap**: The "bootstrap" property accepts an array of the component. The Angular Application can be considered as an inverted tree of components. The root of this tree is provided inside the "bootstrap" property. Generally, we have only one root component, that is, AppComponent. In special cases, we can have multiple root components, and we should mention them inside the "bootstrap" property. In Angular Application, at least one of the module should contain "bootstrap" property with at least one component.

- **entryComponent**: The "entryComponent" property an array of components. If "entryComponent" property is not provided, then all components from "bootstrap" property are passed to "entryComponent" internally. The Angular uses "entryComponent" contained components for dynamically loading views. If we have components that are not part of "declarations" property and we want to use it for dynamically loading or creating web components, then we should pass those components into "entryComponents" property; otherwise, these components shall be dropped out of the build process by tree shaking method.

The `@NgModule()` is a way to provides modularization in Angular Application. The `@NgModule()` decorator is applied to a class that serves as a module. Most of the time, there is no business logic specified inside module class, but while exporting the Angular component as a web component, then we might add to some business logic in module class.

TypeScript Modules versus @NgModule()

The module concept in TypeScript is different than other Object-Oriented languages like C#. The TypeScript file can export an object, class, or method with the "export" keyword. The exported class can be imported into other TypeScript files by using the "import" statement. This "export" and "import" has nothing to do with Angular. If we are building Node.js Application using TypeScript, then we will use similar syntax. The @NgModule() decorator has "imports" and "exports" properties. Many developers get these two properties confused with TypeScript's "import" and "export" keywords. The `@NgModule()` "imports" property accepts TypeScript class with `@NgModule()` decorator. To resolve class names, we need to import it using the "import" statement of TypeScript. Similarly "exports" property of `@NgModule()` accepts TypeScript class with `@Component()`, `@Directive()` or `@Pipe()` decorator. The component class should be marked with an "export" keyword so that other TypeScript file can resolve it.

Types of @NgModule()

There is no special syntax for defining different types of modules in Angular. All module class has same `@NgModule()` decorator applied. The usage of module class defines their type. The following list mentions such different types of modules:

- **Feature Module:** The feature module contains specific feature related components and modules. While building an application, we should try to identify various features of Application based on the user journey. For example, any typical web application has a **Login** page, **Sign-Up** page, **User Account** page, **Dashboard** page, and so on and can be used as a feature module. A well organized Angular application consists of feature modules that follow the Single Responsibility Principle. In *Code 5.7*, we have `InventoryModule`, which can be classified as a feature module.

- **Routing Module:** The module which contains all the routing information can be considered as a Routing module. The Routing module should contain only the route configuration and no other business logic.

- **Service Module:** As Angular Application grows into a large number of feature modules, it results in a large number of Injectable Services, and maintaining them into Application becomes challengings. As a best practice, we should create a shared module that provides application-wide services and exports them for other `@NgModules()` modules.

- **Widget Module:** The widget module contains only the import and export section for existing Angular Application, which should be exported as a library.

- **Shared Module:** The Angular Application might want to use some standard components, pipes, directives, and so on. The best practice is to create a Shared Module which imports all common features and exports them.

The key to building modularized and scalable Angular Application is to identify and divide application features into respective `@NgModule()` modules. The granularity of modules and aggregation should be balanced; otherwise, we might end up creating too many modules, and it might affect the application performance.

Eagerly Loaded @NgModule()

The Angular modules are processed in two different ways by Angular compiler. The default method of loading Angular modules is by eagerly loading them. The Angular compiler start processing `@NgModule()` decorator **"imports"** property and tries to load them one by one recursively. If the imported module contains other modules inside **"imports,"** then the Angular compiler starts loading them. If we are building a small application, then we can use eagerly loaded modules. But if we are trying to build big and complex Applications, then we should consider using lazy loading of modules using routing as discussed in the next section.

Lazy Loaded @NgModule()

The lazy loaded modules get loaded at runtime rather than compile time. While building a big and complex web application, we divide the feature modules into different routes. Each main feature module gets mapped to one of the routes. Whenever browser URL matches with given route in routing configuration, then its associated module is loaded at runtime . Thus if user navigate to "/my-account" URL in browser then MyAccountModule will be loaded and its respective component shall be rendered. This behavior is called lazy loaded modules. *Code 5.11* shows how to load **MyAccountModule** through route **"my-account"**. We will see more about routing in the *Routing* chapter.

```
const routes: Routes = [
        {
                path: 'login',
                component: LoginComponent
        },
        {
                path: 'sign-up',
                component: SignUpComponent
        },
        {
                path: 'my-account',
                        loadChildren: () => import('./my-account/my-account.
module')
                        .then(m => m.MyAccountModule)
        }
];

@NgModule({
                imports: [
                        LoginModule,
                        SignUpModule,
                        RouterModule.forRoot(
                        routes,
                        {
                                enableTracing: false, // Disable it for
production build
                        // preloadingStrategy: NoPreloading
                        preloadingStrategy: PreloadAllModules
                        })
                ],
                exports: [RouterModule]
})
export class AppRoutingModule { }
```

Code 5.11: *Lazy Loading MyAccountModule*

Commonly Used @NgModule()

Angular library exports lots of modules for building an application. These modules are categorized based on their features and domains. The compartmentalization also helps to load fewer angular libraries if not required by Application. There are a few modules that we will be using very often. Here is the list of a few commonly used NgModules:

- **CommonModule**: The CommonModule is exported from the "@angular/common" library. This module exports commonly used components, directives like NgIf, NgFor. In the previous version of Angular, we had to import packages explicitly, but in the newer version, it is out of the box to ease development.

- **FormsModule**: The FormsModule is exported from the "@angular/forms" library. FormsModule provides directives for building Template Driven Forms. For example, if we want to use two-way data binding using [(ngModel)] directive, then we must import the FormsModule.

- **ReactiveFormsModule**: ReactiveFormsModule is also exported from the "@angular/forms" library. For example, if we want to build reactive forms using FormGroup, FormControl classes, then we must import ReactiveFormsModule.

- **RouterModule**: RouterModule is exported from the "@angular/router" library. We must import RouterModule into NgModule, where we have defined routing or inject Router singleton service into a child component.

- **HttpClientModule**: HttpClientModule is exported from "@angular/common/http" library. There is also HttpModule, which was used in the earlier version, but HttpClientModule is recommended for consuming HTTP resources.

- **BrowserModule**: The BrowserModule contains the default infrastructure for running Angular Application into the browser. It is imported into AppModule by default if a project is created using Angular CLI. We do not need to work extensively with this module.

The Angular framework provides lots of modules. It is very important to understand which modules are already present in framework, third-party modules that can be imported by NPM packages, and so on. Please check the official Angular website for more details about modules.

Hands-on

We will build an Angular application without any business functionality but with placeholder modules and routing. Let's get started with building application by the following steps:

1. **Create Application**: Create a new application by running *Command 5.6*:

```
ng new shop-kart
```

***Command 5.6**: Create new Application*

The Angular CLI will prompt if we want to use "routing" in this project to select **"Yes"** as a response, and the following question about stylesheet selection, please select "CSS". Once we have provided answers to questions of Angular CLI wizard, it will create a new project structure and start downloading required NPM packages. The partial output of *Command 5.6* should look like *Figure 5.2*. Once *Command 5.6* is completed, change the current working directory to the new project folder we just created. Let's start the development server by running the command **"ng serve --open"**. The development server shall compile the Application and load browser with a new Application. Let's remove default HTML code from `app.component.html` file except `<router-outlet></router-outlet>` tag. We want to use load output from different route modules; hence we will keep routing tag.

```
→ chapter05-1 ng new shop-cart
? Would you like to add Angular routing? Yes
? Which stylesheet format would you like to use? CSS
CREATE shop-cart/README.md (1025 bytes)
CREATE shop-cart/.editorconfig (246 bytes)
CREATE shop-cart/.gitignore (629 bytes)
CREATE shop-cart/angular.json (3449 bytes)
CREATE shop-cart/package.json (1282 bytes)
CREATE shop-cart/tsconfig.json (543 bytes)
CREATE shop-cart/tslint.json (1988 bytes)
CREATE shop-cart/browserslist (429 bytes)
CREATE shop-cart/karma.conf.js (1021 bytes)
CREATE shop-cart/tsconfig.app.json (210 bytes)
CREATE shop-cart/tsconfig.spec.json (270 bytes)
CREATE shop-cart/src/favicon.ico (5430 bytes)
CREATE shop-cart/src/index.html (295 bytes)
CREATE shop-cart/src/main.ts (372 bytes)
CREATE shop-cart/src/polyfills.ts (2838 bytes)
CREATE shop-cart/src/styles.css (80 bytes)
CREATE shop-cart/src/test.ts (642 bytes)
CREATE shop-cart/src/assets/.gitkeep (0 bytes)
CREATE shop-cart/src/environments/environment.prod.ts (51 bytes)
CREATE shop-cart/src/environments/environment.ts (662 bytes)
CREATE shop-cart/src/app/app-routing.module.ts (246 bytes)
CREATE shop-cart/src/app/app.module.ts (393 bytes)
CREATE shop-cart/src/app/app.component.css (0 bytes)
CREATE shop-cart/src/app/app.component.html (1152 bytes)
CREATE shop-cart/src/app/app.component.spec.ts (1104 bytes)
CREATE shop-cart/src/app/app.component.ts (213 bytes)
CREATE shop-cart/e2e/protractor.conf.js (810 bytes)
CREATE shop-cart/e2e/tsconfig.json (214 bytes)
CREATE shop-cart/e2e/src/app.e2e-spec.ts (638 bytes)
CREATE shop-cart/e2e/src/app.po.ts (251 bytes)
```

***Figure 5.2**: "ng new shop-cart" partial output*

2. **Sign-up Module**: In our Application's user journey, a new user will be required to Sign-up first. Let's create a Sign-up module and Sign-up component with routing. We can create them by running separate two commands. There is a smarter way to do that. Angular CLI 8.1.x provides a shorthand command to generate both modules and components with routing using a single command, as shown in *Figure 5.3*:

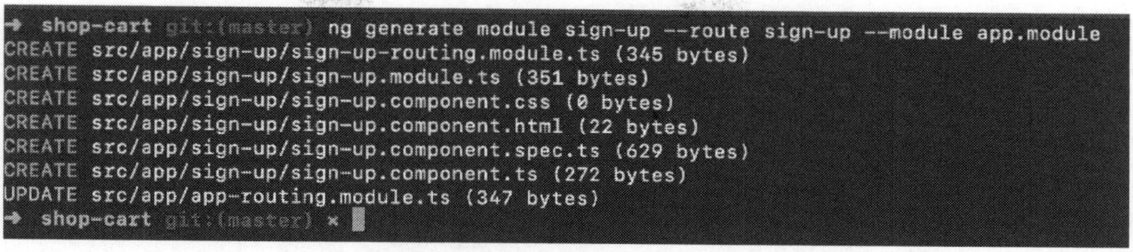

Figure 5.3: *Generate SignUp module with dynamic routing*

In this command **"ng generate module sign-up"** is used for generating SignUpModule, **"--route sign-up"** creates a new component "SignUpComponent" and update "app-routing.module" by adding a new dynamic route for "sign-up" pointing to SignUpModule and "--module app.module" tells Angular CLI that "app-routing.module.ts" should be updated for routing. *Code 5.12* shows how "app-routing.module.ts" looks like after running this command.

```
import { NgModule } from '@angular/core';

import { Routes, RouterModule } from '@angular/router';


const routes: Routes = [
      {
              path: 'sign-up',
              loadChildren: () =>
              import('./sign-up/sign-up.module')
                      .then(m => m.SignUpModule)
      }];


@NgModule({
              imports: [RouterModule.forRoot(routes)],
              exports: [RouterModule]
})
export class AppRoutingModule { }
```

Code 5.12: SignUp route generated by Angular CLI

3. **Login Module**: Another user journey is to allow the user to Login into our Application. We will use a similar command for generating the login component as we did for sign-up, as shown in *Figure 5.4:*

```
→ shop-cart git:(master) × ng generate module login --route login --module app.module
CREATE src/app/login/login-routing.module.ts (340 bytes)
CREATE src/app/login/login.module.ts (342 bytes)
CREATE src/app/login/login.component.css (0 bytes)
CREATE src/app/login/login.component.html (20 bytes)
CREATE src/app/login/login.component.spec.ts (621 bytes)
CREATE src/app/login/login.component.ts (265 bytes)
UPDATE src/app/app-routing.module.ts (457 bytes)
→ shop-cart git:(master) × ▊
```

Figure 5.4: Create Login module with routing and component

4. **Dashboard Module:** Our next user journey is, if the login is successful, then we will take the user to the dashboard page. So let's create a Dashboard module by running the command shown in *Figure 5.5:*

```
→ shop-cart git:(master) × ng generate module dashboard --route dashboard --module app.module
CREATE src/app/dashboard/dashboard-routing.module.ts (356 bytes)
CREATE src/app/dashboard/dashboard.module.ts (370 bytes)
CREATE src/app/dashboard/dashboard.component.css (0 bytes)
CREATE src/app/dashboard/dashboard.component.html (24 bytes)
CREATE src/app/dashboard/dashboard.component.spec.ts (649 bytes)
CREATE src/app/dashboard/dashboard.component.ts (281 bytes)
UPDATE src/app/app-routing.module.ts (571 bytes)
→ shop-cart git:(master) × ▊
```

Figure 5.5: Create Dashboard module with routing and component

5. **UserProfile Component**: The next part of the user journey is that the user can view and edit his/her profile. In our Dashboard, we will have another component called `UserProfile`, which should display the user's profile information. Let's create a new component inside the Dashboard module by running the command shown in *Figure 5.6:*

```
→ shop-cart git:(master) × ng generate component dashboard/user-profile
CREATE src/app/dashboard/user-profile/user-profile.component.css (0 bytes)
CREATE src/app/dashboard/user-profile/user-profile.component.html (27 bytes)
CREATE src/app/dashboard/user-profile/user-profile.component.spec.ts (664 bytes)
CREATE src/app/dashboard/user-profile/user-profile.component.ts (292 bytes)
UPDATE src/app/dashboard/dashboard.module.ts (470 bytes)
→ shop-cart git:(master) × ▊
```

Figure 5.6: Create a UserProfile component inside the Dashboard module

6. **UserProfile Route:** In the previous step, we have just created a component. We have to update the Dashboard module's route configuration for the `UserProfile` component, as shown in *Code 5.13:*

```
import { NgModule } from '@angular/core';

import { Routes, RouterModule } from '@angular/router';
```

```
import { DashboardComponent } from './dashboard.component';
import { UserProfileComponent } from './user-profile/user-profile.
component';


const routes: Routes = [
            { path: '', component: DashboardComponent },
            { path: 'user-profile', component:
UserProfileComponent }
];


@NgModule({
            imports: [RouterModule.forChild(routes)],
            exports: [RouterModule]
})
export class DashboardRoutingModule { }
```

Code 5.13: dashboard-routing.module.ts - add a new route for user-profile

7. **Data Service and Service Module:** The web application needs to consume resources from the server through REST API or other protocols to fetch data. We have seen that Angular provides the HttpClientModule module for accessing HTTP resources. But instead of importing the HttpClientModule module in all feature modules, the best practice is to delegate server communication tasks to Angular service typically called DataService and put it inside a module called ServiceModule. This ServiceModule module can then be imported by other feature modules for accessing HTTP resources. So let's create service and module by running the command shown in *Figure 5.7:*

```
➜  shop-cart git:(master) ✗ ng generate module service
CREATE src/app/service/service.module.ts (193 bytes)
➜  shop-cart git:(master) ✗ ng generate service service/data
CREATE src/app/service/data.service.spec.ts (323 bytes)
CREATE src/app/service/data.service.ts (133 bytes)
➜  shop-cart git:(master) ✗ █
```

Figure 5.7: Generate DataService service and ServiceModule module

8. **Provide Service in ServiceModule**: We need to provide DataService service into ServiceModule. We can do this in two ways. One by providing

DataService into **"providers"** property of **@NgModule()** decorator of ServiceModule module or by specifying `ServiceModule` into **"providedIn"** property of **@Injectable()** decorator of `DataService`. The best practice to do is update the "providedIn" property of @Injectable() decorator applied to the `DataService` class. The updated code should look similar to *Code 5.14:*

```
import { Injectable } from '@angular/core';

import { ServiceModule } from './service.module';


@Injectable({

        providedIn: ServiceModule

})
export class DataService {


        constructor() {

                console.log('DataService initialized...');

        }

}
```

Code 5.14: Provide DataService into ServiceModule

9. **Import ServiceModule**: We would like to have a single instance of `DataService` for all components throughout the Application. Thus we need to import it at the root of the Application, that is, the `AppModule` module. Since `DataService` is provided inside `ServiceModule` and `AppModule` is the root module, `DataService` can be injected into any children of the `AppModule` module. *Code 5.15* shows `AppModule` after importing `ServiceModule`:

```
import { AppRoutingModule } from './app-routing.module';

import { AppComponent } from './app.component';

import { ServiceModule } from './service/service.module';


@NgModule({

        declarations: [

                AppComponent

        ],

        imports: [

                BrowserModule,

                AppRoutingModule,
```

```
            ServiceModule
        ],
        providers: [],
        bootstrap: [AppComponent]
})
export class AppModule { }
```

Code 5.15: Import ServiceModule into AppModule

10. **Inject DataService**: After `DataService` is provided into AppModule, we
     can inject it into any components, for example, Login Component. There are
     different ways of injecting dependency in, for example, Constructor injection,
     method injection, property injection. The Angular framework supports the
     `Constructor` injection method. Injecting service into the component class is
     easy; just declare a variable of type service in component's constructor and
     set it to a member variable of the class. Angular maintains an Injector tree
     for dependency injection. If service is provided and its instance is not found,
     then, Angular will create a new instance and pass it to the component. If
     the instance is already created, then Angular will simply pass it on to the
     component's constructor. *Code 5.16* shows updated `LoginComponent` after
     injecting `DataService`:

```
import { Component, OnInit } from '@angular/core';
import { DataService } from '../service/data.service';


@Component({
        selector: 'app-login',
        templateUrl: './login.component.html',
        styleUrls: ['./login.component.css']
})
export class LoginComponent implements OnInit {

        constructor(private dataService: DataService) { }

        ngOnInit() {}
}
```

Code 5.16: Injecting DataService service into LoginComponent

11. **Verify Output:** We have done the basic setup of our mock Application so far. Let's save all the changes and run **"ng serve --open"** command if not already running. The command shall launch a browser. We will open the browser's **"Inspect"** section (through **Developer** settings). In the browser, let's change the URL to login URL, that is, http://localhost:4200/login and observe the **"Console"** section of the browser. We should see **"DataService initialized…"** message in the console, as shown in *Figure 5.8*. This message is printed from the DataService constructor. When we changed URL to **"/ login",** Login component got initialized, and its constructor got called. In **LoginComponent's** constructor, we have injected **DataService**. Since there was no earlier instance created for the **DataService** class, it's constructor will be called, and the message will be printed in the console. As a homework, try to inject **DataService** into Sign-up component and change browser URL to **"/sign-up" after "/login"**. We should see only one message and not two because the same instance of DataService class should be passed to **SignUpComponent**.

Figure 5.8: Verify DataService is injected in LoginComponent

12. **Augury Extension:** The Augury is a browser extension for Angular Application. It can be downloaded from https://augury.rangle.io/ website or marketplace of browser. It provides lots of debug information during development, and every Angular developer should have this. One of the features of Augury is it lists Angular Application's routing at runtime. In *Figure 5.9*, we can see how the **"/login"** route is mapped to **LoginComponent**. Note that **"login"**, **"sign-up"**, and "dashboard" are suffixed with **"[Lazy]"** keyword, which let us know that these routes are lazy-loaded.

Figure 5.9: LoginModule lazy-loaded with "/login" url

13. **user-profile route:** We can observe that *Figure 5.9* doesn't show a "/user-profile" route though we have defined it in the routing module. It will be loaded at runtime whenever we change the browser URL to "/dashboard/user-profile". Once the URL is changed, observe the change in Augury "Router Tree", as shown in *Figure 5.10*. We should see the child routes of Dashboard modules loaded into memory:

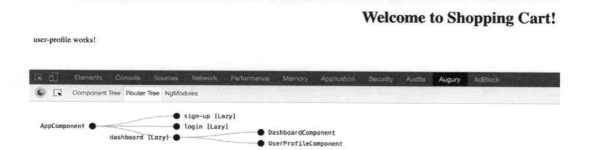

Figure 5.10: Dashboard module lazy-loaded for "dashboard/user-profile" url

14. **NgModules runtime information:** Augury extension also gives us an overview of all NgModules of current Angular Application. *Figure 5.11* shows some of the information captured. We can see for each module what does it imports, exports, providers list, declared classes, and declarations. This information comes very handily when Application is being built by multiple teams, and there are chances of duplicate modules/services/components being defined and exported.

Figure 5.11: Dashboard module lazy-loaded for "dashboard/user-profile" url

15. **Communication between NgModules**: In our Application, we have lazy-loaded feature modules that are activated through routing. Soon we will need to pass data between components and modules. How to do that? One approach is to pass data using injectable service. But best practice is to pass data between lazy loaded modules is either through route parameters or by local storage (or other browser supported storage based on the required scope of data). We will see how to pass data via routes in the routing chapter.

This mock example has given us a chance to model user journey into Angular feature modules and how to map feature modules to their routes. We have also seen how to create lazy loaded modules and use Augury for debug information.

Identifying Different Types of Modules

We have learned that there are different types of modules based on their usage. In our previous example, we have created quite a few modules. Let's try to identify the types of these modules.

- **AppModule**: This is the root module and bootstraps Angular Application with `AppComponent`
- **AppRoutingModule, SignUpRoutingModule, LoginRoutingModule, DashboardRoutingModule**: These are the Routing module defined for their feature modules.
- **LoginModule, SignUpModule, and DashboardModule:** These are feature modules as they contain their functionality and aren't dependent on any other modules explicitly.
- **ServiceModule**: We have picked up the name of this module so that it makes it explicit that it is a Service Module.

Note that there is no defined rule abut types of modules. Per the company, per development team can opt for their naming convention and modularization techniques, but we should follow best practices of Angular guidelines.

Introduction to Angular Ivy

Angular Ivy is a new compilation and renderer engine. Ivy engine compiles Angular Application in a way to reduce build size and faster Application. It depends on the metadata being generated during the build stage and uses this information for building efficient JavaScript code. One of the impacts of Ivy is, NgModule might get obsolete in the future as it emphasis on having `@Component()` decorator most of the metadata and avoid NgModule which creates tree-shaking process ambiguous. Ivy is a default render engine for Angular 9 onward versions. We can create a project with Ivy enabled by running command **"ng new shop-cart-ivy --enable-ivy"**.

Conclusion

In this chapter, we have learned how NgModules are similar to the Namespace concept of C#. We compared C# Application with namespace along with Angular Application with NgModule and saw how the analogy works. After that, we visited @NgModule decorator in detail and understood its metadata properties and their significance. JavaScript Modules are not precisely the same as NgModule, and we saw how they differ. Then we learned that though there is no syntax difference between different types of NgModules, but their usage gives them a different meaning. We briefly saw a difference between eagerly loaded modules versus lazy loaded modules. After that, we visited commonly used NgModules provided by Angular library like CommonModule. With the knowledge gathered about NgModules, we created an application with different types of NgModules. We used Augury extension to see how lazy loaded modules are loaded in runtime along with Application wide NgModules overview. Then we tried to identify different types of NgModules we created based on their usage. We briefly touch base on Angular Ivy, which might reduce the usage of NgModule in the future and make @Component() self-sufficient.

This chapter should allow us to build new Angular Application in a modular way by creating various types of modules, importing/exporting components, identifying modules based on the user journey, and how to map routes to modules.

In the next chapter, we will dive deep into Dependency Injection and Services. We have seen how we can create service and specify where to provide it using either @ NgModule() decorator or @Injectable() decorator. In the next chapter, we will learn more about it.

Questions

1. Can we provide a Component class inside NgModule's "providers" metadata properties?

2. What will happen if we provide injectable service in NgModule, as well as component's providers' metadata properties, declared inside "declarations" of NgModule?

3. Can we have lazy-loaded routing targeting Component class rather than a module?

4. If lazy module gets "imported" into other eagerly loaded NgModules, then will it be a still lazy-loaded module or eagerly loaded module?

5. For using [(ngModel)] across the Application with multiple domain feature modules, how will we provide FormsModule? Will we import FormsModule in each domain feature module?

6. Write a widget module that will export a login and sign-up components that any Angular application can use.

7. If we import modules in multiple domain feature modules, does it create multiple instances of NgModule or share a single instance?

8. What is the difference between the "bootstrap" component and "entryComponents" components which are provided in the NgModule metadata object?

9. Can we have a shared module exporting only Pipes? Explain with example.

10. Write an application with multiple "bootstrap" components.

CHAPTER 6

Dependency Injection (DI) and Services

Dependency Injection (DI) is a very famous design principle used in software development. It enables developing loosely coupled, scalable, and maintainable software systems. In this chapter, we will get a quick overview of DI, how DI is supported in C# and Java. Then we will learn how Angular supports DI and services. We will learn the lifetime and scope of DI ready services based on where they are provided and injected in Angular application. There are different ways we can provide Service, and we will learn them in this chapter. We need to mock data for writing unit test cases; thus, we will see how to write mock services. We will also learn how to build Singleton services; that is, at most, a single instance of Service can exist throughout the application. We will build a small application with the usage of DI and services to get hands-on experience. After reading this chapter, we should be able to understand how DI works in general and Angular and how to write services and the best practices of DI usage.

Structure

- Introduction to Dependency Injection
  - o Problem Statement with an Example
  - o Solution with Dependency Injection
  - o Dependency Injection in C#
  - o Dependency Injection in Java Spring Framework

Objective

This chapter aims to understand core concepts of **Dependency Injections (DI),** which is provided by Angular framework out of the box. Angular maintains different dependency graphs for the `NgModule` hierarchy. Angular Services has a different scope of a lifetime based on where we are providing them, and we will see how it works. Later we will see how DI helps in making code more testable, scalable, and maintainable. With the help of an example, we will learn how to organize code into components, services, and how to provide services at the proper provider level in Angular application.

Introduction to Dependency Injection

Dependency Injection is one of the design principles widely used in many programming languages and technologies. The DI is a technique reverting the dependencies between two or more modules/components. Let's try to understand the problem statement of why DI is required and how to solve it in the next section.

Problem Statement with an Example

Before going deep into DI in Angular, let's have a quick overview of what Dependency Injection is. Dependency Injection is a design pattern to implement **"Inversion of**

Control" (IoC). The IoC in simple terms can be understood as creating an instance of dependent class first and then creating instances of consumer classes by passing dependent instance. Let's try to understand it with the help of a simple example. In our example, we have three classes `Engine`, `Car`, and `Truck`. `Car` and `Truck`, both classes, depends on `Engine` class as direct membership, as shown in *Code 6.1*:

```
export class Engine {
    model: string;
}
export class Car {
    name: string;
    engine: Engine;

    constructor() {
        this.engine = new Engine();
        this.engine.model = "Car Model";
    }
}


export class Truck {
    name: string;
    engine: Engine;
    constructor() {
        this.engine = new Engine();
        this.engine.model = "Truck Model";
    }
}
```

Code 6.1: Dependency between Engine, Car and Truck classes

In the above example, both `Car` and `Truck` class holds a reference to the instance of `Engine` class. Whenever a new instance is created for `Car` and `Truck` class, `Engine` object is also created internally by their constructor. *Code 6.2* shows the creation of instances of `Engine`, `Car`, and `Truck` classes:

```
const engine = new Engine();
engine.model = "Engine1";
console.log(engine)
```

```
const car = new Car();
car.name = "Car1";
console.log(car);


const truck = new Truck();
truck.name = "Truck1";
console.log(truck);
```

Code 6.2: *Creating objects of Engine, Car and Truck classes*

If we compile this TypeScript code and run it with the **"tsc"** compiler, then the output of *Code 6.2* should look similar to *Figure 6.1*. Note that the Car and Truck object structure contains Engine object created in their constructor. The **"console. log()"** internally convert JSON object representation in the output:

```
tsc main.ts && node main.js
Engine { model: 'Engine1' }
Car { engine: Engine { model: 'Car Model' }, name: 'Car1' }
Truck { engine: Engine { model: 'Truck Model' }, name: 'Truck1' }
```

Figure 6.1: *Output of Code 6.2*

Consider this is our product X, and for production release version 1.0, this implementation is tested and validated. Another assumption is the product X version 1.0 has been released to various production servers. Then after a few months, there is a new requirement for amending product X. The requirement states to add a new property to Engine class called **"horsePower"** of type number and should be initialized when the object is created that is, through the constructor. The developer can go to Engine class and update its constructor, as shown in *Code 6.3:*

```
export class Engine {
    model: string;
    horsePower: number;
    constructor(_horsePower:number){
        this.horsePower = _horsePower;
    }
}
```

Code 6.3: *Updated Engine class with new "horsePower" member initialized through a constructor*

Can you guess how this new requirement will impact our existing system? As Car and Truck class initiate Engine class in their constructor and Engine class's constructor has been updated, it will require updating `Car` and `Truck` class's constructor with new `Engine` class instantiation. Imagine having 100s of classes depending on `Engine` class. Every time there is a signature change in Engine class's constructor, then all its dependent classes must update their code for coping with changes. This is the core problem referred to as tight coupling. If we update product X with a new requirement, then we need to compile and deploy all dependent modules and packages which are dependent on `Engine` class. This might introduce breaking changes in modules that are closed for modifications, that is, third-party components whose source code is not available only binaries are. This problem can be solved by inverting control and data flow, as explained in the next section.

Solution with Dependency Injection

There are a few ways to resolve the tight coupling between components and modules. One of the ways to remove tight coupling is **"Inversion of control" (IoC)**. In product X example, `Truck` and `Car` classes are dependent on `Engine` class and control the lifetime of `Engine` instance. If we invert the controls, then we can resolve this tight coupling. We will introduce a new class called "EngineService" in our application. The `EngineService` class is responsible for creating an instance of `Engine` class with proper constructor parameters and provides a getter method to return engine instance to caller/consumer. The next step is to remove the direct dependency between `Car` and `Truck` on `Engine` class. We can do it by removing the instance creation of `Engine` class from `Car` and `Truck` class constructor and ask the `EngineService` class to provide an instance by calling a getter method. The `Car` and `Car` class doesn't know how the instance of Engine class is being created. They simply get an instance. Only `EngineService` knows the constructor signature of Engine class. If we get a new requirement in the future which changes Engine class constructor signature, then we have to change only the `EngineService` class, and the rest of dependent classes like `Car` and `Truck` will be intact. The way we provide EngineService class into `Car` and `Truck` classes is called **Dependency Injection (DI)**. *Code 6.4* shows updated `Car` and `Truck` classes and EngineService class:

```
export class Engine {
    model: string;
    horsePower: number;

    constructor(_horsePower: number) {
        this.horsePower = _horsePower;
    }
}

export class EngineService {
```

```
    private _engine: Engine;

    public getEngine(): Engine {
        return this._engine;
    }

    constructor(horsePower: number) {
        this._engine = new Engine(horsePower);
    }
}

export class Car {
    name: string;
    private engine: Engine;

    constructor(engineService: EngineService) {
        this.engine = engineService.getEngine();
        this.engine.model = "Car Model";
    }
}

export class Truck {
    name: string;
    engine: Engine;

    constructor(engineService: EngineService) {
        this.engine = engineService.getEngine();
        this.engine.model = "Truck Model";
    }
}

const engineService = new EngineService(3000);
const car = new Car(engineService);
car.name = "Car1";
console.log(car);
```

```
const truck = new Truck(engineService);
truck.name = "Truck1";
console.log(truck);
```

Code 6.4: Removing direct coupling by introducing EngineService class

In a nutshell, to remove tight coupling between classes/component/modules, we need to introduce an intermediary service class which wraps the instance creation logic and abstract it for consumers. This is called Dependency Injection by constructor injection. There are other types of DI like method injection, property injection in C#, and Java, but in Angular, we have only constructor injection.

Dependency Injection in C#

The .NET framework provides Dependency Injection out of the box and with the help of packages and libraries. In Windows Forms and WPF C# application, we can use Unity container DI. In ASP.NET MVC and ASP.NET Core Web API, Dependency Injection is provided by the framework, and we don't have to install any libraries like Unity container explicitly. *Code 6.5* shows a Dependency Injection example for .NET Core Web API from MSDN. As shown in the code "ConfigureServices" function gets the "IServiceCollection" service through which we can configure application-level dependencies, which can be injected into controllers later point of time:

```
public void ConfigureServices(IServiceCollection services)
{
    services.AddMvc().SetCompatibilityVersion(CompatibilityVersion.
Version_2_2);


    services.AddScoped<IMyDependency, MyDependency>();
    services.AddTransient<IOperationTransient, Operation>();
    services.AddScoped<IOperationScoped, Operation>();
    services.AddSingleton<IOperationSingleton, Operation>();
    services.AddSingleton<IOperationSingletonInstance>(new
Operation(Guid.Empty));


    // OperationService depends on each of the other Operation types.
    services.AddTransient<OperationService, OperationService>();
}
```

Code 6.5: Dependency Injection snippet for .NET Core Web API through ConfigureServices

The C# applications can have different types of Injection like constructor injection, method injection, or property injection. The interface and DI framework make C# application very robust and maintainable for the long term. Similarly, in Java, we can use DI frameworks for achieving scalability and loose coupling, as discussed in the next section.

Dependency Injection in Java Spring Framework

In the Java Spring framework, the `ApplicationContext` interface provides Inversion of Control. The naming convention used for DI is a bit different, though, like `@Beans` for defining dependencies and `@AutoWired` for injecting dependencies. But core DI functionality remains the same; we can get an instance of bean injected into our class.

Dependency Injection in Angular

Unlike React.js, Angular is not just a library; it is a framework, and one of the features it provides is Dependency Injection out of the box for building applications. Most of the time, we will be providing services for dependency injection, but there are more Angular offers.

Introduction to Angular Services

We have seen how simple Dependency Injection can be implemented with the help of the `EngineService` class. There was nothing special about this class as Service as compared to class syntax. It is the way we have used the `EngineService` class as a Service. Similarly, Angular services are regular Typescript class with `@Injectable()` decorator applied. In the Java Spring framework, we can mark the class method with `@bean` annotation for DI. Similarly, in Angular, we can mark the class with `@Injectable()` decorator to be an Injectable Service.

Automobile application example

We will create a new Angular project using Angular CLI and learn how to implement Dependency Injection in it. Let's build an application by following steps:

1. **Create a new application:** Create a new project by running command "**ng new automobile**". Angular CLI will ask us if we want to use "Angular Routing" in our new project to which respond "**Yes**". Next, we will be prompted to select stylesheet format, select "**CSS**" as a response.

2. **Clean up:** In command prompt, change the current working directory to the new project directory. Open `app.component.html` file and remove boilerplate HTML code and just keep "Welcome to `{{title}}`" `<h1>` tag for simplicity and "`<router></router>`" tag.

3. **Engine class:** Create a new Engine class by running the command "**ng generate class engine**". Let's add "model" and "horsePower" members into this class. `Engine` class is shown in *Code 6.6:*

```
export class Engine {
    private _model: string;
    public get model(): string {
        return this._model;
    }


    private _horsePower: number;
    public get horsePower(): number {
        return this._horsePower;
    }


    constructor(model: string, horsePower: number) {
        this._model = model;
        this._horsePower = horsePower;
    }
}
```

Code 6.6: Engine class definition

4. **Car Component:** Let's create `Car` module and component with their route definition. We can generate these combined items by running the command as shown in *Command 6.1:*

```
ng generate module car --route car --module app.module
```

Command 6.1: Generate truck-suv component

Code 6.7 will generate files and folders for the "Car" component and will update the "app-routing.module.ts" file, as shown in *Figure 6.2*:

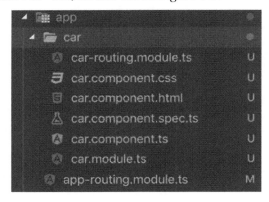

Figure 6.2: Directory structure of "car" component generated by Code 6.7

To see our new "Car" routes work, start the application by running the command "**ng serve --open**" inside command prompt and change browser url to "**http://localhost:4200/car**". We should see **car works**!, message in the browser. Below are the important classes and components we will need going further .

1. **EngineService class:** We will create a new engine service by running the command **ng generate service engine**. This EngineService will be responsible for providing Engine object to its consumer components (CarComponent in this case). The auto-generated code of EngineService will look similar to *Code 6.7*:

```
import { Injectable } from '@angular/core';


@Injectable({
providedIn: 'root'
})
export class EngineService {


constructor() { }
}
```

Code 6.7: Auto generated code of EngineService class

The important part is @Injectable() decorator exported from @angular/core package. @Injectable() decorator tells Angular to mark EngineService class to be injected into the DI injector framework. The providedIn parameter of @Injectable() decorator defines the scope of

Service application-wide. By default, Service is provided in "root" meaning in the AppModule class. The AppModule is the root module of Angular application. By providing EngineService into AppModule, it will be available throughout the application for Injection. In the previous chapter of NgModule, we have seen @NgModule() decorator has a property called "providers" of type array of classes. We can define EngineService inside the "providers" array as well for DI. The best practice of providing Service is in @Injectable() "providedIn" property; this helps Angular compiler to do "**Tree Shaking**" during the build procedure.

Let's add features to in EngineService class. As shown in *Code 6.8,* EngineService creates Engine object and has a getter method to provide already created _engine object:

```
import { Injectable } from '@angular/core';
import { Engine } from './engine';


@Injectable({
    providedIn: 'root'
})
export class EngineService {
    private _engine: Engine;

    constructor() {
        this._engine = new Engine("CarEngine-1", 3000);
    }

    public getEngine(): Engine {
        return this._engine;
    }
}
```

Code 6.8: EngineService with an engine singleton instance

2. **Inject EngineService in CarComponent:** Since EngineService is provided into the AppModule module, we can inject it into CarComponent's constructor. As shown in *Code 6.9,* we can inject Service into components by merely mentioning a variable of type service into the component's

constructor. In Typescript, we can declare class member variables in the constructor as well. Hence when we declare constructor as "constructor(private engineService: EngineService) { }", a private member "engineService" is declared for CarComponent, and the instance is provided from Angular DI injector of type "EngineService". That is why we can use "engineService" in the rest of the member function of CarComponent as used in the ngOnInit() function:

```typescript
import { Component, OnInit } from '@angular/core';
import { EngineService } from '../engine.service';
import { Engine } from '../engine';


@Component({
    selector: 'app-car',
    templateUrl: './car.component.html',
    styleUrls: ['./car.component.css']
})
export class CarComponent implements OnInit {
    private model: string;
    private engine: Engine;

    constructor(private engineService: EngineService) { }

    ngOnInit() {
        this.model = "Car Model";
        this.engine = this.engineService.getEngine();
    }
}
```

Code 6.9: Injecting Engineservice into CarComponent

3. **Display Engine details in CarComponent:** Let's update the Car component's HTML file to display car and engine details. In *Code 6.10*, we can see how we can display values of the "engine" instance provided by EngineService through interpolation binding. By the way, did you observe something different about interpolation binding? The "?." syntax used in {{engine?.model}} binding tells HTML parser to ignore interpreting the "model" property of the "engine" object if "engine" is null or undefined. This way, we can avoid runtime exception if our engine object is null or undefined.

```
<h2>Car Details</h2>

<div>
    Car Model: {{model}}
</div>
<div>
    Engine Model: {{engine?.model}}
</div>
<div>
    Engine HorsePower: {{engine?.horsePower}}
</div>
```

Code 6.10: Displaying Engine details in Car component

5. **Verify Output:** Let's save the changes in all files and make sure our previous "**ng serve --open**" command is still running. If not, then rerun it. The output in the browser should look similar to *Figure 6.3:*

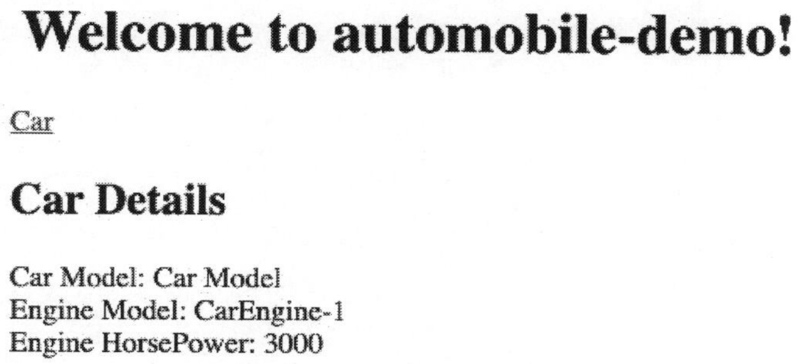

Welcome to automobile-demo!

Car

Car Details

Car Model: Car Model
Engine Model: CarEngine-1
Engine HorsePower: 3000

Figure 6.3: Output of Car component with Engine details

6. **Augury tool analysis:** Augury is an Angular application runtime analysis browser extension. We have briefly got introduced to **Augury** in previous chapters. Let's open Developers Tools in the browser and go to the Augury tab. Next, select **CarComponent** in the **Component Tree** section and verify the **Properties** tab on the right side. We can see the engineService object is part of CarComponent, and the values of the engine object are the same

as created in the `EngineService` constructor and displayed in the browser output. The output of the browser should look similar to *Figure 6.4:*

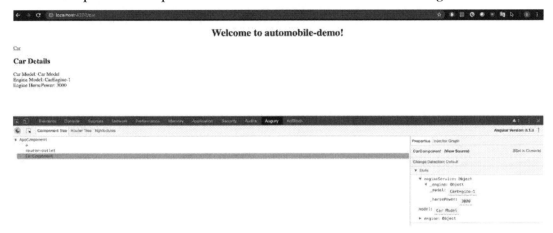

Figure 6.4: *Augury tool inspection of EngineService injection*

Summary

This is a simple example that demonstrates how Angular's Dependency Injection feature can be used. All we have to do is create a service class with `@Injectable()` decorator and mention in which module to provide this Service through `providedIn` property of `@Injectable()` decorator or **providers** property of `@NgModule()` decorator. Then based on the scope of Service, it can be injected into Angular component classes through the **Constructor Injection** mechanism. After injected, Service is ready to be used in component class without worrying about the underlying details of dependencies.

Service Lifetime and Scope

The `@Injectable()` service lifetime and scope are defined by the level of the hierarchy it is provided at. For example, if a service is provided at the root module, then it is a Singleton service available throughout the application's components for Injection. This is a very common case for a "`DataService`" service defined in the application which communicates with the HTTP REST server using HttpClient Service. In this section, we will extend our example to understand more about services.

Injector graph

Angular manages the Dependency Injection mechanism by defining "Injector Graph (Inverted tree)". Angular manages another graph for NgModules/Component (Inverted tree) for defining hierarchy. These two graphs are used to determine the lifetime and scope of Service. If a service is injected into the root module, then it is "root injector's" responsibility to provide an instance of this Service whenever it is asked by the injected component. No matter how deep NgModule/Component tree goes down, you can always get the same instance of your Service from the root injector. In another use case, the child injector object is created, which manages another instance of Service down to its component tree.

> **Note: Merely marking Service with @Injectable() decorator and providing it into @NgModule() injector doesn't create service class's instance. A new instance will be created only when its first Injection is requested by the component's constructor. In our example, the "EngineService" instance will be created only when we navigate to the "http://localhost:4200/car" route; that's when CarComponent is rendered. If another component asks for a service instance, then previously created service instance shall be passed instead of creating new.**

To further understand service lifetime and scope, let's extend our example:

1. **Create Truck Component:** Let's create another component called "TruckComponent" by running *Command 6.2* in the command prompt:

```
ng generate module truck --route truck --module app.module
```

Command 6.2: Generate truck component

Command 6.2 will create another route for the "truck" component along with its NgModule and component. We can verify its output as we did for the "car" route. The next step is to inject EngineService into TruckComponent. This can be done, as shown in *Code 6.11*. As homework, you can try to update the truck.component.html file as a car.component.html file for displaying truck and model details in the browser:

```
import { Component, OnInit } from '@angular/core';
import { EngineService } from '../engine.service';
import { Engine } from '../engine';


@Component({
    selector: 'app-truck',
    templateUrl: './truck.component.html',
    styleUrls: ['./truck.component.css']
})
export class TruckComponent implements OnInit {
    model: string;
```

```
engine: Engine;

constructor(private engineService: EngineService) { }

ngOnInit() {
    this.model = "Truck Model";
    this.engine = this.engineService.getEngine();
}
}
```

Code 6.11: *TruckComponent class with EngineService injected*

2. **Create TruckSUV component:** We will add another component called TruckSuvComponent as a child of the "truck" component. We can do so by running *Command 6.3:*

```
ng generate module truck/truck-suv --route truck-suv --module
truck.module
```

Command 6.3: *Generate truck-suv component*

Command 6.3 is different as compared to previous commands. "module truck/truck-suv" tells Angular CLI to create "truck-suv" as a child of "truck" module and "--module truck.module" tells Angular CLI to update routes for "truck-suv" in the "truck-routing.module.ts" module.

3. **Provide New Instance:** We want to override the root injector's "EngineService" instance for the TruckSuv component. We can do this by providing the "EngineService" service again inside TruckSuvModule, as shown in *Code 6.12:*

```
import { NgModule } from '@angular/core';
import { CommonModule } from '@angular/common';


import { TruckSuvRoutingModule } from './truck-suv-routing.
module';
import { TruckSuvComponent } from './truck-suv.component';
import { EngineService } from 'src/app/engine.service';


@NgModule({
declarations: [TruckSuvComponent],
```

```
imports: [

    CommonModule,

    TruckSuvRoutingModule

],

providers: [EngineService]

})

export class TruckSuvModule { }
```

Code 6.12: Providing EngineService in TruckSuvModule for new instance

4. **Inject EngineService in TruckSuv component:** We would like to inject EngineService new instance inside the TruckSuv component. We can do so using constructor injection shown in *Code 6.13:*

```
import { Component, OnInit } from '@angular/core';

import { EngineService } from 'src/app/engine.service';


@Component({

selector: 'app-truck-suv',

templateUrl: './truck-suv.component.html',

styleUrls: ['./truck-suv.component.css']

})

export class TruckSuvComponent implements OnInit {


    constructor(private engineService: EngineService) { }


    ngOnInit() {  }

}
```

Code 6.13: Injecting EngineService in TruckSuv component

5. **Update EngineService:** For a demonstration of service scope, we will put the "instanceCount" static field inside our EngineService class. Inside the constructor, we will increment instanceCount by one to keep count of a number of instances generated so far. Whenever EngineService is injected into a component, Angular's injector will try to create a new instance for module scope if not created so far and will share the same instance if the component is the same injector hierarchy. *Code 6.14* shows updated EngineService class with instanceCount feature. We will log a message in the browser's console displaying message and instanceCount whenever

EngineService's constructor is run:

```
import { Injectable } from '@angular/core';
import { Engine } from './engine';


@Injectable({
    providedIn: 'root'
})
export class EngineService {
    private _engine: Engine;
    static instanceCount = 0;


    constructor() {
        EngineService.instanceCount++;
        console.log(`EngineService instance created. Instance
Count = ${EngineService.instanceCount}`);
        this._engine = new Engine("CarEngine-1", 3000);
    }


    public getEngine(): Engine {
        return this._engine;
    }
}
```

Code 6.14: EngineService with instanceCount to keep track of instances created so far

6. **Add routes links in the dashboard:** Let's add router links in `app.component.html` for navigating between car, truck, and `truck-suv` components. *Code 6.15* shows updated `app.component.html`:

```
<div style="text-align:center">
    <h1>
        Welcome to {{ title }}!
    </h1>
</div>


<div> <a routerLink="/car">Car</a> </div>
```

```
<div> <a routerLink="/truck">Truck</a> </div>

<div> <a routerLink="/truck/truck-suv">Truck SUV</a> </div>


<router-outlet></router-outlet>
```

Code 6.15: *app.component.html - add routs for Car, Truck and TruckSuv components*

7. **Car route Output:** Let's verify the output in the browser. Let's make sure **"ng serve --open"** command is still running, and if not, then rerun it. Once the application is running a browser, open Developer Tools, and go to the **Console** tab. Now click on the **"Car"** hyperlink in the browser and observe the console output. It should be similar to *Figure 6.5*. We should see the message as **"EngineService instance created. Instance Count = 1"**:

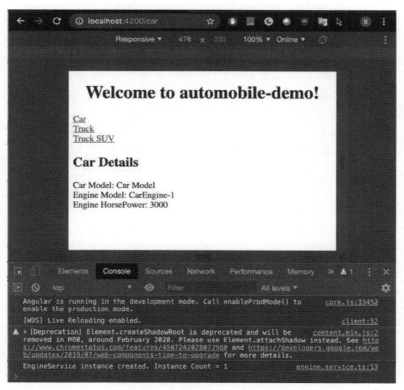

Figure 6.5: *First instance of EngineService created when /car route is activated*

8. **Truck route output:** The next step is to click on the **"Truck"** hyperlink in the browser and observe the output. As an output, we should see the content of **"Truck Component"** is being displayed in the browser, but the console message is the same, and no new instance of EngineService is created for the

Truck component as shown in *Figure 6.6*. This is because TruckComponent is in the same injector graph hierarchy and doesn't override it with the custom provider:

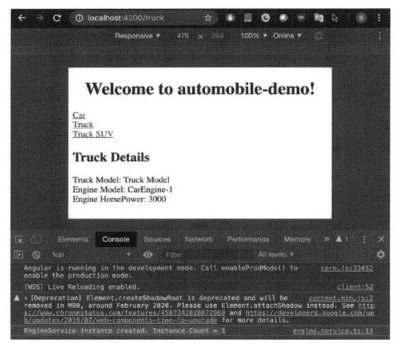

Figure 6.6: *Output of /truck route using the same EngineService instance as of /car route*

9. **TruckSuv route output:** Now click on **"Truck SUV"** hyperlink in browser and observe the changes in the browser console. Something interesting has happened. We can see another message is logged with `instanceCount` set to two in the console from `EngineService` constructor. This is because the child injector of `TruckSuvModule` has created a new instance of `EngineService` when asked by the `TruckSuv` component. This is how we can override the root injector's service instance by child injector. The output of the browser console should look similar to *Figure 6.7*:

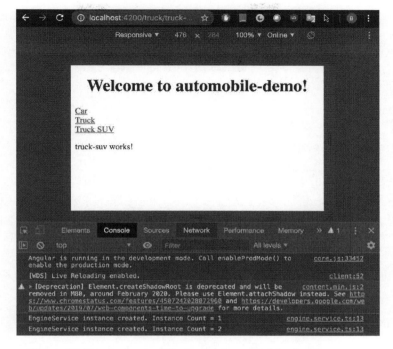

Figure 6.7: *New instance of EngineService created for /truck-suv route*

Summary

We can summaries the lifetime and scope of Service by its provision in injector graph hierarchy. If we inject Service in root injector, then its instance will be shared throughout the application hierarchy unless the child injector overrides it. The child injector's service instance will be shared down to the hierarchy level of its component graph unless some other child overrides it and so on. Sometimes it becomes tricky were to provide Service and might result in subtle bugs, so be mindful where you are providing Service in the component hierarchy.

Injecting Service into Another Service

While building an Angular application, we will come across a situation where one Service has a dependency on another service and needs another service injected into its constructor. A typical example is creating a `DataService` service class for communication with the API server. For `Http` communication, Angular provides two services Http Service and `HttpClient` Service. For general purpose HTTP communication, we should use `HttpClient` Service. Angular components can directly get HttpClient Service injected if `HttpClientModule` is imported into root `AppModule` or in the parent module. But it will be tedious to handle HTTP operations in all feature components. Thus we should create another service class,

"DataService", which will take care of HTTP communication. This `DataService` class can handle all other internal operations before making HTTP calls like defining Http request headers, JWT tokens, security, and so on, in a single place. The `DataService` service class then can be provided at root injector and injected into components for performing HTTP operations:

1. **Create DataService:** Let's create a new service called `DataService` by running *Command 6.4*:

   ```
   ng generate service data
   ```

   Command 6.4: *Create a DataService service*

2. **Import HttpModule:** `HttpClient` service is provided into `HttpModule` module exported from `"@angular/common/http"` package. Thus we need to import HttpModule into AppModule so that HttpClient service will be available throughout the application, as shown in *Code 6.16*:

   ```
   import { BrowserModule } from '@angular/platform-browser';
   import { NgModule } from '@angular/core';
   import { HttpClientModule } from "@angular/common/http";


   import { AppRoutingModule } from './app-routing.module';
   import { AppComponent } from './app.component';

   @NgModule({
   declarations: [
       AppComponent
   ],
   imports: [
       BrowserModule,
       AppRoutingModule,
       HttpClientModule
   ],
   providers: [],
   bootstrap: [AppComponent]
   })
   export class AppModule { }
   ```

   Code 6.16: *Import HttpModule into AppModule for accessing HttpClient service*

3. **Update DataService**: We can inject HttpClient Service into DataService's constructor after HttpClientModule has been imported. After injected, we will try to hit a public **GET HTTP URL** of mock JSON data server, which returns an array of JSON object through a method called "getPosts()" using HttpClient. In this method, we will return Observable, which will hold the HTTP response from the server and pass it on to its caller. *Code 6.17* shows an updated DataService class:

```
import { Injectable } from '@angular/core';
import { HttpClient } from '@angular/common/http';
import { Observable } from 'rxjs';


@Injectable({
            providedIn: 'root'
})
export class DataService {
            constructor(private httpClient: HttpClient) { }


            getPosts(): Observable<any> {
                    const url = 'https://my-json-server.typicode.
com/typicode/demo/posts';
                    return this.httpClient.get(url);
            }
}
```

Code 6.17: Injecting HttpClient service into DataService

4. **Consume DataService**: Next, we will update the Car component constructor for injecting DataService instance. We will call the "getPosts()" method of DataService class and log the result into browser console, as shown in *Code 6.18:*

```
import { Component, OnInit } from '@angular/core';
import { EngineService } from '../engine.service';
import { Engine } from '../engine';
import { DataService } from '../data.service';


@Component({
    selector: 'app-car',
```

```
        templateUrl: './car.component.html',
        styleUrls: ['./car.component.css']
    })
    export class CarComponent implements OnInit {
        private model: string;
        private engine: Engine;

        constructor(private engineService: EngineService,
            private dataService: DataService) { }

        ngOnInit() {
            this.model = "Car Model";
            this.engine = this.engineService.getEngine();

            this.dataService.getPosts().subscribe(posts => {
                console.log(posts);
            })
        }
    }
```

Code 6.18: Injecting DataService into Car component

5. **Verify output:** Let's try to see the output in the browser. Make sure the development server is running and navigate to the "http://localhost:4200/car" route. Then open browser console, and we should see output similar to *Figure 6.8* listing JSON array of **"Posts"** returned by the **"getPosts()"** method of DataService class:

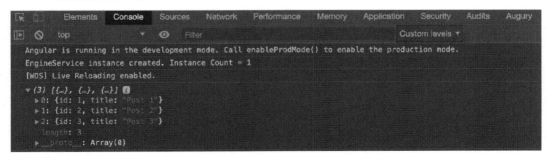

Figure 6.8: Consuming real HTTP API via DataService and log output in the console

The Angular DI framework is very powerful and helps modularizing applications by segregating responsibilities. The services can take responsibilities like fetching data from the server, processing data and updating for visual purpose, and so on. The services can also be broken down into smaller services with interdependencies and injected using the DI framework.

Mock Services for Faster UI Development

Many time frontend team and backend teamwork in separation, focusing on different features. Even though features are supposed to be built in parallel, in reality, it doesn't go hand in hand. A common practice is that the backend team defines a contract for service API and passes contracts to the frontend team for reference. Then the frontend team can start building UI features and build mock data based on future backend service API contracts. We can define a mock data service that will provide backend API mock data to the UI component. Once backend API is published, then we just need to change the service provider from mock Service to real Service. Let's see, in the example, to create a mock data service. In our demo application, we have `DataService`, which fetches `Posts` through the `getPosts()` method from an HTTP server. We have injected this `DataService` into CarComponent and logged posts into the browser console. We will create a new service called `MockDataService`, which will have a hardcoded "`Posts`" array, which will be returned by the `getPosts()` method with the same signature as of `DataService`. Let's follow the following steps for extending our application for mock Service:

1. **Mock Data Service:** Create `MockDataService` by running *Command 6.5:*

   ```
   ng generate service mock-data
   ```

   Command 6.5: *Generate MockDataService*

2. **Update `MockDataService`:** Once `MockDataService` is created, let's add hardcoded `Posts` array and method, as shown in *Code 6.19*. We are using Rxjs operator of(`this.MOCK_POSTS`) returns an Observable because `HttpClient` service's `get()` method returns `Observable<any>` type. This way, we will keep the same contract with mock and real data service.

   ```
   import { Injectable } from '@angular/core';
   import { Observable, of } from 'rxjs';


   @Injectable({
       providedIn: 'root'
   })
   export class MockDataService {
   ```

```
MOCK_POSTS = [
    {
        "id": 1,
        "title": "Mock Post 1"
    },
    {
        "id": 2,
        "title": "Mock Post 2"
    },
    {
        "id": 3,
        "title": "Mock Post 3"
    }
];
getPosts(): Observable<any> {
    return of(this.MOCK_POSTS);
}
}
```

Code 6.19: *MockDataService providing mock POSTS*

3. **Update CarComponent:** Instead of injecting "DataService" into CarComponent, we will inject "MockDataService" in the constructor, as shown in *Code 6.20*. Note that "ngOnInit()" code remained the same for calling "getPosts()" method:

```
import { Component, OnInit } from '@angular/core';
import { EngineService } from '../engine.service';
import { Engine } from '../engine';
import { DataService } from '../data.service';
import { MockDataService } from '../mock-data.service';

@Component({
    selector: 'app-car',
    templateUrl: './car.component.html',
    styleUrls: ['./car.component.css']
```

```
})
export class CarComponent implements OnInit {
    private model: string;
    private engine: Engine;

    constructor(private engineService: EngineService,
        private dataService: MockDataService) { }

    ngOnInit() {
        this.model = "Car Model";
        this.engine = this.engineService.getEngine();

        this.dataService.getPosts().subscribe(posts => {
            console.log(posts);
        })
    }
}
```

Code 6.20: Injecting MockDataService into CarCmponent

4. **Verify Output:** We can verify output by going to http://localhost:4200/car route and open browser console. We should see mock posts logged into the console, as shown in *Figure 6.9*:

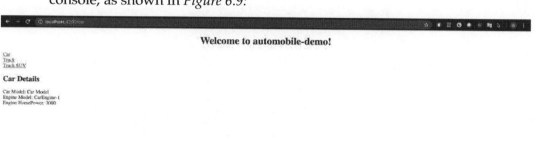

Figure 6.9: *Output of MockDataService injected into CarComponent*

Summary

Angular Services can be used for mocking data into an application for accelerating UI feature development, as shown in the previous example. Though we are injecting `DataService` into `CarComponent` directly instead of `DataService`, we should implement a better approach of using **"Interface"** based Service. The `@NgModule()` decorator has `"providers"` property which accepts an instance of `"{provide: <Service>, useValue:<ServiceName>}"` JSON object. Using this approach, we can define a service interface and inject this interface into the rest of the application components. To change the actual service instance, we should update only the `"useValue"` property of `NgModule` in one place, and all components will get it injected.

ElementInjector – Providing Service into Component

So far, we have seen how we can provide Service into NgModule, and they will be ready for Injection into child components. In some cases, we need Service specific to only a component level and doesn't need to be shared with other components. If we inject such Service into `@NgModule()` module, then Service's instance will be created and maintained until the `@NgModule()` module gets unloaded by the current context. If we could provide Service into components, then the service instance will be removed as soon as the component is destroyed. Thus freeing memory occupied by Service. Such provision and Injection of Service into a component is maintained by `"ElementInjector"` of Angular.

For demonstration purposes, we will extend ours by creating `CarService` and `TruckService`. We shall provide these services into the `Car` and `Truck` component, respectively. Let's follow the following steps:

1. **Create `CarService`:** Let's create CarService by running *Command 6.6:*

   ```
   ng generate service car/car
   ```
   Command 6.6: Generate CarService into Car folder

2. **Update `CarService`:** We will remove the default `"providedIn: root"` property of `@Injector()` decorator of `CarService`. This way, we will not provide `CarService` into AppModule by default. Inside `CarService` class, we will add a property `"fuelType"` and a constructor with `console.log()` message to verify how many times Service has been initialized. The updated `CarService` class should look like *Code 6.21:*

   ```
   import { Injectable } from '@angular/core';
   ```

```
@Injectable()
export class CarService {

    fuelType: string = 'Petrol';

    constructor() {
        console.log('CarService initialized....');
    }
}
```

Code 6.21: Updated CarService service

3. **Provide and Inject CarService:** We will provide CarSerivce into CarComponent's "providers" array and inject CarSerivce into CarComponent's constructor, as shown in *Code 6.22:*

```
import { Component, OnInit } from '@angular/core';
import { EngineService } from '../engine.service';
import { Engine } from '../engine';
import { DataService } from '../data.service';
import { MockDataService } from '../mock-data.service';
import { CarService } from './car.service';

@Component({
    selector: 'app-car',
    templateUrl: './car.component.html',
    styleUrls: ['./car.component.css'],
    providers:[CarService]
})
export class CarComponent implements OnInit {
    private model: string;
    private engine: Engine;

    constructor(private engineService: EngineService,
        private dataService: MockDataService,
        private carService: CarService) { }
```

```
ngOnInit() {
    this.model = "Car Model";
    this.engine = this.engineService.getEngine();

    this.dataService.getPosts().subscribe(posts => {
        console.log(posts);
    })

    console.log(`Fuel Type: ${this.carService.fuelType}`);
}
}
```

Code 6.22: Providing and Injecting CarService into CarComponent

4. **Verify output**: If the Angular development server is not running, then start it. After that, in the browser, change URL to the "http://localhost:4200/car" route and verify output in the browser's developer console. We should see one of the messages in the console as "**CarService initialized....**" logged by CarService constructor, which means a new CarService instance has been created. Now let's navigate to other routes "http://localhost:4200/truck" and navigate back to the "http://localhost:4200/car" route and observe the output in the browser console. We will have another message logged by CarService constructor, which means another new instance has been created of CarService, unlike EngineService. We have only one message logged by EventService constructor no matter on which route we navigate because we have provided it into AppModule, and the same instance is shared by child components. We should see output similar to *Figure 6.10*:

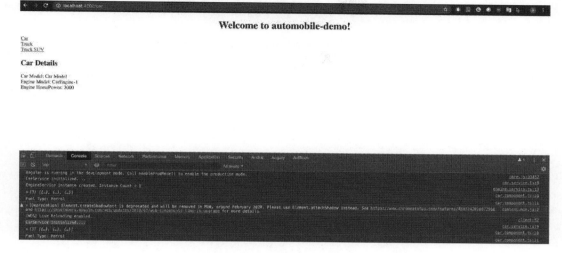

Figure 6.10: Multiple log message from CarService constructor

Summary

When the Angular component needs a specific service functionality that cannot be shared or doesn't require to be shared with other components, then we should provide such Service into component's **"Providers"** array. This way, we can limit the scope of Service and reduce memory leaks. Another important point is, if Service is available to more than one component, then other components can change the service state, which is an unwanted effect for component-specific Service. Note that component provided Service will be available to its child component, though.

Angular Ivy note: The new renderer engine, Angular Ivy, tries to evaluate all dependencies of components during compilation for building efficient production binaries and better tree shaking. Angular Ivy prefers Services to be injected into @Component() decorator metadata rather than @NgModule so that while rendering component, its dependencies are resolved correctly and injected into injector tree.

Different Types of Providers

The @NgModule() and @Component() decorators have a property called "providers," which accepts value array of type "Provider" class. We have seen how to provide a service into @NgModule() and @Component() by passing the name of the Service into "providers" array. There are situations where we want to customize this configuration. In this section, we will see different types of providers option passed to injector tree and how they get injected into components.

The Provider with "useValue"

Whenever we provide a service class name or injectable token name in "providers" array of @NgModule() or @Component(), Angular register class name in injector graph and create a new instance whenever Injection is requested at runtime. If we do not want Angular to create a new instance of the injected type and pass a fixed constant value, then we can use the "useValue" feature. Let's try to understand "useValue" with an example. We will define a constant array called "Cars" with mocked car names, as shown in *Code 6.23*:

```
export const Cars = [
    'Car 1',
    'Car 2',
    'Car 3',
    'Car 4',
    'Car 5'
]
```

Code 6.23: cars.ts - Mocked car names array

Next, define "Trucks" constant array with mocked truck names, as shown in *Code 6.24*:

```
export const Trucks = [
    'Truck 1',
    'Truck 2',
    'Truck 3',
    'Truck 4',
    'Truck 5'
]
```

Code 6.24: trucks.ts - Mocked truck names array

The "Cars" and "Trucks" are the values that we would like to inject into components. But we cannot directly inject values into components. We need to provide some token to the Angular injector graph for mapping value. Thus we will create a "Vehicle" token. The InjectionToken class accepts the type of token value as a generic type argument and token name as a string in its constructor. In our case, we would like to register a token called "Vehicles" of an array of strings, as shown in *Code 6.25*:

```
import { InjectionToken } from '@angular/core';

export const Vehicles = new
InjectionToken<Array<string>>('Vehicles');
```

Code 6.25: vehicles.ts - Vehicle injection token created

Once the token is created, we can provide it into `@NgModule()`. In our AppModule, we will provide `Vehicle` token with the value of trucks, as shown in *Code 6.26*. In `"providers"` array instead of the passing service name, we are passing an object with key-value pair of `"provide"` and `"useValue"`. The "provide" key accepts a token name, which is the object of InjectionToken class or any `@Injectable()` service name. The "useValue" key accepts an object whose type matches with InjectionToken. The "useValue" accepts only compile-time value; we can not specify any expression which will compute the value at runtime.

```typescript
import { BrowserModule } from '@angular/platform-browser';
import { NgModule } from '@angular/core';
import { HttpClientModule } from "@angular/common/http";

import { AppRoutingModule } from './app-routing.module';
import { AppComponent } from './app.component';
import { Vehicles } from './vehicles';
import { Cars } from './cars';
import { Trucks } from './trucks';

@NgModule({
    declarations: [
        AppComponent
    ],
    imports: [
        BrowserModule,
        AppRoutingModule,
        HttpClientModule
    ],
    providers: [
        {
            provide: Vehicles, useValue: Trucks
        }
    ],
    bootstrap: [AppComponent]
})
export class AppModule { }
```

Code 6.26: app.module.ts - *Providing "Vehicle" injection token into AppModule*

We are now ready to inject the "Vehicles" injection token into the rest of our application. As shown in *Code 6.27*, in AppComponent, we will inject Vehicle using @Inject() decorator exported from the "@angular/core" package. The injection syntax is a bit different from the service injection. If we need to inject token into component, then we must call @Inject() decorator and ask the injector graph to find this token in and use the value specified in "useValue" key of "providers" property:

```
import { Component, Inject } from '@angular/core';
import { Vehicles } from "./vehicles";
@Component({
    selector: 'app-root',
    templateUrl: './app.component.html',
    styleUrls: ['./app.component.css']
})
export class AppComponent {
    title = 'automobile-demo';


    constructor(@Inject(Vehicles)private vehicles: Array<string>) {
    }


    ngOnInit(){
        console.log(this.vehicles);
    }
}
```

Code 6.27: *app.component.ts - Injecting "Vehicle" injection token into AppComponent*

In AppModule, we have used "Trucks" as "useValue" value; hence if we run this application and observe the browser console output, then we should see the "Trucks" array being printed as shown in *Figure 6.11*. As an exercise, print "Cars" mock array instead of "Trucks":

Figure 6.11: *Mocked truck names injected through "useValue"*

There are situations while building Angular application where we would like to provide constant values as @Injectable() like VERSION_NUMBER or PRODUCT_NAME, which should be the same for the rest of the application but defined only once as constant. In such cases "useValue" provider option is very helpful.

C# Analogy

In C#, we can achieve similar functionality using the "RegisterInstance()" method of UnityContainer. In *Code 6.28,* we are creating an object of "Audi" class that implements interface ICar, and we are registering this instance with Unity container. Now we will try to resolve ICar using UnityContainer then we will get the same object that we have registered, UnityContainer won't create a new instance:

```
var container = new UnityContainer();

ICar audi = new Audi();

container.RegisterInstance<ICar>(audi);
```

Code 6.28: Registering instance in UnityContainer and C#

The Provider with "useClass"

In the previous section, we have seen how to inject "DataService" and "MockDataService" into CarComponent by switching in the "providers" section of CarModule and changes in CarComponent constructor. This is not an effective way of handling services. For example, if we have an application where lots of components are using DataService, and we want to change it to MockDataService for local development or testing purpose, then it will involve changes in all component's constructor. We have discussed a better approach to solve this issue, and now we will see how to implement it. Let's create an abstract class called "IDataService" which we will use an interface, as shown in *Code 6.29:*

```
import { Observable } from 'rxjs';


export abstract class IDataService {
    abstract getPosts(): Observable<any>;
}
```

Code 6.29: idata.service.ts - IDataService interface

Next, we will implement IDataService into MockDataService, as shown in *Code 6.30:*

```
@Injectable()
export class MockDataService implements IDataService {


    getPosts(): Observable<any> {
        return of(this.MOCK_POSTS);
    }
}
```

Code 6.30: mock-data.service.ts - implement IDataService interface

Similarly, we will implement IDataService into DataService, as shown in *Code 6.31:*

```
@Injectable()
export class DataService implements IDataService {


    getPosts(): Observable<any> {
            const url = 'https://my-json-server.typicode.com/typicode/
demo/posts';
            return this.httpClient.get(url);
```

```
    }
}
```

Code 6.31: *data.service.ts - implement IDataService interface*

> **Note: It is not required to implement the IDataService interface into DataService and MockDataService for using them as "useClass" value, but it is a best practice. It prevents a situation where a function is defined inside the interface but not implemented into a service class. If such a function gets called by component, then it will throw a runtime exception.**

In CarModule, we will provide IDataService with the value of DataService class inside "providers" property with "useClass" property, as shown in *Code 6.32:*

```
import { NgModule } from '@angular/core';
import { CommonModule } from '@angular/common';


import { CarRoutingModule } from './car-routing.module';
import { CarComponent } from './car.component';
import { MockDataService } from '../mock-data.service';
import { IDataService } from '../idata.service';
import { DataService } from '../data.service';


@NgModule({
    declarations: [CarComponent],
    imports: [
        CommonModule,
        CarRoutingModule
    ],
    providers: [
        { provide: IDataService, useClass: DataService }
    ]
})
export class CarModule { }
```

Code 6.32: *car.module.ts – Provide DataService class for IDataService service*

Finally, we will update the `CarComponent` constructor by injecting `IDataService`, and the rest of the code will be the same as shown in *Code 6.33*:

```
import { DataService } from '../data.service';
import { MockDataService } from '../mock-data.service';
import { CarService } from './car.service';
import { IDataService } from '../idata.service';


@Component({
    selector: 'app-car',
    templateUrl: './car.component.html',
    styleUrls: ['./car.component.css'],
    providers: [CarService]
})
export class CarComponent implements OnInit {
    constructor(private engineService: EngineService,
        private dataService: IDataService,
        private carService: CarService) { }


    ngOnInit() {
        this.dataService.getPosts().subscribe(posts => {
            console.log(posts);
        });
    }
}
```

Code 6.33: car.component.ts – Inject IDataService into CarComponent

Let's save all the changes and verify the browser output. We should see the output of the `"getPosts()"` function of `"DataService"` in the browser's console logged since we have used it as a `"useClass"` property value. As an exercise update code for getting output from `MockDataService's` "getPosts()" function.

C# Analogy

In C# we could achieve similar functionality using UnityContainer "register()" and "resolve()" methods. In *Code 6.34* we are registering DataService and MockDataService for IDataService interface with token string. While resolving specific instance this token is used to get instance of class from dependency injection object. It is pretty straight forward in C# whereas in Angular syntax is a bit complex but analogy is same. The important thing is we are getting power of Dependency Injection and features in JavaScript framework which is pretty cool.

```
IUnityContainer container = new UnityContainer();

container.RegisterType<IDataService, DataService>("DataService");

container.RegisterType<IDataService,
MockDataService>("MockDataService");


IDataService service = container.
Resolve<IDataService>("DataService");

service.GetPosts();
```

Code 6.34: "useClass" reference code for C# and UnityContainer

The Provider with "useFactory"

So far, we have provided services with a service class having default constructors. When Service is injected into a component, the Angular injector graph calls the default constructor of service class and returns the new instance if not cached earlier. But what if our Service has a parameterized constructor? Angular injector graph cannot create a new instance of Service as it doesn't know how to invoke the parameterized constructor. That's where the "useFactory" property comes into the picture. We have to define a factory function that will call the parameterized constructor of Service. We will pass this factory function as a value to "useFactory" property. Let's try to understand "useFactory" by an example. We will create a new service class called "TruckService" by running *Command 6.6:*

```
ng generate service truck
```

Command 6.6: Generate TruckService service

In the "truck.service.ts" file, we will define factory function and parameterized TruckService class constructor, as shown in *Code 6.35*. Note that we have also removed @Injector(), decorator, from TruckService service class as we are going to define its injection strategy. TruckService service class constructor accepts two parameters and initializes its member variables. The TruckServiceFactory function is responsible for creating a new instance of TruckService service class. It accepts "stroke" and "capacity" parameters and returns an inner function, which returns a new instance of type "TruckService" class:

```
export function TruckServiceFactory(stroke: number, capacity: number)
{
    return (): TruckService => {
```

```
        return new TruckService(stroke, capacity);
    }
}


export class TruckService {

    private _stroke: number;
    private _capacity: number;

    constructor(stroke: number, capacity: number) {
        this._stroke = stroke;
        this._capacity = capacity;
    }

    getStroke() {
        return this._stroke;
    }

    getCapacity() {
        return this._capacity;
    }
}
```

Code 6.35: truck.service.ts - TruckService class and TruckServiceFactory factory method

In the TruckModule module, we will provide TruckService service class with the factory method, as shown in *Code 6.36*. The "providers" section has got more interesting now! We are asking the Angular DI framework to register class "TruckService" for Injection by invoking factory function. Whenever any component requests for TruckService instance to be injected, then the "useFactory" function (in this case TruckServiceFactory) will be called with parameters if any and instance will be injected into component's constructor.

```
import { NgModule } from '@angular/core';
import { CommonModule } from '@angular/common';


import { TruckRoutingModule } from './truck-routing.module';
```

```
import { TruckComponent } from './truck.component';
import { TruckService, TruckServiceFactory } from '../truck.service';


@NgModule({
    declarations: [TruckComponent],
    imports: [
        CommonModule,
        TruckRoutingModule
    ],
    providers: [
        {
            provide: TruckService, useFactory:
TruckServiceFactory(62, 449)
        }
    ]
})
export class TruckModule { }
```

Code 6.36: Providing TruckService class using TruckServiceFactory function

Summary

If injectable service class has parameterized constructor or Injection Token value should be computed by custom function, then we can use the "useFactory" provision mechanism of DI. This becomes very handy while defining custom business logic or services has dependencies on other dependencies. While writing unit tests, we need to define some mock data, and "useFactory" can be very useful there as well. Throughout this chapter, we have seen how to inject services into components or other services. But we can inject services into Angular pipes, directives, modules, and any other declarable classes as well.

Organizing services

The Angular commercial application will involve many feature modules, different routes, components, pipes, directives, and lots of services. It is very important to organize code structure for application maintainability. Different practices are being followed on how to organize services in the application.

- **Service Modules:** One approach is to keep all services provided for the "root" module into a separate folder called "services" and provide them into an @NgModule() decorated class called "ServiceModule". The ServiceModule is then imported into AppModule (root module). Similarly, specific feature related services are wrapped into FeatureServiceModule(s) and imported into other feature modules.

- **Co-located Services:** In co-located services approach, features related Service(s) are kept into feature modules and provided there itself. This makes easy to find Service and maintain code. The downside of this approach is if feature service is injected into two different feature modules, then we need to keep feature service into one of the modules or their parent module. If the parent module has more feature modules, then other modules will get this feature service unnecessarily.

- **Facade service:** The Facade software design pattern states that it keeps one wrapper class, which provides access to many other classes. Imagine in our application we have 50 features and 40 feature services. Maintaining these services will be challenging as there might be more than one team developing similar Service or duplicate Service. Maintaining provider section and Injection of Service into components will be tricky as there are lots of services names to be aware of. In such a case, we can use a Facade design pattern for services.

The idea of façade service is it will encapsulate all feature services as class members. Facade service constructor and member function will make sure how to inject all feature services and provide access to these services. In the rest of the application, we can inject only one Service—FacadeService Service into feature components. Since there is only one Service to work with, it is easier to maintain code.

The challenge of this approach is to maintain the life and scope of wrapped services instances. We must create and destroy the instance of each Service, which is no longer required by feature components. *Figure 6.12* shows how we can architect Facade service patterns in Angular application. In this example, FacadeService holds a reference to AccountService, DashboardService, LoginService, ProductService, and SignupService instances. Facade service class also provides wrapper methods of facade services like "getOrderList()", "getProductDetails()", and so on. The OrderComponent can invoke one of these methods by injecting the FacadeService service class and being unaware of which Service is being called internally. In the future, if we want to change ProductService to

SalesServices providing the same signature method, then changes will take place into FacadeService class only, and the consumer component will not change.

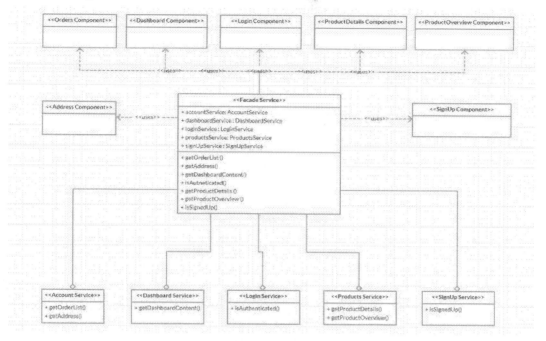

Figure 6.12: Facade design pattern for Angular services

The Facade service class has its advantages and disadvantages. Based on the problem we have to solve, we can opt Façade service patter or any other method. There is no hard and fast rule which pattern to use.

Conclusion

In this chapter, we have learned quite a few things about **Dependency Injection (DI)** and Services in Angular. We first tried to understand what problem Dependency Injection tries to solve and how does it work in C# and Java framework. Then We have seen how DI works in Angular via Injectable services, which are merely simple TypeScript classes with @Injectable() decorator. We have implemented a very basic automobile application to explore DI and Service concepts. Lifetime and scope of Angular services are defined by the "providers" section and hierarchy of injector graph. We have seen how service scope changes based on where Service is provided at the different module and component level. Then we have written a service that has a dependency on another injectable service. Writing unit test cases for components and services consuming HTTP resources can be handled by creating mock data services. If HTTP resource is not available, then local development can continue using such mock data services. The `ElementInjector` comes into the picture when Service is provided and injected into a component. This will become a best practice in the coming future as the Angular Ivy renderer engine gets matures enough. The real-world web application involves writing services with parameterized constructor and custom business functionality. For providing such services, Angular provides different ways of how to provide injectable token through `useValue, useClass, useExisting,` and `useFactory` options. Finally, we have learned how to organize services in Angular application. There is no right or wrong way of organizing services, and it depends on the type of application and developer teams. We have seen a few best practices like creating service modules and importing service modules, placing services into the same folder as of feature modules, and finally facade service design pattern.

After reading this chapter, we should be able to orchestrate the Angular application into different components, modules, and services. We should be able to identify how many services we should create, where to provide them, and which mechanism to opt for providing services. We should be able to create mock data services for writing unit test cases and mock demo application for quick prototypes.

In the next chapter, we will see how to build Angular forms. The forms are key to any Angular application. Any interactive web application needs to collect inputs from users and process them. The Angular forms allow us to write a neat and scalable data-bound application. We will continue discussing Angular forms in the next chapter.

Questions

1. Consider we have two components in the parent-child relationship; for example, `OrderComponent` renders `AccountComponent`. If we provide a service into the parent component inside the "`providers`" property of @ `Component()` decorator, then do we need to inject the same Service into the child component's "`providers`" property of `@Component()` decorator as well?

2. Implement a `MessageService` service class in Angular application. The `MessageService` class will pass data between components without worrying about their relationship. We can pass data between child and parent components, but what if we want to pass data between two components that are not in the same feature modules? Here our MessageService will come into the picture. Using `MessageService`, component A can pass data to B and vice versa even if they are not related.

3. Write a simple `TranslateService` service class. The `TranslateService` service class will have a function "`translate(string text)`" which accepts a string in English and will return its translated text in German. You can keep some hardcoded English-German keywords for testing purposes. Create a new pipe using Angular CLI called "`MyTranslatePipe`". Then inject `TranslateService` into the "`MyTranslatePipe`" pipe. Use `MyTranslatePipe` pipe in any component's HTML text field and observe the output. The browser should render text in German even though at design time, we have specified text in English.

4. Write an Angular application that will have a fixed/constant base URL for HTTP resources. Create a new InjectableToken "`BASE_URL`" and provide it into `AppModule`. This token can be resolved for consuming HTTP resources into `DataService` using `HttpClientService`. The purpose of this token is to maintain the base URL in one place and make it easy for changing between "development" and "production" base URL.

5. Create a small e-commerce website with various feature components and services. Write a FacadeService to encapsulate feature services like `OrderService, ProductService`, as shown in *Figure 6.11,* and feel free to extend it.

CHAPTER 7

Building Forms

The Web forms are core components of any web application. We will hardly come across a website that doesn't have any web forms. Typical website at least has a **"Contact us", "Login", "Sign-in"** or similar small forms. The HTML provides a web form out of the box for collecting user inputs. Angular provides a rich form's functionality on top of it. In this chapter, we will learn about how to build Angular forms, different types of forms, how to do basic validation and error handling. We will build a demo application and learn these concepts while building the same.

Structure

- HTML Forms
- ASP.NET Forms
- AngularJS Forms
- Angular Forms
- Template Driven Forms
- Template-driven form validations
- Template-driven form – custom validations
- Reactive forms
- Reactive form validations

- Reactive forms custom validations
- Template-driven forms versus Reactive forms

Objective

This chapter aims to learn Angular Forms in detail. There are two types of forms in Angular:

- Template-driven forms
- Reactive forms.

We will learn by example how these forms are built. We will also see the key differences between these types of forms and which scenarios are best suited for the specific application type. We will learn how to validate form inputs and track changes. At the end of this chapter, we should be able to build an Angular application with Template-driven forms and Reactive forms.

HTML Forms

The HTML standard components provide <form> control out of the box with basic functionalities. Using <form> tag, we can encapsulate form controls in a group and operate them as a single logical entity. The basic form validations (for example., required field validation, number validation, and so on) are also provided by form control attributes out of the box. *Code 7.1* shows the simple subscription form. This form has two <input> controls one for entering "**username**" and another for user "email address". The third <input> control is interesting. If we check its type, it is of "submit," which will render this <input> element as a default button on a web page. Whenever a user has entered data into controls and press "*Enter*/Return" key, then <input> with "submit" type will get executed. A click on **Submit** button will trigger "action" HTTP request on <form> tag. The HTTP method type will be decided by the "method" attribute, which is by default "GET". There are attributes for <form> control for other functionalities which the reader should explore as an exercise.

```
<form action="" method="post" class="form-example">
    <div class="form-example">
        <label for="name">Enter your name: </label>
        <input type="text" name="name" id="name" required>
    </div>
    <div class="form-example">
        <label for="email">Enter your email: </label>
        <input type="email" name="email" id="email" required>
```

```
        </div>
        <div class="form-example">
            <input type="submit" value="Subscribe!">
        </div>
    </form>
```

Code 7.1: *app.component.html - Simple HTML subscription form*

The output of *Code 7.1* will be similar to *Figure 7.1*, shown as follows:

Figure 7.1: *Simple HTML subscription form output*

The `<input>` tag for username and email address has **required** form validation. If the user doesn't provide value for the "required" input field and tries to submit the form, then the browser will throw validation error and form submit action will be canceled as shown in *Figure 7.2*:

Figure 7.2: *HTML Form "required" field validation error output*

The HTML `<form>` has been heavily used until React.js, AngularJs introduced extended version of `<form>` control. These new JavaScript frameworks have written wrapper over native `<form>` element providing fine control and abstraction over low-level API for the web developer. There is no form layout that we cannot build with native HTML `<form>` tag. But doing so will be tedious and time-consuming. That's why we have new JavaScript frameworks like Angular to make a web developer's life easy!

ASP.NET Forms

The .NET framework has Windows Forms and WPF Forms for building powerful desktop applications. The ASP.NET Forms are also capable of building complex web forms. But when it comes to JavaScript integration, ASP.NET forms get messy. The ASP.NET forms have their form tags and attributes mixed with native HTML attributes. *Code 7.2* shows the simple ASP.NET form code. In this code, native `<form>` control is used, and submitted values are displayed with ASP.NET binding "@companyname" and "@contactname" whose values are extracted from incoming requests. Again, ASP.NET has Web Pages, MVC forms, and Web Forms as three different models of creating forms to make things more complicated.

```
<html>
    <body>
        @{
        if (IsPost) {
        string companyname = Request["CompanyName"];
        string contactname = Request["ContactName"];
        <p>You entered: <br />
            Company Name: @companyname <br />
            Contact Name: @contactname </p>
        }
        else
        {
        <form method="post" action="">
            Company Name:<br />
            <input type="text" name="CompanyName" value="" /><br />
            Contact Name:<br />
            <input type="text" name="ContactName" value="" /><br
/><br />
            <input type="submit" value="Submit" class="submit" />
        </form>
        }
        }
    </body>

    </html>
```

Code 7.2: Simple ASP.NET form

AngularJS Forms

Angular previous version "AngularJS" has introduced forms with powerful data bindings. AngularJS forms were very popular and used heavily. Still, there were few problems like accessing right scoped variables, the complexity of form validation with promise, intervals, watchers, resolves, and so on, `$apply` and `$digest` flow, and many more. If not implemented correctly, AngularJS forms can become a victim of sporadic bugs. Also, the two-way data binding causes memory leak if a component is not destroyed correctly. The good thing is that in the new implementation Angular team has written forms of functionality in a better way.

Angular Forms

The angular framework provides extended form features. As an Angular developer, you can leverage on two types of forms—Template-driven forms, and Reactive forms. Based on the complexity of the forms we want to build, we can choose which forms type to use. If we want to build a very basic form that we might not reuse or won't scale in the future, then we can go for Template-driven forms. Whereas if we want to build a complex form with rigorous form validations and want to reuse and scale forms throughout the application, then we should choose Reactive forms. Template-driven forms are easy to implement but difficult to scale. Reactive forms learning curve is a bit steep but provides benefits in maintaining code and testable. We will take a look at both of these types of forms in the next sections.

Template-driven Forms

As the name suggests, Template-driven forms provide forms functionality via Angular template directives. The HTML code defines the form layout, validations, data bindings, and so on. Let's try to build a simple login form with a Template-driven form. In our login form, we will have two input fields for username and password. For completing the login process, we will have a submit button. Let's generate a new module and component for template-login-form by running *Command 7.1:*

```
ng generate module template-login-form

ng generate component template-login-form
```

Command 7.1: Generating template is driven login form module and component

We need to update `TemplateLoginFormModule`'s metadata to export components, as shown in *Code 7.3*. If we don't export components, then other modules importing `TemplateLoginFormModule` can't use component:

```
@NgModule({

declarations: [TemplateLoginFormComponent],
```

```
exports: [TemplateLoginFormComponent],
imports: [
    CommonModule
]
})
export class TemplateLoginFormModule { }
```

Code 7.3: *Export TemplateLoginFormComponent from module*

Now we will import `TemplateLoginFormsModule` into AppModule, as shown in *Code 7.4:*

```
import { TemplateLoginFormModule } from './template-login-form/
template-login-form.module';


@NgModule({
declarations: [
    AppComponent
],
imports: [
    BrowserModule,
    TemplateLoginFormModule
],
providers: [],
bootstrap: [AppComponent]
})
export class AppModule { }
```

Code 7.4: *Import TemplateLoginFormModule into AppModule*

Once imported, we can use `<app-template-login-form>` selector inside `app.component.html` to render components inside our root AppComponent as shown in *Code 7.5:*

```
<div style="text-align:center">
    <h1>
        Angular Forms!
    </h1>
</div>
```

```
<app-template-login-form></app-template-login-form>
```

Code 7.5: Render TemplateLoginFormComponent inside AppComponent

With the above steps, we should see "**template-login-form works!**" inside the browser. Now we can start building our Login form using Template-driven forms. Template-driven forms directives are exported by package "**@angular/forms**" through "**FormsModule**". We have already used this module in our previous chapters, do you recall? When we have learned about two-way data bindings through [**(ngModel)**] directive, we had imported "**FormsModule**". The NgModel directive is a very powerful directive, amongst others, while working with Template-driven forms. We will see how we can use it soon. So, let's import FormsModule into TemplateLoginFormModule, as shown in *Code 7.6:*

```
import { FormsModule } from "@angular/forms";


@NgModule({
    declarations: [TemplateLoginFormComponent],
    exports: [TemplateLoginFormComponent],
    imports: [
        CommonModule,
        FormsModule
    ]})
export class TemplateLoginFormModule { }
```

Code 7.6: Import FormsModule into TemplateLoginFormModule

For our login form, we will define a model class "**AuthModel**" to hold username and password, which should be sent to the backend for authentication. Run *Command 7.2* to generate **AuthModel** class:

```
ng generate class auth-model
```

Command 7.2: Create AuthModel class

Let's put the username and password fields inside the model class, as shown in *Code 7.7:*

```
export class AuthModel {
    username = '';
    password = '';
}
```

Code 7.7: AuthModel with user information

We will create a member variable of type `AuthModel` inside `TempalteLoginForm` Component for binding username and password into HTML, as shown in *Code 7.8*:

```
import { AuthModel } from '../auth-model';


@Component({
    selector: 'app-template-login-form',
    templateUrl: './template-login-form.component.html',
    styleUrls: ['./template-login-form.component.css']
})
export class TemplateLoginFormComponent implements OnInit {
    authModel: AuthModel;


    constructor() { }


    ngOnInit() {
        this.authModel = new AuthModel();
    }
}
```

Code 7.8: Creating authModel member inside the component

All we have done so far is configuration to hold **authModel** information. Now we will start defining our HTML form. As a first step, we will define plain HTML form without any Angular construct as shown in *Code 7.9*:

```
<div>
    <h1>Template Login Form</h1>
    <form>
        <div>
            <label for="username">User name</label>
            <input type="text" id="username" required>
        </div>

        <div>
            <label for="password">Password</label>
            <input type="password" id="password" required>
```

```
        </div>

        <button type="submit">Sign-in</button>

    </form>
  </div>
```

Code 7.9: Plain HTML form

The output of the plain HTML form will look similar to *Figure 7.3* shown as follows:

Angular Forms!

Template Login Form

Figure 7.3: Plain HTML form

As we can see, it is not looking at any beautiful. We can use the Bootstrap CSS library to make our form look nice. There are different ways of integrating Bootstrap with Angular like through NPM, CDN server. We will use the CDN approach. Open styles.css file and add the CDN URL of bootstrap as shown in *Code 7.10*:

```
@import url('https://unpkg.com/bootstrap@3.3.7/dist/css/bootstrap.
min.css');
```

Code 7.10: styles.css - adding Bootstrap CDN url

Once Bootstrap is added, we will update our HTML form code by adding CSS classes provided by the Bootstrap library, as shown in *Code 7.11*:

```
    <div class="container">
        <h1>Template Login Form</h1>
        <form>
            <div class="form-group">
                <label for="username">User name</label>
                <input type="text" class="form-control" id="username"
required>
            </div>
```

```
        <div class="form-group">
            <label for="password">Password</label>
            <input type="password" class="form-control"
id="password" required>
        </div>


        <button type="submit" class="btn btn-success">Sign-in</
button>


    </form>
  </div>
```

Code 7.11: *template-login-form.component.html - adding Bootstrap CSS classes*

After saving the changes, the browser should display a beautiful form as compared to without Bootstrap, as shown in *Figure 7.4:*

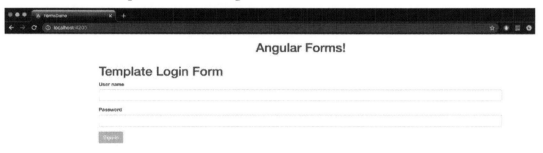

Figure 7.4: *Template login form with Bootstrap CSS classes*

We are all set to implement a Template-driven form now. In plain form we have <form> tag, we will attach "ngForm" directive to it and store a local HTML reference variable as <form #loginForm = "ngForm">. The ngForm directive is exported from the FormsModule; hence if we do not import it, we will get a runtime error. In HTML form, we have the "action" attribute, which is executed whenever a "submit" button is pressed. In Angular Template-driven form, we will add an event handler for "submit" event by setting "ngSubmit" event exported by FormsModule as <form #loginForm = "ngForm" (ngSubmit) = "onSubmit()">. The **onSubmit()** method should be defined in the component class. Whenever a Submit button is pressed, then the onSubmit() method shall be executed if there are no validations error. The local HTML reference is very useful in checking the aggregated form status. We will see it later on how to use this variable for form validations.

We have set `<form>` directives; now, we will set the input fields directive. For "username" and "password" input fields, we will add [(ngModel)] directive for two-way data bindings. With newer Angular version we should provide "name" attribute or set [ngModelOptions] = "{standalone: true}" attribute on `<input>` tag. In our case, we will simply provide the "name" attribute. The updated HTML code with Template-driven forms looks like *Code 7.12*:

```
<div class="container">

    <h1>Template Login Form</h1>

    <form #loginForm="ngForm" (ngSubmit)="onSubmit()">

        <div class="form-group">

            <label for="username">User name</label>

            <input type="text" [(ngModel)]="authModel.username"
class="form-control" id="username" required>

        </div>

        <div class="form-group">

            <label for="password">Password</label>

                <input type="password" [(ngModel)]="authModel.
password" name="password" class="form-control" id="password" required>

        </div>

        <button type="submit" class="btn btn-success">Sign-in</
button>

    </form>

</div>
```

Code 7.12: Template login form with FormsModule directives

As we can see there are only HTML tag changed - `<form>` tag and `<input>` tags with directives. We need to define the `onSubmit()` method into our component class; otherwise, an error will be thrown at runtime. *Code 7.13* shows the component code with the `authModel` member variable and `onSubmit()` method:

```
import { AuthModel } from '../auth-model';


@Component({
    selector: 'app-template-login-form',
    templateUrl: './template-login-form.component.html',
    styleUrls: ['./template-login-form.component.css']
})
```

```
export class TemplateLoginFormComponent implements OnInit {

    authModel: AuthModel;

    constructor() { }

    ngOnInit() {
        this.authModel = new AuthModel();
    }

    onSubmit() {
        alert(this.authModel.username + ' ' + this.authModel.
password);
    }
}
```

Code 7.13: template-login-form.component.ts - authModel and onSubmit method

The code is simple. We have a member variable of type AuthModel holding username and password. During application initialization, we are creating a new instance of AuthModel inside "ngOnInit()" so that the [(ngModel)] directives don't throw runtime error such as **"cannot read the username and password property of undefined"**. The onSubmit() method is simply showing user-entered values in the alert box. Note that we are not reading values from <input> element using jQuery or document.getElementById() construct as a legacy JavaScript application. The [(ngModel)] directives make sure that the latest value is updated on view as well as in the model. After saving all changes, we can test the output in the browser, and output should be similar to *Figure 7.5:*

Figure 7.5: Output of template-driven login form

Since we have the **"Sign-in"** button as a **"submit"**, if the user presses the *"Enter/ Return"* key, then it will fire the ngSubmit event, and we will get similar output.

Template-driven Form Validations

In simple HTML forms, we have seen that if we add "required" validation attribute on the input field, then submit action will not be triggered until the value is provided, and visual error is shown in the browser to the user. In our login form, our validation will not work out of the box. If we try to submit the form without providing username and password, then we will get an empty alert box, which is not good user experience. In this section, we will see how to enforce validation on form.

1. **Disable sign-in button:** Our first simple validation is whenever a username and password are both provided by the user, then only the **"Sign-in"** button should be enabled; otherwise, the button should stay in disabled mode. We can apply this rule by adding "disabled" attribute binding on the **Submit** button and querying form status from local HTML reference variable loginForm, as shown in *Code 7.14*:

```
<form #loginForm="ngForm" (ngSubmit)="onSubmit()">


        <button type="submit" class="btn btn-success"
[disabled]="!loginForm.valid">Sign-in</button>


    </form>
```

Code 7.14: *Sign-in button validation*

The loginForm variable hold the reference of FormGroup object through #loginForm = "ngForm" binding on <form> tag. Using this reference, we can query the properties of FormGroup object, and one of them is "valid" boolean property, which is set to true if all form validations are passed by encapsulating controls. If any of the validation error is failing, then this property will be set to false. Once this "valid" property is bound to an [disabled] attribute of <button> of type "submit," then the "**sign-**

in" button will be disabled if username and password are not provided as shown in *Figure 7.6:*

Figure 7.6: Sign-in button disabled when username and password are not provided

Once the user provides both **username** and **password**, then the "**sign-in**" button will get enabled, as shown in *Figure 7.7:*

Figure 7.7: Sign-in button enabled when username and password are provided

2. **Display validation error message**: We have made sure that an empty alert box is not shown if the username and password are not provided by the disabling sign-in button on validation error. But to the user, it is not intuitive why the button is disabled and what action the user should take to enable the sign-in button. We should show the error message to the user whenever there is a validation error. Let's start with the **username** input field. If the username is empty, we should display an error message that means we need to get access to the value of <input> field and validation status as well. All this information can be provided by [(ngModel)] directive. The ngModel directive doesn't just do two-way data binding, but it also provide more details about validations. The ngModel directive holds the reference of FormControl object internally, and FormControl contains validations property. We will show an error message in <div>, which should be visible only if there is a validation error. We will create a local HTML reference variable on <input> tag from the ngModel directive and then use this local variable to check validation properties as we did with the ngForm directive. *Code 7.15* shows how to display the validation messages. We are binding "hidden" attribute of <div> to "username.valid" expression which will be evaluated whenever user types in <input> field. If there is no input, then the user will see an error message, and as he starts typing error will be hidden.

```
<div class="container">
<h1>Template Login Form</h1>
<form #loginForm="ngForm" (ngSubmit)="onSubmit()">
    <div class="form-group">
        <label for="username">User name</label>
        <input type="text" [(ngModel)]="authModel.
username" name="username" class="form-control" id="username"
            #username="ngModel" required>


        <div [hidden]="username.valid" class="alert
alert-danger">
            Username is required
        </div>
    </div>


    <div class="form-group">
        <label for="password">Password</label>
        <input type="password" [(ngModel)]="authModel.
password" name="password" class="form-control" id="password"
            #password="ngModel" required>
        <div [hidden]="password.valid" class="alert
alert-danger">
            Password is required
        </div>
    </div>


    <button type="submit" class="btn btn-success"
[disabled]="!loginForm.valid">Sign-in</button>

</form>
</div>
```

Code 7.15: Display required field validation messages

The output of the above code should look similar to *Figure 7.8* when the **username** is provided, but the **password** is not:

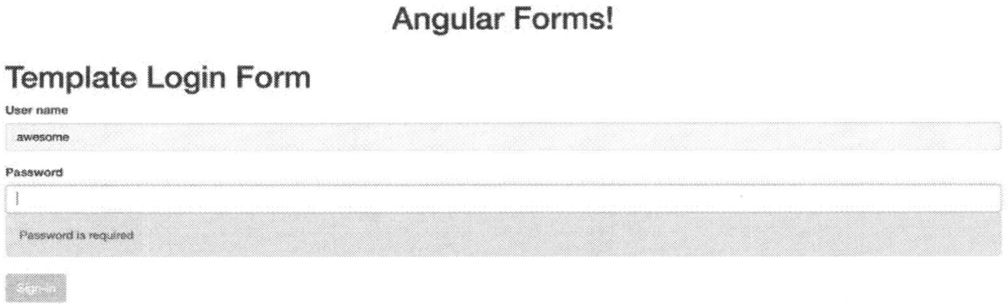

Angular Forms!

Template Login Form

User name

awesome

Password

Password is required

Figure 7.8: Password field required error message

3. **Track control state:** Our required field validations work as expected, but there is one user experience problem. When the application is started, we can see validation messages before the user visited controls. Ideally, the validation message should be shown when the user has clicked on `<input>` and left the focus from it without providing any value. Angular provides a set of CSS classes that are automatically set to a different value based on control's state. *Table 7.1* shows these CSS classes with a summary:

CSS Class name	Control state
ng-untouched	When the user has not visited control by clicking or tab navigation
ng-touched	When the user has visited control by clicking or tab navigation
ng-pristine	When control's value has not been changed
ng-dirty	When control's value is modified by the user
ng-valid	When control's value is valid as per applied validations
ng-invalid	When controls' value is invalid due to any of the validation failing

Table 7.1: CSS classes for tracking control state and validation

We have already used "ng-valid" class in our example by binding it [hidden] attribute of error message `<div>` tag. As we do not want to show error message until the user has visited and changed the value of control, we can use the "ng-touched" class along with "ng-valid," as shown in *Code 7.16:*

```
<div [hidden]="username.valid || username.untouched" class =
"alert alert-danger">
                Username is required
        </div>
```

```
<div [hidden]="password.valid || password.untouched" class =
"alert alert-danger">
                    Password is required
        </div>
```

Code 7.16: Using ng-pristine and ng-valid class to hide the validation error message

Template-driven form Custom Validations

Using ngModel directive and CSS validation classes, we can perform business validations on the form. In complex form applications, we might need to apply custom validation logic. Angular provides a set of validator functions out of the box, and we can also write our validator function. For example, we would like to add requirements that username should not start with a special character "@". Adding custom validator is a bit complicated for Template-driven forms as compared to Reactive forms. The Template forms abstract away the FormControl instance and doesn't allow us to work with built-in validators. We need to write a new validator directive with validator function and apply this directive on target <input> tag. Let's create a new directive called "invalid-username" by running *Command 7.3*:

```
ng generate directive invalid-username
```

Command 7.3: Generate directive for custom validator

We need to tell the Angular compiler that this directive will be used as a validator through @Directive() decorator, as in *Code 7.17*. This metadata allows Angular parser to treat "appInvalidUsername" as a validator when applied on <input> tag.

```
@Directive({
    selector: '[appInvalidUsername]',
    providers: [
        {
            provide: NG_VALIDATORS,
            useExisting: InvalidUsernameDirective,
            multi: true
        }]
})
export class InvalidUsernameDirective {
}
```

Code 7.17: Specify validator metadata into @Directive decorator

The next step is to implement the "Validator" interface on the directive and provide custom validator function implementation. *Code 7.18* shows the complete implementation of the custom validator directive. Whenever Angular runs a validation check, it will call "validate()" function and "control" argument will have value of target <input> tag applied. The "invalidCharacter" member variable is the argument passed to directive by target <input> tag. In our case, we will set the "@" character as an input to the "appInvalidUsername" directive. The "validate()" function checks if value is present for control's value and input invalidCharacter variable. If true then it calls a global function "invalidUsernameValidator()" which is a curry function. Curry function is a JavaScript concept where a function parameter can be passed in different phases. invalidUsernameValidator() function checks if controls' value starts with invalidCharacter string. If true, then returns an object, which means validation failed. If validation is successful, then it simply returns "null" to signal no error.

```
import { Directive, Input } from '@angular/core';

import { NG_VALIDATORS, Validator, AbstractControl, ValidatorFn }
from '@angular/forms';


export function invalidUsernameValidator(invalidCharacter: string):
ValidatorFn {
    return (control: AbstractControl): { [key: string]: any } | null
=> {
        const invalid = control.value.startsWith(invalidCharacter);
        return invalid ? { 'invalidCharacter': { value: control.
value } } : null;
    };
}


@Directive({
    selector: '[appInvalidUsername]',
    providers: [
        {
            provide: NG_VALIDATORS,
            useExisting: InvalidUsernameDirective,
            multi: true
        }]
})
```

```
export class InvalidUsernameDirective implements Validator {

    @Input('appInvalidUsername') invalidCharacter = "@";

    constructor() { }

    validate(control: AbstractControl) {
        console.log(this.invalidCharacter);
        console.log(control.value);

        return control.value && this.invalidCharacter ?
invalidUsernameValidator(this.invalidCharacter)(control) : null;
    }

}
```

Code 7.18: Complete implementation of custom validator directive

Now we can use custom validator directive inside our Template-driven login form. The first step is to import InvalidUsernameDirective into TemplateLoginFormModule and remove it from AppModule if present, as shown in *Code 7.19*:

```
import { InvalidUsernameDirective } from '../invalid-username.
directive';

@NgModule({
    declarations: [
        TemplateLoginFormComponent,
        InvalidUsernameDirective
    ],
    exports: [TemplateLoginFormComponent],
    imports: [
        CommonModule,
        FormsModule]
})
export class TemplateLoginFormModule { }
```

Code 7.19: Import InvalidUsernameDirective into module

Finally, we can apply "appInvalidUsername" directive on our "**username**" <input> tag. In *Code 7.20*, we can see we are passing **"@"** character as invalid username character to appInvalidUsername. Whenever the user starts typing username with the first character being "@" then "invalidCharacter" validation will fail. We would like to show different error messages for the invalid character. We can check which validation has failed from the ngModel directive's "errors" array. For example, "username?.errors?.invalidCharacter" will be true if invalidCharacter validation has failed. Note that "invalidCharacter" is a key value of the object returned by the "invalidUsernameValidator()" function.

```
<div class="form-group">
        <label for="username">User name</label>
        <input type="text" [(ngModel)]="authModel.username"
name="username" class="form-control" id="username"
            #username="ngModel" appInvalidUsername="@" required>


        <div *ngIf="username?.errors?.invalidCharacter" class="alert
alert-danger">
            Username cannot start with @
        </div>
        <div [hidden]="username.valid || username.untouched"
class="alert alert-danger">
            Username is required
        </div>
    </div>
```

Code 7.20: Import InvalidUsernameDirective into the module

If the user starts typing **username** starting with **"@"** character, then the browser will show error message as shown in *Figure 7.9*:

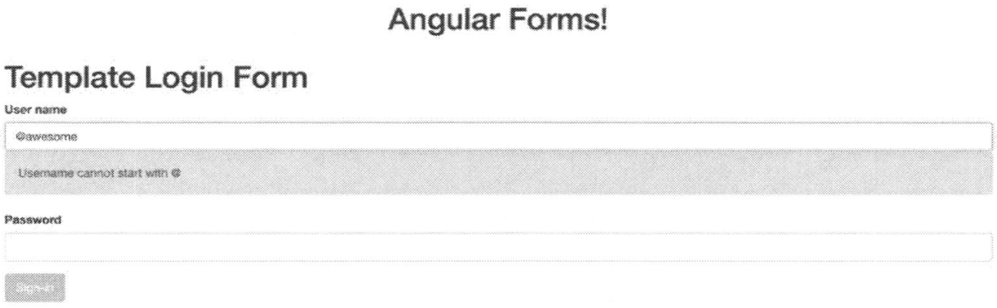

Figure 7.9: Custom validation error message for username starting with @ character

As mentioned in the introduction of this chapter, Template-driven forms are a bit complicated to structure and hard to reuse. We should use Template-driven forms only for very basic forms, and for complex and scalable forms, we should use Reactive forms.

Reactive Forms

The Reactive forms allow us to define form in a model-driven approach. In this approach, we have access to FormControl instance directly, and there is no abstraction like ngModel directives. This allows synchronous data flow between view and model as compared to the Template-driven form where data flows asynchronously. We will see a detailed comparison soon.

C# **Analogy**: Though there is not a direct Windows Forms analogy, we can consider Template-driven form as if we are defining windows form through form.designer.cs file or using IDE and drag-drop component over form. We can also create a Control class object and set "children" properties of the control to define form layout as well, which is similar to Reactive forms.

We will build a similar login form using a Reactive form. Let's generate a new module and component for reactive login form as shown in *Command 7.4*:

```
ng generate module reactive-login-form
ng generate component reactive-login-form
```

Command 7.4: Generate reactive-login-form module and component

The Reactive forms controls are exported through the ReactiveFormsModule module from the "@angular/forms" package. We will import ReactiveFormsModule and export ReactiveLoginFormComponent so that we can use it in AppComponent, as shown in *Code 7.21*:

```
import { ReactiveLoginFormComponent } from './reactive-login-form.component';

import { ReactiveFormsModule } from "@angular/forms";


@NgModule({

declarations: [ReactiveLoginFormComponent],

exports: [ReactiveLoginFormComponent],

imports: [

    CommonModule,

    ReactiveFormsModule

]})
```

```
export class ReactiveLoginFormModule { }
```
Code 7.21: *Import ReactiveFormsModule into ReactiveLoginFormModule*

Next step is to import `ReactiveLoginFormsModule` into AppModule's imports property as shown in *Code 7.22*:

```
import { ReactiveLoginFormModule } from './reactive-login-form/
reactive-login-form.module';
@NgModule({
    declarations: [
        AppComponent],
    imports: [
        BrowserModule,
        TemplateLoginFormModule,
        ReactiveLoginFormModule
    ],
    providers: [],
    bootstrap: [AppComponent]
})
export class AppModule { }
```
Code 7.22: *Import ReactiveLoginFormModule into AppModule*

Finally, add `<app-reactive-login-form>` tag into the `app.component.html` file for rendering component in the browser, as shown in *Code 7.23*. You should see **"reactive-login-form works!"** message below our `TemplateLoginForm` output in the browser.

```
<div style="text-align:center">
    <h1>
        Angular Forms!
    </h1>
</div>
<app-template-login-form></app-template-login-form>
<app-reactive-login-form></app-reactive-login-form>
```
Code 7.23: *Render ReactiveLoginFormComponent*

The configuration we have done so far allows us to use Reactive form controls. Let's start building a login form now. In Reactive forms, we can create an object of `FormControl` for each control inside our form and manage its value. For example, we can create two `FormControl` objects for username and password. The best practice is to use `FormGroup` objects, which encapsulate all `FormControl` objects. In *Code 7.24*, we have a `loginForm` member variable of type `FormGroup` class. Angular provides DI ready service called `FormBuilder`, which has a factory method to create `FormGroup` object. We can directly import `FormBuilder` service and get a new instance of a group by specifying a form control configuration JSON object. We can specify a control group either by creating a new object of `FormControl` as we did for a username or by specifying an array of the parameter for `FormControl` constructor as we did for a password. The constructor of `FormControl` class accepts default value, validator function, async validator function as optional arguments. In our code, we are setting the default value to an empty string by passing it to `FormControl` constructor and the first element of an array.

```
import { Component, OnInit } from '@angular/core';

import { FormGroup, FormBuilder, FormControl } from '@angular/forms';

import { AuthModel } from '../auth-model';


@Component({
    selector: 'app-reactive-login-form',
    templateUrl: './reactive-login-form.component.html',
    styleUrls: ['./reactive-login-form.component.css']
})
export class ReactiveLoginFormComponent implements OnInit {

    loginForm: FormGroup;
    authModel: AuthModel;


    constructor(private formBuilder: FormBuilder) { }


    ngOnInit() {
        this.authModel = new AuthModel();
        this.loginForm = this.formBuilder.group({
            username: new FormControl(''),
            password: ['']
        });
    }
```

```
onSubmit() {
        this.authModel.username = this.loginForm.
controls["username"].value;
        this.authModel.password = this.loginForm.
controls["password"].value;
        alert(this.authModel.username + ' ' + this.authModel.
password);
    }
}
```

Code 7.24: reactive-login-form-component.ts - Reactive login form

Similar to the Template-driven login form, the "onSumit()" method will be executed whenever (ngSubmit) event is fired by submit type button on the form. Unlike the ngModel directive, where value is updated in a two-way direction, the Reactive form always returns a new state value of control as it is immutable. Hence, we can get control's value by accessing direct FormControl instance's "value" property. In onSubmit() method we can either get individual controls value from the group by accessing their key specified in control configuration inside "group()" function of FormBuilder or we can get complete form value as a JSON object by accessing "value" property of FormGroup object, for example, "this.loginForm.value".

The HTML configuration for Reactive forms is also very straight forward. In *Code 7.25*, we can see how to specify data binding with Reactive forms. We can see the difference in <form> tag as we are doing directive binding of [formGroup] = "loginForm" instead of creating local HTML reference. Next, change in <input> tag where instead of [(ngModel)], we are using formControlName = "username" binding where "**username**" is a key specified in FromGroup configuration. For the "**password**" field, we have done similar changes.

```
<div class="container">
    <h1>Reactive Login Form</h1>
    <form [formGroup]="loginForm" (ngSubmit)="onSubmit()">
        <div class="form-group">
            <label for="username">User name</label>
            <input type="text" formControlName="username"
name="reactive-username" class="form-control" id="reactive-username">
        </div>

        <div class="form-group">
```

```
        <label for="password">Password</label>

        <input type="password" formControlName="password"
name="reactive-password" class="form-control" id="reactive-password">

        </div>


        <button type="submit" class="btn btn-success"
[disabled]="!loginForm.valid">Sign-in</button>


    </form>
</div>
```

Code 7.25: reactive-login-form-component.html - HTML data binding with Reactive forms

The output of changes should be similar to *Figure 7.10* without any validations:

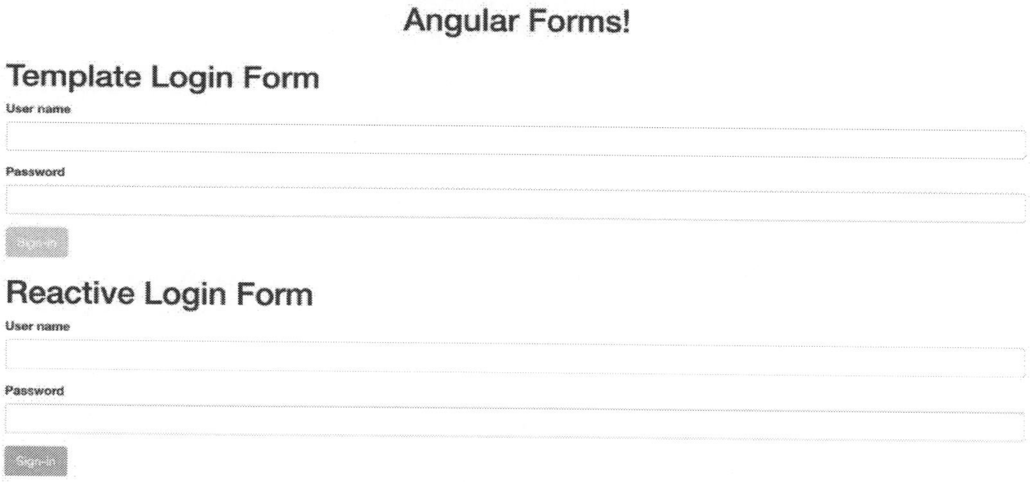

Figure 7.10: Reactive and Template-driven form output side by side

Reactive Form Validations

Adding validations in Reactive forms is very easy. The FormControl constructor takes second and third arguments for sync and async validator functions, respectively. Angular also provides a set of predefined validators. We can add the "required" field validator to the **username** and **password** field, as shown in *Code 7.26:*

```
ngOnInit() {
    this.authModel = new AuthModel();
    this.loginForm = this.formBuilder.group({
```

```
            "username": new FormControl('', Validators.required),
            "password": ['', Validators.required]
      });
}
```

Code 7.26: Adding Required field validator to username and password

In HTML, we will check form control state and display error message with Bootstrap classes, as shown in *Code 7.27*. Note that we are not creating any local reference of ngModel directive and accessing control state through CSS classes, unlike Template-driven forms. We are directly accessing FormControl properties to show validation error messages.

```
      <div class="form-group">
            <label for="username">User name</label>
            <input type="text" formControlName="username"
name="reactive-username" class="form-control" id="reactive-username">
            <div *ngIf="loginForm.controls['username'].invalid &&
            (loginForm.controls['username'].dirty || loginForm.
controls['username'].touched)"
                  class="alert alert-danger">
                  Username is required
            </div>
      </div>


      <div class="form-group">
            <label for="password">Password</label>
            <input type="password" formControlName="password"
name="reactive-password" class="form-control" id="reactive-password">
            <div *ngIf="loginForm.controls['password'].invalid &&
            (loginForm.controls['password'].dirty || loginForm.
controls['password'].touched)"
                  class="alert alert-danger">
                  Password is required
            </div>
      </div>
```

Code 7.27: Showing validation error message by tracking FormControl state

If the user visits our Reactive login form and doesn't provide values for username and password field, then the user shall be prompted with error messages and sign-in button will be disabled as shown in *Figure 7.11:*

Reactive Login Form

User name

Username is required

Password

Password is required

Sign-in

Figure 7.11: Error message shown to the user if username and password left blank

Reactive Form Custom Validator

Adding custom validation to the Reactive form is fairly easy as compared to Template-driven form. In the Template-driven form, we had to create a new directive, and then we could use it in HTML for custom validation. For Reactive form, we can directly use custom validator function without creating any new directive, as shown in *Code 7.28.* Here we have passed "`invalidUsernameValidator()`" function with "**@**" character to `FormControl`'s constructor. We can pass any other character instead of "**@**" and verify if validation is working or not. Note that the second argument is passed as an array means we can apply more than one validation on given `FormControl`.

```
ngOnInit() {
    this.authModel = new AuthModel();
    this.loginForm = this.formBuilder.group({
        "username": new FormControl('', [Validators.required,
invalidUsernameValidator("@")]),
        "password": ['', Validators.required]
    });
}
```

Code 7.28: Passing custom validator function to FormControl

The HTML changes are required only to display an error message as we do not have any directive to apply on `<input>` as shown in *Code 7.29:*

```
<div class="form-group">
    <label for="username">User name</label>
```

```
        <input type="text" formControlName="username"
name="reactive-username" class="form-control"
        id="reactive-username">
        <div *ngIf="loginForm.controls['username'].invalid &&
        (loginForm.controls['username'].dirty || loginForm.
controls['username'].touched)"
        class="alert alert-danger">
        Username is required
        </div>
        <div *ngIf="loginForm.controls['username']?.errors?.
invalidCharacter" class="alert alert-danger">
        Username cannot start with @
        </div>
    </div>
```

Code 7.29: Display validation error message for custom validator

The output of the Template-driven form and Reactive form is shown in *Figure 7.12:*

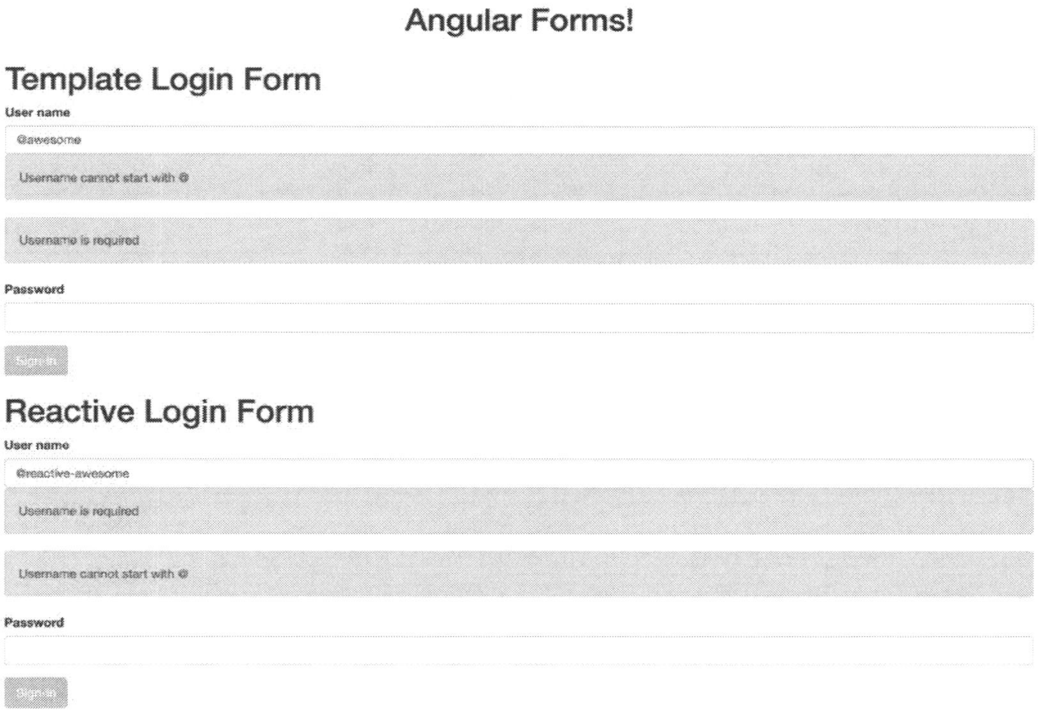

Figure 7.12: Validation error messages for Template-driven and Reactive forms

The validation error messages order for username field has been switched for visual differentiation only. Now, if the user enters username and password in either of the forms and submits the form, then he will get alert with fed data. If there are any validation errors, the message will be displayed in the browser. These two examples show the same login form can be built using either Template-driven forms or Reactive Forms; it is up to the developer to decide which one to use based on the complexity and nature of the application.

Template-driven Forms versus Reactive Forms

We have seen how to build Template-driven and Reactive forms in previous sections. There are a number of differences between both of these form building approaches. In the following list, we will highlight a few significant differences:

- **Setup**: In Template-driven form, forms directives are used in the HTML template, making it less explicit as code contains CSS classes, data binding, and other rendering logic. In the Reactive form, the component class holds the form definition in terms of objects and makes it easy to separate HTML and code.

- **Data Model:** Reactive forms data model is structured within `FormGroup`. We can work on all `FormControl` objects as a group and as an individual element as well. In Template-driven form, NgModel directive abstract underlying `FormControl` making it unstructured data model to query `FormControl` state and value.

- **Data Flow:** Both `[(ngModel)]` and `"formControlName"` directives provide two-way data binding. There is two possible data flow as follows:

  a. The data can be updated by user in view, and new value should be propagated to model

  b. Model value updated by backend or business logic and view should refresh to show new value to the user

- **Data Flow in Template Driven Forms:** Template driven form does an asynchronous update between view and model, as shown in *Figure 7.13*. The NgModel directive applied on `<input>` field creates an instance of

FormControl class internally and manages events to publish new values for the view to the model data flow:

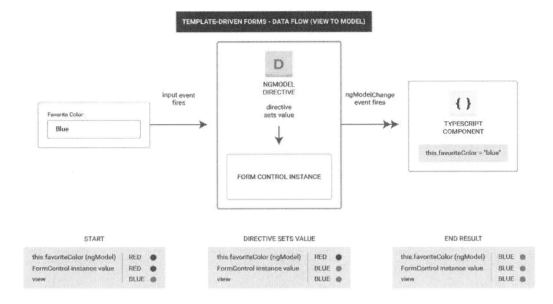

Figure 7.13: *View to the Model data flow in Template-driven forms (source: https://angular.io/guide/forms-overview#data-flow-in-template-driven-forms)*

Figure 7.14 shows data flow from model to view in Template-driven forms. Angular runs lifecycle events periodically like ngOnInit(), ngAfterContentInit(), and so on. One such event is ngOnChanges(), which is like the "tick" event where Angular check if any of the data-bound values have been changed. If the model value is changed, then the NgModel directive updates the value of `FormControl` state and refreshes view with the new value:

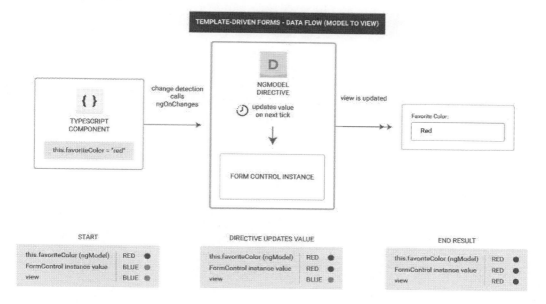

Figure 7.14: *Model to the View data flow in Template-driven forms (source: https://angular.io/guide/forms-overview#data-flow-in-template-driven-forms)*

- **Data Flow in Reactive Forms**: In Reactive forms, view element, for example, `<input>` is directly bound to `FormControl` instance through `formControlName` directive, and there is no middleman like NgModel directive to abstract things. This allows both view and model to update values synchronously without waiting for the next change detection cycle. *Figure 7.15* shows how data is updated from view to model in Reactive Forms. When value gets updated in `<input>` field then an event is fired by

<input>. This event is subscribed by the FormControlName directive, and underlying FormControl's value gets updated immediately.

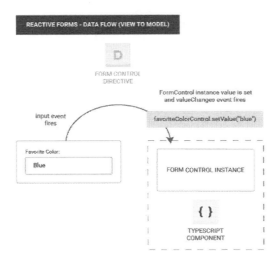

Figure 7.15: *View to the Model data flow in Reactive forms (source: https://angular.io/guide/forms-overview# data-flow-in-reactive-forms)*

Similarly, when FormControls value is updated in component class, that is, the model is updated, then bound HTML control value gets updated by event subscription, as shown in *Figure 7.16*:

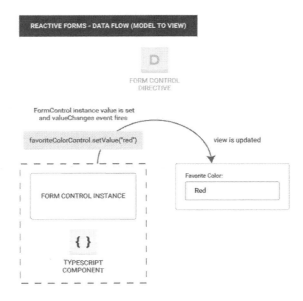

Figure 7.16: *Model to the View data flow in Reactive forms (source: https://angular.io/guide/forms-overview# data-flow-in-reactive-forms)*

The data flow is an essential criterion to select between Template-driven forms versus Reactive Forms. We have seen that Reactive Forms have a better data flow model as compared to Template forms.

- **Form Validations:** Validation is an essential part of any web application. If our application requires built-in validations, then using any form approach is fine. But if we want to write custom validations, then there is a difference. We have seen in the Login form that for building custom username validation, Template-driven forms had to create a new directive along with validation function. For Reactive forms, we just created a validation function and passed it to `FormControl`'s constructor. Thus, Reactive forms superior here as well as compared to Template-driven forms.

- **Mutability**: In Template-driven forms, model value is modified whenever there is a change in view. In Reactive forms, a new value `FormControl` value instance is returned, making it immutable. Thus, change tracking is efficient in Reactive forms as compared to Template-driven forms.

- **Scalability**: In Reactive forms, we define forms definition as `FormGroup` and can be reused in other applications or modules; we cannot reuse Template-driven forms definitions. Also, the NgModel abstraction level makes it difficult for Template-driven form to write validation code, custom validators, and so on. When it comes to unit testing, writing unit test cases for asynchronous code is always challenging. Since Template-driven forms do asynchronous data exchange, writing unit test case makes it difficult. We have to make sure that new changes are detected by calling "detectChanges()," and new events are fired by "`tick()`" functions in the unit test case. For Reactive forms, unit test cases can be written straightforward. In Reactive forms, we have access to a direct instance of `FormControl` and `FormGroup`, which gives us flexibility in terms of writing code.

Conclusion

In this chapter, we have seen two types of form building options as Template-driven forms and Reactive forms. As per the application requirements, we can go for Template-driven forms if we are building a very simple and easy form without much validations like "**Login**", "**Subscribe**", "**Contact Us**", and more forms. If we are building complex form like "**User profile**", "**Account settings**", and so on, then we should consider using Reactive forms to make sure code is scalable and maintainable. We have seen how these two forms differ with their advantages and disadvantages.

After reading this chapter, we should be able to build data entry forms using Template-driven forms and Reactive forms with various validations.

In the next chapter, we will learn how to pass data between components. Angular components can be at a different level; for example, they can be in the parent-child relationship, siblings, or not connected at all. We will learn how to communicate with such components in the next chapter.

Questions

1. In Angular, which module should be imported for using Reactive forms?
2. Build a sign-up form using Template-driven forms with the custom validator.
3. Build a sign-up form using Reactive forms with the custom validator.
4. How can you make a Reactive sign-up form reusable so that you can use it in other component/application?
5. Create a Reactive sign-up form from JSON shown in *Code 7.30*. In this JSON, "**sign-up-form**" is form configuration, which is an array of objects. Each object has a "**key**" property, which is the name of the control to be created in the form. Different validations are specified in the "**validators**" array where each object is a validator. Your task is to parse this JSON file from the "**assets**" folder and create a sign-up form by creating a `FormGroup` object with the configuration from the JSON file with all validations.

```
{
    "sign-up-form": [
        {
            "key": "username",
            "validators": [
                {
                    "required": true
                },
                {
                    "minlen": 8
                }
            ]
        },
        {
            "key": "password",
            "validators": [
                {
                    "required": true
                },
```

```
            {
                "minlen": 6
            }
        ]
    },
    {
        "key": "firstName"
    },
    {
        "key": "lastName"
    },
    {
        "key": "age"
    },
    {
        "key": "email",
        "validators": [
            {
                "required": true
            },
            {
                "custom": "email"
            }
        ]
    }
  ]
}
```

Code 7.30: *Assignment JSON to build dynamic sign-up form*

CHAPTER 8

Communication Between Components

The components are the basic building blocks of any Angular application. Each component should follow the single responsibility principle, that is, doing only one thing and not the multiple things at a time. A simple feature like "sign-in", "sign-up", can be implemented by an individual component. Still, when we have to build a complex feature, we might need to aggregate multiple components, for example, "dashboard", "shopping cart", and so on. The composition of components creates a need for communication between components. There are various ways Angular components can communicate with each other, and in this chapter, we will learn about these techniques.

Structure

- C# Windows Form Communicators
- Parent-Child communication using @Input() and @Output()
- Parent-Child communication using a local variable reference
- Parent-Child communication using @ViewChild() decorator
- Passing data between components through Service
- Passing data between components through LocalStorage

Objective

In this chapter, we will learn about how to pass data between components. As components can be in different hierarchy levels, the mode of communication is also different. For example, if two components are in a parent-child relationship, then we can use @Input(), @Output(), and @ViewChild() decorators provided by Angular framework for passing data. If two components are at the same hierarchical level, then we can either use a parent to pass data between them, or we can use Events through service to communicate. The moral is, based on the requirements, we should be able to select the most suitable communication models available to us, and we will explore it in this chapter.

C# Windows Form Communications

In C# Windows forms, two forms can communicate with each other in different ways. One of the approaches is **Object Containment,** where form's instance is created into parent form, and public methods and member variables are invoked. Another approach is events and delegates where events are registered, and data is passed by invoking events and passing event arguments. We can also pass data by marking member variables, properties, the method as static and invoking them from the outside world, but this is not a good object-oriented approach. We can also use Dependency Injection with service class with singleton instance and resolve it other forms for storing and retrieving data between forms. In Angular, we do not create a component class's instance directly as in C#. A component instance is created when its selector tag is rendered inside the browser; for example, when the browser encounters a tag `<app-login></app-login>`, it will create a new instance of `LoginComponent` class with "`app-login`" selector metadata in its `@Component()` decorator. We will see how to pass data between parent-child components in the next section.

Parent-Child Communication Using @ Input() and @Output()

Angular application is organized into an inverted tree of components. The default root component is AppComponent, which is specified in AppModule's "bootstrap" property. Of course, we can mark any other component as root component other than AppComponent if required. The parent-child relationship is formed when one component's selector ID is rendered into another component's HTML file. In that case, the component in which the selector is used will be considered as parent component, and components rendered inside will be considered as a child component. In a parent-child relationship, we might need to pass data from parent component to child and vice versa. We can achieve such communication by using @

Input() and @Output() decorator. The @Input() decorator is used for passing data from parent to child using property binding. We will define a property inside a child component with @Input() decorator, and we will set this property in parent component HTML as an attribute to selector tag. The @Output() decorator is used for passing data from child component to parent component. The child component shall have an event member field of type EventEmitter class, and @Output() decorator shall be applied to this field. The parent component will subscribe to the child component event using Angular event subscription syntax in HTML. The child component can pass data to the parent component by raising the event and passing data as an event argument. The parent component's event handler will receive event argument data and can process it further.

Let's try to build a simple example to see how to pass data. In this example, we would like to have a child component with `<div>` tag whose background color is being set by the parent component. Also, the child component will have a button; upon click, it will set the same color as the background color of the parent's `<div>` tag.

Let's create a new Angular project and generate a new component, as shown in *Command 8.1*:

```
ng new ng-communication-demo
```

```
ng generate component color-demo
```

Command 8.1: *Create a new project and generate ColorDemoComponent component*

We will render ColorDemoComponent component inside AppComponent component. In `color-demo.component.html` file, we will have a `<div>` tag with a label and a button. This `<div>` tag background color should be changed by parent component, that is, by AppComponent component. We will define a "[style.backgroundColor]" data binding with "inputColor" string variable of ColorDemoComponent class. *Code 8.1* shows a complete `color-demo.component.html` file code:

```
<div style="text-align:center" [style.backgroundColor]="inputColor"
class="bg-color-test">

    <h3>Child</h3>

    <button (click)="updateParent()">Update Parent</button>

</div>
```

Code 8.1: *color-demo.component.html - <div> with background color data binding*

We will also set some height and width for `<div>` in "bg-color-test" CSS class, as shown in *Code 8.2*:

```css
.bg-color-test {
    width:200px;
    height:100px;
    text-align:center;
}
```

Code 8.2: color-demo.component.css - child <div> CSS styling definition

The `ColorDemoComponent` class definition is shown in *Code 8.3*. There are two new decorators used in this code—`@Input()` and `@Output()` prefixing component's member variables. When `@Input()` decorator is used in front of a member variable of component, then that member can accept value from its parent component through "**property binding**" (that is, [ ] binding notation) syntax. The `@Output()` decorator is used to send data from child to parent via raising an event. This event can be handled by the parent with optional event arguments. In our case, the `outputColorChanged` event will be fired with event argument of type `<string>`. The "`emit()`" method of EventEmitter will accept only a string parameter if another data type value is passed, then a compile-time error will be thrown.

Thus whenever the "`inputColor`" member receives any new value from its parent, it will update the background color of the `<div>` tag of the child. If the user clicks on the Update Parent button, then the "outputColorChanged" event will be fired by passing "`inputColor`" as an event argument. In a nutshell, our child component is ready for communication with the parent.

```typescript
import { Component, OnInit, Input, Output, EventEmitter } from '@angular/core';


@Component({
    selector: 'app-color-demo',
    templateUrl: './color-demo.component.html',
    styleUrls: ['./color-demo.component.css']
})
export class ColorDemoComponent implements OnInit {

    @Input() inputColor = '';
    @Output() outputColorChanged = new EventEmitter<string>();


    constructor() { }
```

```
    ngOnInit() {
        this.inputColor = 'gray';
    }


    updateParent() {
        this.outputColorChanged.emit(this.inputColor);
    }

}
```

Code 8.3: color-demo.component.ts definition

In `AppComponent`, we will render `ColorDemoComponent` by its selector tag. In *Code 8.4*, we can see that app.component.html has a `<input>` tag with type "color". We have used two-way data binding on this `<input>` tag using `[(ngModel)]`; hence don't forget to import "`FormsModule`" into AppModule otherwise runtime error will be thrown in the browser for `[(ngModel)]` binding. Whenever the user clicks on color input, a color palette will be shown, and selected color value will be stored into the "`backgroundColor`" member. Notice how we have used `<app-color-demo></app-color-demo>` tag inside `app.component.html` file. The `[inputColor]` = "`backgroundColor`" is property data binding. In `ColorDemoComponent` class "`inputColor`" member is defined with prefix `@Input()` decorator; thus, we can pass the value of "`backgroundColor`" member value to "`inputColor`" through property binding:

```
    <div style="text-align:center">
        <h1>
            Communication Demo
        </h1>
    </div>


    <div>
        <label for="childBGColor">Select child background color: </label>
        <input id="childBGColor" type="color"
[(ngModel)]="backgroundColor">
    </div>


    <div [style.backgroundColor]="newColor" class="parent-bg-color-test">
        <h3>Parent</h3>
    </div>
```

```
<app-color-demo [inputColor]="backgroundColor"
(outputColorChanged)="onOutputColorChanged($event)"></app-color-demo>


<router-outlet></router-outlet>
```

Code 8.4: app.component.html definition

The workflow will be as follow:

1. User clicks on `color <input>` tag and select color palette.
2. As soon as the user-selected value, the new color value will be stored inside the "`backgroundColor`" member of the `AppComponent` class.
3. Since "`backgroundColor`" is used in property binding of `<app-color-demo>` tag, its value will be passed to "`inputColor`" member of `ColorDemoComponent` class.
4. In `color-demo.component.html`, we have used property binding for `[style.backgroundColor]` = "`inputColor`" on `<div>`. As soon as the "`inputColor`" value is updated inside `ColorDemoComponent`, this style data binding will be executed, and the child's `<div>` background color will be changed to a new color passed from AppComponent.
5. *Figure 8.1* shows the output of changing the background color from parent to child. As the user keeps changing the color palette, the child `<div>` background color will keep updating as well.

Figure 8.1: Changing child <div> background color from parent

In summary, `@Input()` decorator is used to accept data from the parent component into a child component. The member variable on which `@Input()` decorator is applied will be exposed for the property binding. We can provide a different name for input data-binding syntax as well. In *Code 8.5*, we have passed a string '`inputBGColor`' to `@Input()` decorator inside `ColorDemoComponent` class:

```
@Input('inputBGColor') inputColor = '';
```

Code 8.5: color-demo.component.ts - passing argument to @Input() decorator

In `app.component.html,` we will have to bind to "`inputBGColor`" property and not "`inputColor,`" as shown in *Code 8.6*:

```
<app-color-demo [inputBGColor]="backgroundColor"
(outputColorChanged)="onOutputColorChanged($event)"></app-color-demo>
```

<div align="center">*Code 8.6*: *app.component.html - passing data to child component*</div>

Passing data from parent to child is simple as the parent knows its children through module import and declaration. But the child doesn't know anything about its parents, thus passing data from child to parent is a bit different.

Angular provides `@Output(),` property decorator. The `@Output()` decorator is applied to the member variable of type EventEmitter class. In *Code 8.3* we have "`outputColorChanged`" member of type `EventEmitter<string>` with `@Output` decorator prefixed. The `ColorDemoComponent` HTML has a button **Update Parent.** When this button is clicked, then the "`updateParent()`" method is executed. In this method, we will raise an event by calling the "`emit()`" method and passing the "`inputColor`" parameter as an event argument.

Since we have used `@Output()` decorator on "`outputColorChanged`", in `app.component.html` we can listen to this event by subscription syntax as `(outputColorChanged)= "onOutputColorChanged($event)`".

Note that if we do not pass the "`$event`" as a parameter, then we won't be able to receive event arguments in the event handler. In "`onOutputColorChanged()`" function, we are setting "`newColor`" member variable of `AppComponent` class. This "`newColor`" is used in style background color data binding inside `AppComponent` HTML. Thus whenever the user presses the **Update   Parent** button inside the `ColorDemoComponent` component, then the event is fired and "`onOutputColorchanged()`" handler is executed with "`newColor`" holding event argument. This `newColor` updates the background color of `<div>` inside `AppComponent`. The output of updating the parent's `<div>` background color from the child component will be similar to *Figure 8.2*:

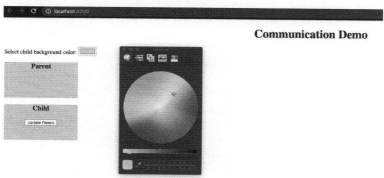

<div align="center">*Figure 8.2*: *Updating parent <div> background color from child component*</div>

In summary, @Input() decorator should be applied to a member variable of child component for receiving data from the parent component. Parent component should pass data using property binding syntax, that is, [property-name] = "expression" to child component. In C# windows forms, child form's public properties can be directly accessed by parent form using child form object; we don't need any specific syntax for such communication.

For a child to parent data communication, @Output() decorator should be applied on member variable of type EventEmitter<type> of child component and "emit()" method should be invoked to send data to the parent component. The parent component should subscribe to this event as if any standard HTML event using expression (event-name) = "eventHandler($event)". Note that passing the "$event" is very important as it holds the event argument passed by the child component. If not passed here, then parents won't receive data from the child.

Parent-Child communication through a local variable reference

In the previous chapter of *Template Driven Forms*, we have seen how to create local HTML references using "#reference" syntax, for example, . <form #loginForm = "ngForm">. Using a local variable, we can access HTML tag's properties and method in the template, that is, HTML code. We can use apply the local variable concept to parent-child communication as well.

Let's extend our example further. We will define two new methods inside ColorDemoComponent namely "showColorName()" and "setNewColor()". The showColorName() method will show current background color name by reading "inputColor" property. When setNewColor(newColor) is called, new background color will be set. *Code 8.7* shows the updated color-demo.component.html file:

```
import { Component, OnInit, Input, Output, EventEmitter } from '@
angular/core';


@Component({
    selector: 'app-color-demo',
    templateUrl: './color-demo.component.html',
    styleUrls: ['./color-demo.component.css']
})
export class ColorDemoComponent implements OnInit {


    @Input('inputBGColor') inputColor = '';
```

```
@Output() outputColorChanged = new EventEmitter<string>();

constructor() { }

ngOnInit() {
    this.inputColor = 'gray';
}

updateParent() {
    this.outputColorChanged.emit(this.inputColor);
}

showColorName() {
    alert(this.inputColor);
}

setNewColor(newColor: string) {
    this.inputColor = newColor;
}
}
```

Code 8.7: *color-demo.component.html – showColorName and setNewColor methods added*

In the `app.component.html` file, we will create a local variable named "childComponent" on <app-color-demo> component, as shown in *Code 8.8*:

```
<app-color-demo #childComponent [inputBGColor]="backgroundColor"
(outputColorChanged)="onOutputColorChanged($event)">

</app-color-demo>
```

Code 8.8: *app.component.html – creating a local variable of the child component*

Next, we will have a text field in the parent component to ask the user a new color name for the child component. On click of the **Set Color** button, the child component will have background color the same as passed in the text field. We will also have a button to show the current background color name of the child component. *Code 8.9* shows these new HTML content. For the sake of local variable explanations, we are creating a "colorInput" local variable on <input> tag of type "text" where the user can type the new color name and its value is retrieved using local variable and passed as an argument to `childComponent.setNewColor()` method.

```html
<input type="text" #colorInput placeholder="Enter color name">
<button (click)="childComponent.setNewColor(colorInput.value)">Set
Color</button>
<button (click)="childComponent.showColorName()">Show Color</button>
```

Code 8.9: app.component.html – HTML content to update child component's background color

When a browser renders `<app-color-demo>` tag with a local variable, it creates new instances and alias with name `childComponent`. It can be referred to as the instance object of **ColorDemoComponent** class. Using `childComponent` local variable we can invoke `setNewColor()` and `showColorName` methods. *Code 8.10* shows complete:

```html
<div style="text-align:center">
    <h1>
        Communication Demo
    </h1>
</div>


<div>
    <label for="childBGColor">Select child background color: </
label>
    <input id="childBGColor" type="color"
[(ngModel)]="backgroundColor">
</div>


<div [style.backgroundColor]="newColor" class="parent-bg-color-
test">
    <h3>Parent</h3>
</div>


<br>


<input type="text" #colorInput placeholder="Enter color name">
<button (click)="childComponent.setNewColor(colorInput.value)">Set
Color</button>
<button (click)="childComponent.showColorName()">Show Color</button>


<app-color-demo #childComponent [inputBGColor]="backgroundColor"
```

```
(outputColorChanged)="onOutputColorChanged($event)">

    </app-color-demo>


<router-outlet></router-outlet>
```

Code 8.10: *app.component.html – complete code with a local variable for a child component*

Having all code being saved, make sure **ng serve --open** command is running and verify output in the browser. Enter the color name in a text box, for example, "**red**" and click on the **Set Color** button. As an output child component's background color should be set to "**red**" color. Now click on **Show Color** button, it should show an alert in browser with color name **red** similar to *Figure 8.2:*

Figure 8.3: *Updating child component background color using a local variable reference*

Parent-Child communication through @ ViewChild() decorator

In C# Windows Forms communications, we can register an instance of child form in Dependency Injector and resolve the same instance in parent component for accessing the child component's properties and methods. On a similar note, we can do the same in Angular as well. In the previous section, we have seen how to use child component instance in the parent component's template using a local variable. But the problem with the local variable approach is that we cannot access it inside the parent component class. If we have a requirement where child component instance should be accessed by parent component class, then we can use @ViewChild(), decorator.

We will update our example for similar functionality but with @ViewChild() decorator instead of the local reference variable. In AppComponent class, we will create a new member variable for holding a reference of the ColorDemoComponent

component, and we will apply **@ViewChild()** decorator on this variable as shown in *Code 8.11*. We have also defined two wrapper methods inside AppComponent component namely **setNewColor()** and **showColorName()** which invokes methods of ColorDemoComponent class:

```
import { Component, OnInit, ViewChild } from '@angular/core';

import { ColorDemoComponent } from './color-demo/color-demo.
component';


@Component({
    selector: 'app-root',
    templateUrl: './app.component.html',
    styleUrls: ['./app.component.css']
})
export class AppComponent implements OnInit {


    @ViewChild(ColorDemoComponent, {static: false}) private
childComponent: ColorDemoComponent;


    setNewColor(newColor: string) {
        this.childComponent.setNewColor(newColor);
    }


    showColorName() {
        this.childComponent.showColorName();
    }
}
```

Code 8.11: app.component.ts – referencing child component using @ViewChild() decorator

The **@ViewChild()** decorator accepts two arguments—selector of component class and options metadata. *Code 8.12* shows a declaration of **@ViewChildDecorator()** from Angular official documentation. In our case, we have used component type as a selector, but it can be string or function as well. Second argument {**static: false**} tells Angular not to resolve query results before change detection runs.

```
export declare interface ViewChildDecorator {
    (selector: Type<any> | Function | string, opts: {
        read?: any;
```

```
    static: boolean;
}): any;
new (selector: Type<any> | Function | string, opts: {
    read?: any;
    static: boolean;
}): ViewChild;
}
```

Code 8.12: @ViewChild() decorator declaration

As shown in *Code 8.13*, we have removed the local reference variable from the app. component.html file. When the user clicks **Set Color** and **Show Color** buttons, then we will call the child component's method using the **@ViewChild()** reference variable. Let's save the changes and verify the output in the browser. We should have similar output as of local variable, that is, *Figure 8.3*:

```
<input type="text" #colorInput placeholder="Enter color name">

<button (click)="setNewColor(colorInput.value)">Set Color</button>

<button (click)="showColorName()">Show Color</button>


<app-color-demo [inputBGColor]="backgroundColor"
(outputColorChanged)="onOutputColorChanged($event)">

</app-color-demo>
```

Code 8.13: app.component.html – removed local variable

Passing Data between Components through Service

Passing data using Dependency Injectable service is one of the most straightforward approaches of communication between components in Angular. In the C# Windows Form, we can have a service class injected into the Dependency Injection framework and resolve its instance in the rest of the program to pass and retrieve data. Similarly, in Angular, we can create and provide a common service into the root module and then inject this service class in the rest of the components and other elements of Angular application to resolve its instance.

Let's update our example with the use of service. We will create a DataService service class that is injected into the root module by default. The DataService service class will provide methods for updating the background color of child and parent, respectively.

In *Code 8.14*, we have declared a `Subject` and `Observable` variables each for parent and child color change notification. A Subject is a type exported from the 'rxjs' package and used for asynchronous processing. It can return an observable instance which we will hold in another variable. The parent and child components will subscribe to these observable variables through service instance.

```
private parentColorChangedSource: Subject<string>;

private childColorChangedSource: Subject<string>;


parentColorChanged$: Observable<string>;

childColorChanged$: Observable<string>;


constructor() {
    this.parentColorChangedSource = new Subject<string>();
    this.parentColorChanged$ = this.parentColorChangedSource.
asObservable();


    this.childColorChangedSource = new Subject<string>();
    this.childColorChanged$ = this.childColorChangedSource.
asObservable();
}
```

Code 8.14: data.service.ts – declaring Subject and Observables

In *Code 8.15*, we have defined two methods inside `DataService` class, `updateParentColor()` and `updateChildColor()` respectively. Whenever parent wants to update the background color of child component, it can call a method "updateChildColor()" of `DataService` and "next()" method of Subject will be executed causing a new data in observable. Any subscription to observable will get newColor value, which is passed to the "next()" method.

```
updateParentColor(newColor: string) {
    this.parentColorChangedSource.next(newColor);
}


updateChildColor(newColor: string) {
    this.childColorChangedSource.next(newColor);
}
```

Code 8.15: data.service.ts – methods for updating child and parent color

In *Code 8.16* shows the complete source code of the `DataService` service class:

```
import { Injectable } from '@angular/core';
import { Subject, Observable } from 'rxjs';


@Injectable({
    providedIn: 'root'
})
export class DataService {

    private parentColorChangedSource: Subject<string>;
    private childColorChangedSource: Subject<string>;

    parentColorChanged$: Observable<string>;
    childColorChanged$: Observable<string>;

    constructor() {
        this.parentColorChangedSource = new Subject<string>();
        this.parentColorChanged$ = this.parentColorChangedSource.
asObservable();

        this.childColorChangedSource = new Subject<string>();
        this.childColorChanged$ = this.childColorChangedSource.
asObservable();
    }

    updateParentColor(newColor: string) {
        this.parentColorChangedSource.next(newColor);
    }

    updateChildColor(newColor: string) {
        this.childColorChangedSource.next(newColor);
    }
}
```

Code 8.16: *data.service.ts*

Let's update child background color from the parent component using `DataService`. We will inject the `DataService` service class into the `AppComponent` component. When the **Set Color** button is clicked, the "setNewColor()" event handler will be executed, and the `updateChildColor()` method of `DataService` will be executed as shown in *Code 8.17*:

```
constructor(private dataService: DataService) {

}


setNewColor(newColor: string) {
    this.dataService.updateChildColor(newColor);
}
```

Code 8.17: *app.component.ts – using DataService to update the child background-color*

In `ColorDemoComponent`, we will inject `DataService` class and subscribe to `childColorChanged$` subscriber, as shown in *Code 8.18*:

```
constructor(private dataService: DataService) { }


ngOnInit() {
    this.inputColor = 'gray';


    this.dataService.childColorChanged$.subscribe((newColor: string)
=> {
        this.inputColor = newColor;
    });
}
```

Code 8.18: *color-demo.component.ts – using DataService to update child background color*

The workflow will be as follow:

1. When the user enters the new color name in the text field and click on the **Set Color** button of `AppComponent` class then `setNewColor()` method will be executed and will call `updateChildColor()` method of `DataService`.

2. The `updateChildColor()` method will call `next()` method on `childColorChangedSource` subject with `newColor` parameter and will put a data item in `childColorChanged$` observable stream.

3. Since `ColorDemoComponent` has subscribed to this observable, its `subscribe()` method will get executed, and the `newColor` will be set to `inputColor` property of `ColorDemoComponent` class completing the workflow.

Code 8.19 shows the complete source code of the `app.component.ts` file. The commented code is from the previous approach for parent-child communication and can be ignored. We have kept it for reference purposes only:

```
import { Component, OnInit, ViewChild } from '@angular/core';

import { ColorDemoComponent } from './color-demo/color-demo.
component';

import { DataService } from './data.service';


@Component({
    selector: 'app-root',
    templateUrl: './app.component.html',
    styleUrls: ['./app.component.css']
})
export class AppComponent implements OnInit {


    backgroundColor = '';


    newColor = '';


    // @ViewChild(ColorDemoComponent, { static: false }) private
childComponent: ColorDemoComponent;


    constructor(private dataService: DataService) {
    }


    ngOnInit() {
        this.newColor = 'gray';


        this.dataService.parentColorChanged$.subscribe((newColor:
string) => {
            this.newColor = newColor;
        });
    }
```

```
    onOutputColorChanged(newColor: string) {
        this.newColor = newColor;
    }


    setNewColor(newColor: string) {
        // this.childComponent.setNewColor(newColor);
        // this.dataService.childColor = newColor;


        this.dataService.updateChildColor(newColor);
    }


    showColorName() {
        // this.childComponent.showColorName();
        // alert(this.parentColor);
    }
}
```

Code 8.19: app.component.ts – Updating child background color using service

Complete source code ColorDemoComponent is shown in Code 8.20. This code also includes how to set parent component background color using service.

```
import { Component, OnInit, Input, Output, EventEmitter } from '@
angular/core';
import { DataService } from '../data.service';

@Component({
    selector: 'app-color-demo',
    templateUrl: './color-demo.component.html',
    styleUrls: ['./color-demo.component.css']
})
export class ColorDemoComponent implements OnInit {

    @Input('inputBGColor') inputColor = '';
    @Output() outputColorChanged = new EventEmitter<string>();

    newParentColor: string;
```

```
constructor(private dataService: DataService) { }

ngOnInit() {
    this.inputColor = 'gray';

    this.dataService.childColorChanged$.subscribe((newColor:
string) => {
        this.inputColor = newColor;
    });
}

updateParent() {
    // this.outputColorChanged.emit(this.inputColor);
}

updateParentColor(newColor: string) {
    this.dataService.updateParentColor(newColor);
}

showColorName() {
    alert(this.inputColor);
}

setNewColor(newColor: string) {
    this.inputColor = newColor;
}
}
```

Code 8.20: color-demo.component.ts – Updating child background color using service

Passing Data between Components through LocalStorage

The browser has small storage capacity, and web application can store application-specific data there. A web application can store data into LocalStorage,

ApplicationStorage, Cookies, or in IndexDB database. We can leverage these storages for passing data between components. The LocalStorage, for example, has methods to save data using key-value pairs where the key is string and value can be serialized JSON object. We can query the saved object into another component by passing the key name. `LocalStorage` is generally used for storing authentication token and session information, but if there is a special case, we can pass data between components using `LocalStorage` as well.

Conclusion

Passing data between components is a very important task. Angular provides various ways of such communication to take place. Based on the application requirement, we can decide we should use `@Input()` and `@Output()` decorator for passing data via template syntax or use local variable syntax to invoke the child component's method from parent component template file. If we want to access the child component's method(s) from the parent component class, then we can use `@ViewChild()`, decorator. `@ViewChild()` decorator doesn't need parent component to have a local variable of the child component. We can use Dependency Injection for injecting service class into parent and child component classes for communication. The Service class can notify the parent and/or child component of data change using Subject, Observable, EventEmitter types. Once we identify the flow of the data, we can choose the right way of passing data between components.

After reading this chapter, we can devise a communication strategy for components in our Angular application.

In the next chapter, we will learn how to consume HTTP resources inside an Angular application. Angular provides various DI ready services and packages for consuming server data like Http service, `HttpClientService`, and so on. We will dive deep into HTTP communication in the next chapter.

Questions

1. Create an Angular application having a component hierarchy, as shown in *Figure 8.4*. Pass data between components D and C back and forth. Also, send data from D and E as well:

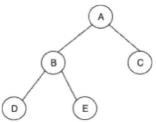

Figure 8.4: Angular application – component hierarchy

2. Can we pass data between components using the `localStorage` mechanism? If yes, create an Angular application demonstrating usage of `localStorage` for data passing between components.

3. Create an Angular application with routing. How can data be passed between routes?

4. Create an Angular application and pass data between components using local variables.

5. Create an Angular application and pass data between components using @ `ViewChild()` decorator.

CHAPTER 9

Being Alive By Consuming HTTP Resources

The web applications are meant to be a thin client. A typical single page web application should not contain any business logic and should collect data from users and present them in easy to access the form. The application's core business logic resides in the server code, which is then exposed via various web protocols like HTTP, web services, and so on. In this chapter, we will see how to consume HTTP based REST, **Representational State Transfer (REST)** services through Angular application.

Structure

- Introduction to HTTP methods
    - o The GET method
    - o The POST method
    - o The PUT method
    - o The DELETE method
- Fetch posts through GET method
- Using async/await for blocking the GET method
- Deletegate HTTP operations to Angular service
- Create a new post using the POST method

- Update post through PUT method
- Delete post via DELETE method
- Handling HTTP errors
- Retry HTTP operation
- Passing parameters in HTTP requests
- Passing HTTP Headers
- Organizing server URLs
- Switching between Mock and Real data service
- Introduction to HTTP Interceptors

Objective

In this chapter, we will learn how about HTTP libraries and modules for consuming REST services. Then we will learn how to use Observables and operators for processing stream-based responses. Then we will learn how to add HTTP headers in requests, which is the most common practice for sending JWT/OAuth tokens for session management on the server-side. Generally, the data sent from the server needs to be stored in the model class and then use it for binding in HTML code; we will learn how to do so as well. We will learn about how to organize Angular services for consuming data and best practices. Error handling is an essential part, and we will learn how to handle error situations if requests fail and how to retry them. We shall use https://jsonplaceholder.typicode.com/ REST services throughout our examples in this chapter.

Introduction to HTTP Methods

The HTTP request methods allow clients to access resources from the server. The client can be a browser, mobile device, another HTTP server, and so on. There are several HTTP methods, but we will be focusing on only CRUD methods like GET, PUT, POST, DELETE in this chapter:

- **The GET Method:** The GET method is used to get data from the server. The request contains a resource URL and optional parameters and query strings. It is the most common method for accessing resources. All native browsers support the **GET** method.
- **The POST Method**: The POST method is used to send the data to the server for creating a new resource. The request contains the resource URL and "body" object parameter and optional request parameters. Browser doesn't support POST method by default, but we can use **POSTMAN** like tools for sending a POST request.
- **The PUT Method**: The PUT method is used to modify existing resources on the server. The request contains the resource URL and updated "body" object

parameter and optional request parameters. Similar to POST, specialized tools are needed for sending PUT requests.

- **The DELETE Method**: The DELETE method is used to delete the resource on the server. The request contains the resource URL and optional parameters. POSTMAN like tools is required to send DELETE request.

Fetch Posts through the GET Method

In this section, we will create a new application and learn how to consume GET endpoint and display data in HTML code. Run *Command 9.1* in the terminal window for creating a new project:

```
ng new http-demo
```

Command 9.1: *Create a new project*

We will hit the GET endpoint of https://jsonplaceholder.typicode.com/posts URL, which returns an array of "Post" model. The browser shall display plain JSON response if https://jsonplaceholder.typicode.com/posts URL is hit. The partial response array is shown in *Code 9.2*. Note that this mock data and it can be different for multiple GET requests:

```
[
    {
        "userId": 1,
        "id": 1,
        "title": "sunt aut facere repellat provident occaecati excepturi optio reprehenderit",
        "body": "quia et suscipit\nsuscipit recusandae consequuntur expedita et cum"
    },
    {
        "userId": 1,
        "id": 2,
        "title": "qui est esse",
        "body": "est rerum tempore vitae\nsequi sint nihil reprehenderit dolor beatae ea dolores neque"
    }
]
```

Code 9.2: *GET endpoint response returning an array of Posts model*

Let's create a TypeScript class for holding this model information. It is best practice to hold response data into a model class for type safety and code maintenance. As we can see, there is four data members of the GET response, we can create "PostModel" class as shown in *Code 9.3*:

```
export class PostModel {
    id: number;
    userId: number;
    title: string;
    body: string;
}
```

Code 9.3: post.model.ts – PostModel for holding Posts data structure

The Angular library contains a **"@angular/common/http"** package, which exports the **"HttpClientModule"** module. We need to import this module into root AppModule, as shown in *Code 9.4*:

```
import { BrowserModule } from '@angular/platform-browser';
import { NgModule } from '@angular/core';
import { HttpClientModule } from '@angular/common/http';
import { AppRoutingModule } from './app-routing.module';
import { AppComponent } from './app.component';
@NgModule({
declarations: [
    AppComponent
],
imports: [
    BrowserModule,
    AppRoutingModule,
    HttpClientModule
],
providers: [],
bootstrap: [AppComponent]
})
export class AppModule { }
```

Code 9.4: app.module.ts – import HttpClientModule for cosuming HTTP resources

The HttpClientModule contains HttpClient service, which is injectable into components for accessing HTTP resources. We will inject this service into AppComponent component, as shown in *Code 9.5*:

```
export class AppComponent implements OnInit {


    constructor(private http: HttpClient) {

    }

}
```

Code 9.5: app.component.ts – Inject HttpClient service

The HttpClient service has **get()** method for sending **GET** request to the server. We will request all posts data from the server and typecast them into an array of **PostModel** class, as shown in *Code 9.6*:

```
import { PostModel } from './post.model';

export class AppComponent implements OnInit {

    posts: Array<PostModel> = [];

    url = 'https://jsonplaceholder.typicode.com/posts';

    ngOnInit() {

        this.http.get<Array<PostModel>>(this.url).subscribe(data =>
{

            this.posts = data;

            console.log(this.posts);

        });

    }

}
```

Code 9.6: app.component.ts – Get all Posts data and store in Posts array

In *Code 9.3*, we have declared an array of PostModel and put all posts resource endpoints into the "url" member variable. In ngOnInit() function we are firing GET request. It is best practice not to use the constructor for processing HTTP requests but ngOnInit(). All data initialization and data acquisition should take place in ngOnInit() and other lifecycle events. The most interesting part is the "get()" function call. We will break it down in a small part to understand in a better way. *Code 9.7* shows get() function declaration from Angular library. The get() function is a generic type; hence in its declaration, it is "get<T>()". What does it mean is the return type of this function will be of the type "Observable<T>". As we are using Array<PostModel> for "get<T>()" in our case, we will receive "Observable of

Array<Post>" that is, Observable<Array<PostModel>>:

```
get<T>(url: string, options?: {
        headers?: HttpHeaders | {
            [header: string]: string | string[];
        };
        observe?: 'body';
        params?: HttpParams | {
            [param: string]: string | string[];
        };
        reportProgress?: boolean;
        responseType?: 'json';
        withCredentials?: boolean;
    }): Observable<T>;
```

Code 9.7: http.d.ts – HttpClient's get() method declaration

Note that passing type to get() function is optional. If we do not pass any type, then the result will be of type "Observable<any>". But it is best practice to specify the type to get() function.

The next part is passing the GET endpoint URL. We are passing "this.url" variable to get() function as an argument, which is https://jsonplaceholder.typicode. com/posts address. We are skipping other parameters of get() function as they are not required for our requirement. So that's our HttpClient.get() function. Next part of code is pipe operation on result returned by get() function which is of type Observable<Array<PostModel>>. The subscribe() method subscribes to Observable returned by GET and executes code when a request is resolved. The "data" parameter of subscribe() function will be of type Array<PostModel>, and we are assigning it to a class member variable of "this.posts". For debugging purposes, we are also printing results to browser console using console.log().

We can verify output by running the command "**ng serve –open**" in the project directory. In the browser, go to the developer console window, and we should have output similar to *Figure 9.1:*

Figure 9.1: Browser console output displaying GET results of PostModel array

As a next step, we will display the result of the GET request in the browser. In the HTML file, we can run a simple "ngFor" loop and bind the properties of PostModel, as shown in *Code 9.8*:

```html
<h2>All Posts:</h2>


<div *ngFor="let post of posts">
    <p>
        <b>Title: </b>
        {{post.title}}
    </p>
    <p>
        <b>Body: </b>
        {{post.body}}
    </p>
</div>


<router-outlet></router-outlet>
```

Code 9.8: *app.component.html – Display PostModel array in browser*

Once changes are saved and angular development server recompiles, the browser should show output similar to *Figure 9.2*. The content being sent from the mock server might vary so you can get different outputs while running this code on your machine:

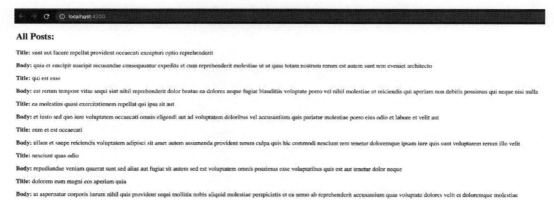

Figure 9.2: *All Posts displayed in a browser*

We can check the "**Network**" tab of browser for GET request being fired, as shown in *Figure 9.3*. It is a handy tool for debugging as it gives detailed information about requests and responses. We can see request and response headers in the "**Headers**" tab.

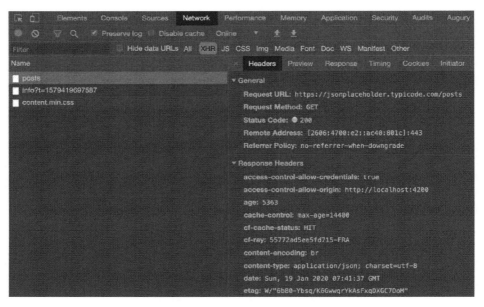

Figure 9.3: *Google Chrome – Developer tool's Network - Headers tab view*

To check the response being sent from the server, click on the "**Response**" tab, and it will show the actual response being sent from the server, as shown in *Figure 9.4*. While debugging, it helps validate if server data is received or not and whether client-side code couldn't process data.

Figure 9.4: *Google Chrome – Developer tool's Network - Response tab view*

Using async/await for Blocking the GET Method

Let's update our code to show the total post objects received. We will declare the "postCount" numeric variable in the AppComponent class and set it in subscribe() function, as shown in *Code 9.9*:

```
export class AppComponent implements OnInit {


    postCount = 0;


    ngOnInit() {
        this.http.get<Array<PostModel>>(this.url).subscribe(data =>
{

            this.posts = data;
            this.postCount = data.length;

            console.log(this.posts);
        });


        console.log(`Post count = ${this.postCount}`);


    }
```

Code 9.9: app.component.ts – Get total post count

The code looks correct, isn't it? Let's save the changes and run the application if not running already. Go to the browser and check the console output; it should be similar to *Figure 9.5:*

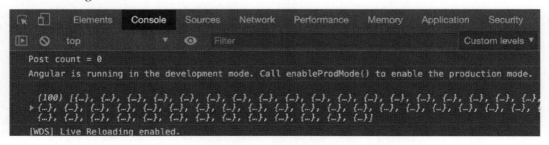

Figure 9.5: Non-blocking call of GET prints postCount zero

Snap! PageCount is displayed as zero though we have 100 objects in an array. What could have happened? This is a common mistake people run into while working with Observable and HttpClient. The `subscribe()` method of Observable will be executed when get() function returns data asynchronously. Since `subscribe()` function call is not a blocker, the `console.log()` for printing `postCount` executes with its default value of zero.

We can make a blocking HTTP call by using the `async/await` feature, as shown in *Code 9.10*. As mentioned earlier the `get()` function returns `Observable<T>` type. Observable has another method "`toPromise(),`" which converts Observable into vanilla JavaScript Promise. We can put the "`await`" keyword in front of our `get()` function, as shown in code. Note that to use `await` keyword, the function must be declared as an `async`; hence we have updated `ngOnInit()` to `async`:

```
async ngOnInit() {
    // this.http.get<Array<PostModel>>(this.url).subscribe(data
=> {
    //      this.posts = data;
    //      this.postCount = data.length;
    //      console.log(this.posts);
    // });
    // console.log(`Post count = ${this.postCount}`);

    this.posts = await this.http.get<Array<PostModel>>(this.
url).toPromise();
    this.postCount = this.posts.length;
    console.log(this.posts);

    console.log(`Post count = ${this.postCount}`);
}
```

Code 9.10: app.component.ts – async/await usage for blocking HTTP GET call

With async/await, the GET request will block further code execution. Once the server responds with data, it will be stored into `this.posts` and `this.postCount` can query a number of posts from an array. As shown in *Figure 9.6,* we can see "`posts`" are logged first, and "`postCount`" is logged after that in the browser console:

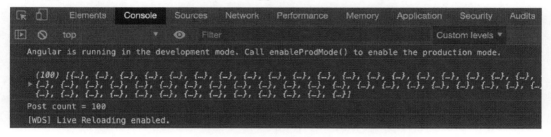

Figure 9.6: Blocking call of GET prints postCount 100 after posts

> **Note: To use async/await, we have to convert Observable to promise. We should be mindful of the difference between Observable and promise features; one of them is that promise will be executed only once even though the server is sending data in a stream. So, if stream-based continuous data is expected, then converting it to promise will give the only first response. But in most of the HTTP CRUD operations, we are interested in request/ response, so this should suffice.**

Delegate HTTP Operations to Angular Service

In our simple example, we have consumed GET endpoint in AppComponent directly for the sake of simplicity. Ideally, we should create a service that is responsible for handling HTTP requests to follow the Single Responsibility Principle. Let's create a new data service by running *Command 9.2:*

```
ng generate service posts
```

Command 9.2: Generate Posts Angular service

In PostsService, we will move HTTP requests related code as shown in *Code 9.11*. We have written `getPosts()` function which will make GET request and return server response by typecasting it into `Observable<Array<PostModel>>`:

```
import { Injectable } from '@angular/core';

import { Observable } from 'rxjs';

import { HttpClient } from '@angular/common/http';


import { PostModel } from './post.model';


@Injectable({
```

```
        providedIn: 'root'
})
export class PostsService {

    url = 'https://jsonplaceholder.typicode.com/posts';

    constructor(private http: HttpClient) { }

    public getPosts(): Observable<Array<PostModel>> {
        return this.http.get<Array<PostModel>>(this.url);
    }
}
```

Code 9.11: posts.service.ts – PostsService for handling HTTP requests

Since we have moved HTTP code to PostsService, we will update our AppComponent code. We will use PostsService for getting all posts, as shown in *Code 9.12*. The benefit of using PostsService rather than direct HttpService is loose coupling and testability. AppComponent doesn't know how posts are being fetched by getPosts(). We can return mocked data from this function without changing AppComponent. Thus it is best practice to create a separate service for handling HTTP resources rather than consuming them from Components/Pipes/Directives.

```
export class AppComponent implements OnInit {
posts: Array<PostModel> = [];

constructor(private postsService: PostsService) {
}

ngOnInit() {
    this.postsService.getPosts().subscribe(data => {
        this.posts = data;
        this.postCount = data.length;
        console.log(this.posts);
    });
}
}
```

Code 9.12: app.component.ts – Using PostsService for getting all posts

Create a New Post Using the POST Method

In this section, we will create a new post object by a firing POST request. We will create a very basic form for getting new post data from the user and send it to the mock server. Import `FormsModule` module into AppModule's import section for using `[(ngModel)]`. As shown in *Code 9.13*, we are creating text boxes for accepting new post fields like title and body. We have used two-way data binding for title and body field. We are using Angular form, and the "**Create Post**" button is marked as a "**submit**" type. On click of the "**Create Post**" button, the ngSubmit event will be fired, and the "`createPost()`" function will be executed.

```html
<form #postForm="ngForm" (ngSubmit)="createPost()">

    <div>Create New Post</div>

    <div>

        <input type="text" name="title" placeholder="Enter title"
[(ngModel)]="newPost.title">

    </div>

    <div>

        <textarea rows="4" name="body" placeholder="Enter content"
[(ngModel)]="newPost.body"></textarea>

    </div>

    <button type="submit">Create Post</button>

</form>
```

Code 9.13: app.component.html – Simple form for creating a new post

After AppComponent's HTML code is updated, we will update its component class. As shown in *Code 9.14*, we have a new member, "`newPost`" of type `PostModel` class. We are initializing it in `ngOnInit()` function. If we do not initialize, then `[(ngModel)]` binding will throw runtime error. In the `createPost()` function, we have left the "`id`" field empty as generally it is filled by database or backend service and won't ask the user to provide it. The last property "`userId`" will have hardcoded, but generally, it should be read from local storage or cache for an active session. We are passing this "newPost" object to the "createPost()" method of PostsService, which returns an Observable of type PostModel. In subscribe() function, we will receive the newly created Post object as a parameter. We are printing new objects into the browser console and will alert for success.

```typescript
export class AppComponent implements OnInit {

    newPost: PostModel;
```

```
    ngOnInit() {
        this.newPost = new PostModel();
    }


    createPost(): void {
        this.newPost.userId = 52;
        this.postsService.createPost(this.newPost).subscribe(newPostData
=> {
            alert('New post created!');
            console.log(newPostData);
        });
    }
}
```

Code 9.14: app.component.ts – Simple form for creating a new post

The createPost() method inside PostsService class simply calls post() method of HttpClient and pass PostModel as generic type argument so that return type of post() is Observable<PostModel>. The post() method accepts POST resource URL and body object, which are passed as of this.url and newPost, respectively, as shown in *Code 9.15:*   export class PostsService {

```
    public createPost(newPost: PostModel): Observable<PostModel> {
        return this.http.post<PostModel>(this.url, newPost);
    }
}
```

Code 9.15: posts.service.ts – Create new post using a POST request

Let's verify the output by saving changes in all files and open developer console in the browser. Enter content for title and body fields in the form and click on the **"Create Post"** button. We should see an alert in the browser, and in the console, we will have a new post object logged similar to *Figure 9.7*. If we observe, the "id" field has been set to 101, whereas we left it empty while sending a POST request. The mock server has updated this field on the server and sent us back. Nevertheless, the GET result will not include our new post object as the given mock server doesn't preserve the changes.

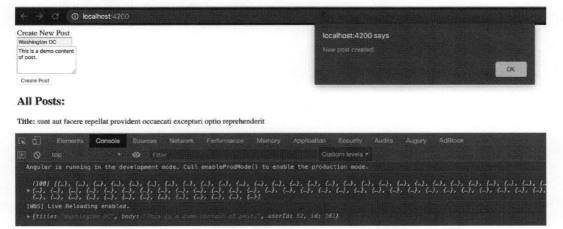

Figure 9.7: New post object created and logged in the browser console

Update post through PUT method

The PUT request is used for updating existing resources on a server. A typical PUT request contains a URL to the exact resource and modified body object. We will update our HTML code for accepting the "id" field of PostModel from the user so that we can pass it to our fake server and a new button for updating resources, as shown in *Code 9.16*:

```html
<form #postForm="ngForm" (ngSubmit)="createPost()">

    <div>Create New Post</div>

    <div>

        <input type="number" name="id" placeholder="Enter id"
[(ngModel)]="newPost.id">

    </div>

    <div>

        <input type="text" name="title" placeholder="Enter title"
[(ngModel)]="newPost.title">

    </div>

    <div>

        <textarea rows="4" name="body" placeholder="Enter content"
[(ngModel)]="newPost.body"></textarea>

    </div>
```

```
        <button type="submit">Create Post</button>
        <button type="button" (click)="udpatePost()">Update Post</
button>
    </form>
```

Code 9.16: app.component.html – accept "id" field of PostModel and Update Post button

The "**Update Post**" is a regular button and not of type submit; hence we have added (click) event handler. In `AppComponent` class we have `updatePost()` function which calls `updatePost()` method of `PostsService` as shown in *Code 9.17:*

```
export class AppComponent implements OnInit {


    udpatePost(): void {
        this.postsService.updatePost(this.newPost).
subscribe(updatedPost => {
            console.log(updatedPost);
        });
    }

}
```

Code 9.17: app.component.ts – call updatePost() of PostsService

In PostsService, we have written `updatePost()` function, which forms the url with resource id. A `POST` request can update one resource at a time; hence we need to specify which resource we are targeting. For type safety reasons, we are passing PostModel type to `put()` method of HttpClient and `postUrl` and `modifiedPost` object are passed as an argument, as shown in *Code 9.18:*

```
export class PostsService {


    public updatePost(modifiedPost: PostModel): Observable<PostModel>
{
        const postUrl = this.url + '/' + modifiedPost.id;
        return this.http.put<PostModel>(postUrl, modifiedPost);
    }

}
```

Code 9.18: posts.service.ts– send PUT request for updating the post

We can verify the output in the browser by saving changes in all files and opening the console window in the browser. In the "id" text field, enter valid id from given posts array and modified title and body fields in other text fields. Then click on the

Update Post button and observe the console window. The output should look like *Figure 9.8*:

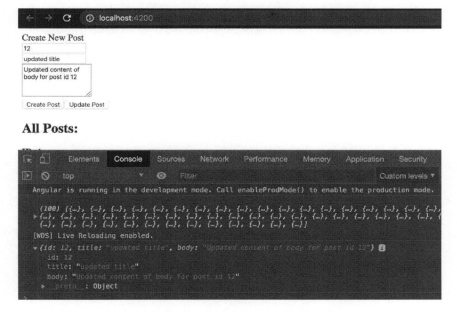

Figure 9.8: *Update post output from a fake server*

As we are using a fake server, it responds with the same updated post object upon success. We can also verify the Network tab of the browser and check the **Status Code** of request to be **200 (OK)**, as shown in *Figure 9.9*:

Figure 9.9: *PUT request Network tab output*

Delete post through DELETE method

One of the most commonly used CRUD related methods is `DELETE` used for the deletion of HTTP resources. We will add another button in HTML for deleting post by its "id". We have also added event handler "`deletePost()`" onclick event, as shown in *Code 9.19*:

```
<form #postForm="ngForm" (ngSubmit)="createPost()">

    <div>Create New Post</div>

    <div>

        <input type="number" name="id" placeholder="Enter id"
[(ngModel)]="newPost.id">

    </div>

    <div>

        <input type="text" name="title" placeholder="Enter title"
[(ngModel)]="newPost.title">

    </div>

    <div>

        <textarea rows="4" name="body" placeholder="Enter content"
[(ngModel)]="newPost.body"></textarea>

    </div>

    <button type="submit">Create Post</button>

    <button type="button" (click)="udpatePost()">Update Post</
button>

    <button type="button" (click)="deletePost()">Delete Post</
button>

    </form>
```

Code 9.19: app.component.html– *Delete Post button added*

In `AppComponent` class, we will add `deletePost()` function, which will call the `deletePost()` function of PostsService by passing post "`id`" to be deleted as shown in Code 9.20. We are not doing any validation here for the sake of simplicity, but in a real application, right validations should be added, for example, checking null, valid id range, and so on. The `subscribe()` method just display an alert for success and logs message:

```
export class AppComponent implements OnInit {


deletePost(): void {
```

```
        this.postsService.deletePost(this.newPost.id).
subscribe(response => {
            console.log(response);
            alert('Post deleted!');
        });
    }
}
```

Code 9.20: *app.component.ts– deletePost() for deleting post by id*

The PostsService has the `deletePost()` method, which calls the `delete()` method of HttpClient service and passes the URL of a resource to be deleted. We are using string interpolation for `deleteUrl` rather than just string concatenation to show as an option. We are not doing any typecasting of return type here as our fake server just responds with an empty JSON object when DELETE request is successful as shown in *Code 9.21:*

```
export class PostsService {

    public deletePost(postId: number) {
        const deleteUrl = this.url + `/${postId}`;
        return this.http.delete(deleteUrl);
    }
}
```

Code 9.21: *posts.service.ts– calling delete() method of HttpClient for deleting post*

We can verify output in the browser by entering the id of the post to be deleted and clicking on the "Delete Post" button. In the **Network** tab, we can see the **Status Code** is 200 for **DELETE** request, as shown in *Figure 9.10:*

Figure 9.10: *DELETE request Network tab output*

Handling HTTP Errors

In a client-server architecture, errors are bound to happen due to many factors, for example, bad network connection, invalid client request, server error, and many more. It is wise to handle the error and show the user some useful information. Let's try to handle **404**, that is, resource not found error. We will update the URL in PostsService to some invalid address as shown in *Code 9.22*:

```
export class PostsService {


    url = 'https://jsonplaceholder.typicode.com/invalid-url';


    constructor(private http: HttpClient) { }
}
```

Code 9.22: posts.service.ts – Invalid URL address for mocking 404 error

So far, we have used only the first parameter of subscribe() method, which gets executed whenever the next() method of subscribed Observer is executed. If there is an error, then we can pass a function as the second parameter to subscribe() method for error handling. In AppComponent class, we are simply displaying an error message in alert to inform the user as shown in *Code 9.23*:

```
export class AppComponent implements OnInit {


    constructor(private postsService: PostsService) {
    }


    ngOnInit() {

        this.postsService.getPosts().subscribe(data => {
            this.posts = data;
            this.postCount = data.length;
            console.log(this.posts);
        },
            errors => alert('Something went wrong!'));
        }
}
```

Code 9.23: app.component.ts – Handling error condition and displaying an alert

Let's save the changes in all files and observe the output in the browser. It should be similar to *Figure 9.11*:

Figure 9.11: *Display alert for HTTP errors*

We have seen a simple case of error handling to show an alert. But in the real-life application, we would like to inform the user why the request failed and some user-friendly messages. Angular provides a detailed error message in an object of type `HttpErrorResponse`. *Code 9.24* shows the official declaration from the Angular library. We can see it contains lots of details like status code, status text, url, and so on.

```
    export declare class HttpErrorResponse extends HttpResponseBase
implements Error {
        readonly name = "HttpErrorResponse";
        readonly message: string;
        readonly error: any | null;
        /**
        * Errors are never okay, even when the status code is in the
2xx success range.
        */
        readonly ok = false;
        constructor(init: {
            error?: any;
            headers?: HttpHeaders;
            status?: number;
```

```
        statusText?: string;
        url?: string;
    });
}
```

Code 9.24: *http.d.ts – HttpErrorResponse class declaration from Angular library*

Let's update the `AppComponent` code for logging more details about the error, as shown in *Code 9.25*. We are printing error status code, status text, and error message in the browser console:

```
export class AppComponent implements OnInit {


    ngOnInit() {
        this.newPost = new PostModel();

        this.postsService.getPosts().subscribe(data => {
            this.posts = data;
            this.postCount = data.length;
            console.log(this.posts);
        },
            (errors: HttpErrorResponse) => {
                console.error(`Status: ${errors.status}`);
                console.error(`Status Text: ${errors.statusText}`);
                console.error(`Message: ${errors.message}`);
                alert('Something went wrong!');
            }
        );
    }
}
```

Code 9.25: *app.component.ts – Logging more error details into the browser console*

After saving changes in all files, observe the output in the browser's console. We should see output similar to *Figure 9.12* with more error details:

Figure 9.12: *Logging error details in the browser console.*

Retry HTTP Operation

Sometimes due to poor network connection, requests may get failed, and if we try again, there are chances of getting through. There is a "retry()" operator from the rxjs library, which is designed for this exact purpose. It tries to connect to the server for a given number of times until a successful request is resolved or the number of retries exceeded. Let's update our code for retrying. In *Code 9.26*, we are trying to retry getPosts operation five times. The pipe() function is another useful thing from rxjs for passing the output of one function as an input to another function:

```
export class PostsService {

    url = 'https://jsonplaceholder.typicode.com/invalid-url';

    constructor(private http: HttpClient) { }


    public getPosts(): Observable<Array<PostModel>> {
        return this.http.get<Array<PostModel>>(this.url).
pipe(retry(5));
    }
}
```

Code 9.26: *app.component.ts – Logging more error details into the browser console*

After saving the changes, open the browser console and go to the **Network** tab. We should see six requests (1 original request + 5 retries) being fired and failed, as shown in *Figure 9.13:*

Figure 9.13: Multiple requests being sent to the server by retry() operator

Passing Parameters in HTTP Requests

So far, we have seen simple HTTP requests being fired and handled. We can also pass additional query string parameters along with GET request. We will update our example to search posts by user id. We will have a text box where user can enter user id and on click on search button click all the posts created by that user will be searched over server. The HTML code for search form is shown in *Code 9.27:*

```
<form #searchForm="ngForm" (ngSubmit)="searchPost()">

    <div>Search posts by user id</div>

    <div>

        <input type="number" name="userId" placeholder="Enter user
ID" [(ngModel)]="searchUserId">

    </div>

    <button type="submit">Search Post</button>

</form>
```

Code 9.27: app.component.html – search posts by user id HTML form

The search posts form submit action will call the `searchPost()` function from `AppComponent`, as shown in *Code 9.28.* We are passing the `searchUserId` member variable to the `searchPost()` method of PostsService to find posts. If posts are found then inside `subscribe()` block we are logging them into browser console:

```
export class AppComponent implements OnInit {
searchUserId = 0;


constructor(private postsService: PostsService) {
}


searchPost(): void {
     this.postsService.searchPost(this.searchUserId).
subscribe(foundPost =>{
          console.log(foundPost);
     });
}
}
```

Code 9.28: app.component.ts – search posts by user id HTML form

The `PostsService` creates a query string for finding posts inside `searchPosts()` function in the format of https://jsonplaceholder.typicode.com/posts?userId=2. *Code 9.29* shows how the query string is built, and the request is sent to the server:

```
export class PostsService {


url = 'https://jsonplaceholder.typicode.com/posts';


constructor(private http: HttpClient) { }


public searchPost(postId: number): Observable<Array<PostModel>>
{
     const searchPostUrl = this.url + `?userId=${postId}`;
     return this.http.get<Array<PostModel>>(searchPostUrl);
}
}
```

Code 9.29: posts.service.ts – Build query string for finding posts by user id

To verify the output, save the changes in all files and go to the browser. In the search text field, enter a valid user id and click on the search post button. Open browser console and check the logs as well as the **Network** tab for request details. We should see found posts in browser console similar to *Figure 9.14:*

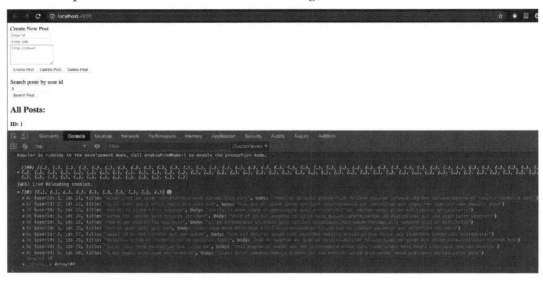

Figure 9.14: Displaying found posts by user id in the browser console

Passing HTTP Headers

The HTTP requests contain headers and body section which server can process. For simple requests, default HTTP headers suffice, but if the server needs additional information, then we can send those in to HTTP request headers. One of the common examples is sending JWT/OAuth token for session management. When a user tries to log on to the system by passing his credentials, the server sends back unique JWT/OAuth token to the client, and the client is supposed to send this token along with all further requests to get data. We will update our example code by passing mock auth-token into the HTTP header. The HttpHeaders class exported by **@angular/ common/http** package provides a way to pass headers in the HTTP request. In *Code 9.30*, we are creating a JSON object with the "headers" key of type HttpHeaders. We are passing a JSON object with key-value pair where the key is token name and value is token value. We are sending an "**Authorization**" token with mock value and a custom token as an example to send any token to serer. The get() method of HttpClient class accepts HTTP options as a second argument which we are passing to its "**headers**" property.

```
import { HttpClient, HttpHeaders } from '@angular/common/http';


@Injectable({
```

```
        providedIn: 'root'
})
export class PostsService {

    url = 'https://jsonplaceholder.typicode.com/posts';

    httpOptions: any;

    constructor(private http: HttpClient) {
        this.httpOptions = {
            headers: new HttpHeaders({
                'Authorization': 'jwt-mock-token',
                'My-Custom-Header' : 'custom-header-value'
            })
        };
    }

    public getPosts(): Observable<Array<PostModel>> {
        return this.http.get<Array<PostModel>>(this.url,
            { headers: this.httpOptions.headers }).pipe(retry(5));
    }
}
```

Code 9.30: posts.service.ts – Sending headers in GET request

We can verify whether our headers are being sent to the server or not. Let's save all the changes and refresh the browser to fire a new request. Next, open the developer tool and go to the **Network** tab and click on **"posts"** request to see its details. As highlighted in *Figure 9.15*, our two headers are present in request details **"authorization"** and **"my-custom-header":**

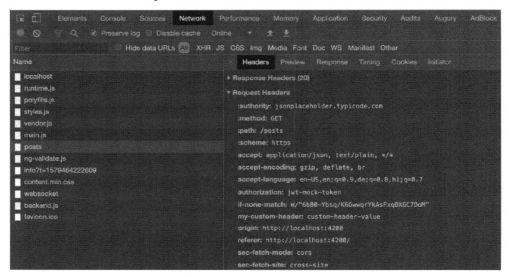

Figure 9.15: Sending HTTP headers in GET posts request

Organizing server URLs

We have used https://jsonplaceholder.typicode.com/posts URL directly in our `PostsService`. For demo purposes, it is okay, but for production, we should not hard code server URLs into TypeScript code but rather make them configurable. When a new Angular project is created, there is a folder created named "environments" with two files (a) `environment.ts` and (b) `environment.prod.ts`. By default, `environment.ts` file is used during development mode. When the application is built for production mode using the command **"ng build --prod,"** then the content of environment.ts file gets overridden by `environment.prod.ts`. We can put the base server URL into the environment.ts file. For development purposes, we can use the development server URL (if any), and once the application is ready to be deployed, we can put the production server URL into `environment.prod.ts`.

Let's add a new property in the environment object of `environment.ts` file, as shown in *Code 9.31:*

```
export const environment = {
    production: false,
```

```
        baseUrl: 'https://jsonplaceholder.typicode.com'
};
```

Code 9.31: environment.ts – Setting the base URL in development mode

Also, update environment.prod.ts file for the same property as shown in Code 9.32:

```
export const environment = {
    production: true,
    baseUrl: 'https://jsonplaceholder.typicode.com'
};
```

Code 9.32: environment.prod.ts – Setting the base URL in production mode

Next, we can update our PostsService to remove the hardcoded base URL and use the environment variable, as shown in *Code 9.33*. Here we are using environment. baseUrl for forming a complete URL of posts. We should get the same output with new changes if everything is okay.

```
    export class PostsService {

    url = environment.baseUrl + '/posts';

    httpOptions: any;

    constructor(private http: HttpClient) {
        this.httpOptions = {
            headers: new HttpHeaders({
                'Authorization': 'jwt-mock-token',
                'My-Custom-Header': 'custom-header-value'
            })
        };
    }
}
```

Code 9.33: posts.service.ts – Using environment variable for resolving base URL

Switching Between Mock and Real Data Service

During development mode, we often want to use some mock data to test our changes rather than directly consuming production service while keeping the same data structure. We will update our example to have a mock service for sending mock data and switch to the live JSON server. We will create a `DataService` abstract class to serve as an interface, as shown in *Code 9.34*. We will keep the only signature of methods which we have implemented in PostsService:

```
import { Observable } from 'rxjs';
import { PostModel } from './post.model';


export abstract class DataService {
    abstract getPosts(): Observable<Array<PostModel>>;
    abstract createPost(newPost: PostModel): Observable<PostModel>;
    abstract updatePost(modifiedPost: PostModel):
Observable<PostModel>;
    abstract deletePost(postId: number);
    abstract searchPost(postId: number):
Observable<Array<PostModel>>;
}
```

Code 9.34: data.service.ts – Using environment variable for resolving base URL

Next, we will create another service called `MockPostsService` by running *Command 9.3*:

```
ng generate mock-posts
```

Command 9.3: Create mock posts service

We will extend the `DataService` abstract class into `MockPostsService`. The `MockPostsService` class will hold an array of PostModel type for mock data. In the constructor, we will fill a few objects into this array. The `MockPostsService` class defines methods for getting, creating, updating, deleting, and searching posts but with mock data. The "of()" operator from the `rxjs` library converts a normal array into an Observable. We are using this "of()" operator to return mock post data to match the same return type as of HttpClient `get/post/delete/put` methods.

```
import { Injectable } from '@angular/core';
import { PostModel } from './post.model';
```

```typescript
import { Observable, of } from 'rxjs';
import { DataService } from './data.service';


export class MockPostsService implements DataService {

    mockPosts: Array<PostModel> = [];

    constructor() {
        let post = new PostModel();
        post.id = 1;
        post.userId = 1;
        post.title = 'Mock post 1';
        post.body = 'Mock body of post 1';
        this.mockPosts.push(post);

        post = new PostModel();
        post.id = 2;
        post.userId = 2;
        post.title = 'Mock post 2';
        post.body = 'Mock body of post 2';
        this.mockPosts.push(post);

        post = new PostModel();
        post.id = 3;
        post.userId = 3;
        post.title = 'Mock post 3';
        post.body = 'Mock body of post 3';
        this.mockPosts.push(post);

        post = new PostModel();
        post.id = 4;
        post.userId = 4;
```

```
            post.title = 'Mock post 4';
            post.body = 'Mock body of post 4';
            this.mockPosts.push(post);

            post = new PostModel();
            post.id = 5;
            post.userId = 5;
            post.title = 'Mock post 5';
            post.body = 'Mock body of post 5';
            this.mockPosts.push(post);
        }


        public getPosts(): Observable<Array<PostModel>> {
            return of(this.mockPosts);
        }
        public createPost(newPost: PostModel): Observable<PostModel> {
            return of(this.mockPosts[0]);
        }
        public updatePost(modifiedPost: PostModel): Observable<PostModel>
{
            return of(this.mockPosts[0]);
        }
        public deletePost(postId: number) {
            return {};
        }
        public searchPost(postId: number): Observable<Array<PostModel>>
{
            return of(this.mockPosts.filter(x => x.id === postId));
        }
    }
```

Code 9.35: *mock-posts.service.ts – Mock posts data service implementing DataService*

The PostsService class also implements `DataService` class, but its implementation remains the same to fetch data from remote servers, as shown in *Code 9.36:*

```
import { DataService } from './data.service';


@Injectable({
    providedIn: 'root'
})
export class PostsService implements DataService {

    url = environment.baseUrl + '/posts';


    public getPosts(): Observable<Array<PostModel>> {
        return this.http.get<Array<PostModel>>(this.url,
            { headers: this.httpOptions.headers }).pipe(retry(5));
    }
}
```

Code 9.36: *posts.service.ts – PostsService implementing DataService*

The AppModule's **@NgModule** decorator has "providers" property for specifying dependency injection. As shown in *Code 9.37*, we can specify how an instance can be resolved to the DI framework by passing a custom provider object with key-value pair. Here we are passing **DataService** as a type to be injected into the rest of the component classes. Whenever an instance is required for DataService, we are specifying to "useClass" property where we have specified **MockPostsService** class. Thus MockPostsService will be injected. This will act as a switch whether to pass **MockPostsService** or PostsService to the rest of the application:

```
import { DataService } from './data.service';
import { PostsService } from './posts.service';
import { MockPostsService } from './mock-posts.service';


@NgModule({
    declarations: [
        AppComponent
    ],
    imports: [
        BrowserModule,
```

```
        AppRoutingModule,
        HttpClientModule,
        FormsModule
    ],
    providers: [
        {
            provide: DataService,
            useClass: MockPostsService
        }
    ],
    bootstrap: [AppComponent]
})
export class AppModule {


}
```

Code 9.37: app.module.ts – Specify provider for DataService

In the **AppComponent** class, we can remove the dependency injection of PostsService and provide DataService. Nothing else needs to be changed apart from constructor injection, as shown in *Code 9.38:*

```
import { DataService } from './data.service';


export class AppComponent implements OnInit {


    constructor(private postsService: DataService) {
    }


    ngOnInit() {
        this.newPost = new PostModel();


        this.postsService.getPosts().subscribe(data => {
            this.posts = data;
            this.postCount = data.length;
            console.log(this.posts);
```

```
        },
        (errors: HttpErrorResponse) => {
            console.error(`Status: ${errors.status}`);
            console.error(`Status Text: ${errors.statusText}`);
            console.error(`Message: ${errors.message}`);
        }
    );
    }


}
```

***Code 9.38**: app.component.ts – Injecting DataService class*

Let's verify the output in the browser by saving changes in all the files. In the browser, we should see mock posts objects being rendered, as shown in *Figure 9.16*:

***Figure 9.16**: Displaying mock posts objects*

We can easily switch to live server posts just changing the `useClass` property of provider from `MockPostsService` to PostsService, as shown in Code 9.39. To verify outputs, save the changes, and the browser should show the server sent posts data.

```
import { DataService } from './data.service';

import { PostsService } from './posts.service';

import { MockPostsService } from './mock-posts.service';


@NgModule({


    providers: [
        {
            provide: DataService,
            useClass: PostsService
        }
    ],


})
export class AppModule {
}
```

Code 9.39: *app.module.ts – Specify provider for DataService*

Introduction to HTTP Interceptors

Angular HTTP traffic can be monitored and altered by the HttpInterceptor interface. This interface has only one method, "`intercept()`," which should be implemented by the custom interceptor. The purpose of the interceptor is to inspect all output going HTTP requests and, if required, modify them. One of the common use cases of the interceptor is to add JWT/OAuth token to outgoing requests rather than asking data service(s) to add a token. The interceptor can also inspect incoming traffic from the server and modify it. This is a good place for error handling of HTTP requests and leaving the rest of the application to focus on business logic.

We will write a very simple interceptor to understand the concept. Let's create a new service by running *Command 9.4:*

```
ng generate service posts-interceptor
```

Command 9.4: *Create interceptor service*

The purpose of PostsInterceptor is to tap into all outgoing HTTP method type and log them into the browser console. To do so, the `PostsInterceptor` class should implement the `HttpInterceptor` interface, as shown in *Code 9.40*. The `intercept()` method has two parameter of type (a) `HttpRequest` and (b) `HttpHandler`. The `HttpRequest` parameter contains the current outgoing request, and `HttpHandler` represents the next request in the chain. We can get the HTTP method type from the `HttpRequest` object, as shown in the code by accessing "`request.method`" variable.

```
import { Injectable } from '@angular/core';

import { HttpInterceptor, HttpRequest, HttpHandler, HttpEvent } from '@angular/common/http';

import { Observable } from 'rxjs';


@Injectable()
export class PostsInterceptor implements HttpInterceptor {


    constructor() { }


    intercept(request: HttpRequest<any>, next: HttpHandler):
Observable<HttpEvent<any>> {
        console.log(`Intercepted HTTP method: ${request.method}`);


        return next.handle(request);
    }
}
```

Code 9.40: posts-interceptor.service.ts – Implement simple HTTP interceptor

The PostsInterceptor needs to be registered with the root module—AppModule, as shown in *Code 9.41*. We are passing `HTTP_INTERCEPTORS` as a type that is internally used by Angular framework, and `useClass` property takes PostsInterceptor as an argument. The last parameter, "`multi`," tells Angular that `HTTP_INTERCEPTORS` should inject an array rather than a single value:

```
import { PostsInterceptor } from './posts-interceptor.service';


@NgModule({
    declarations: [
        AppComponent
```

```
        ],
        imports: [


        ],
        providers: [
            {
                provide: DataService,
                useClass: PostsService
            },
            { provide: HTTP_INTERCEPTORS, useClass: PostsInterceptor,
multi: true },


        ],
        bootstrap: [AppComponent]
    })
    export class AppModule {}
```

Code 9.41: *app.module.ts – Provide PostsInterceptor into AppModule providers*

Now we can verify output by saving changes in all the files and opening browser console window. The first request we are sending is GET, and we can see it is being logged in browser console by our interceptor, as shown in *Figure 9.17*. We can enter a value in the "`postId`" field and click on the **Delete Post** button. The interceptor should log the DELETE method type for this action, and so for the POST method:

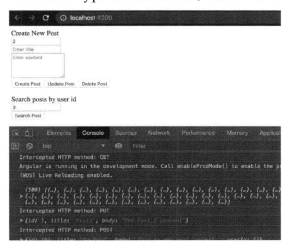

Figure 9.17: *Http method type intercepted and logged in the browser console*

Conclusion

The HttpClient module from the Angular library provides a rich set of methods, and the rxjs library provides nice stream-based operators and methods to work with HTTP resources. In this chapter, we have seen how we can send various HTTP requests and process the response. We have also seen how to handle the error(s) and retry for operation again if required. We have learned the best practices of how to mock server data into local service and how to switch between them using interface-based dependency injection. We have also seen how to store server URL into environment variables and their benefits in maintenance of the application.

Questions

1. Extend our application to send HEAD and PATCH HTTP requests to the server and process them.

2. Can we consume non-REST data using HttpClient? If yes, implement an example.

3. Extend our application to show a progress report during HTTP operation by modifying PostsInterceptor.

4. Can we make nested HTTP calls? For example, As soon as the post() method's is done, call get() method using rxjs operators/functions?

5. Implement a JWT token example by creating your REST API server and send the token to the client. Use Interceptor for passing this token for each request being sent to the server.

6. Can we create an environment file apart from auto-generated? For example, we would like to have a QA server, and its configuration should go in the environment.qa.ts file. Can you implement a solution to handle to generate output for the QA environment?

CHAPTER 10

Routing in Angular

Introduction

In a web application, routing is used for telling the browser to change its current web location (URL) to a new URL. Based on the server's response for a new URL, the browser shall display a new web page or take a different action, for example, download a file. The routing is an efficient way to modularize a web application into different features. In this chapter, we will learn how Angular manages the client-side routing by serving different pages. There are different types of routing in Angular and more features related to routing. Let's get started.

Structure

- What and Why Angular Routing?
- Overview of Angular Routing
- Building Ecommerce web application with routing
- Adding Angular material design library
- Create feature modules with routes
- Navigating to routes through a link
- Set the default route of the application
- Custom 404 Page-Not-Found page

- Route configuration ordering
- Navigate to route through code
- Create Child routes
- Enable debug trace for route configuration
- Routing life cycle events
- Passing route parameter
- Passing data between routes
- Securing the route path
- CanDeactivate guard
- Prefetching Product details
- Asynchronous routes
- Generating child asynchronous routes through CLI
- Inspect Router Tree in Augury
- Module Preloading strategy

Objective

Angular routing is a very vast and powerful feature of the framework. The Angular library contains lots of modules and services which are ready to use in application with little effort. In this chapter, we will see how to configure routing in an application using Angular CLI, how to create new modules and components, and how to link them with routing. Then we will see how to pass data between routes, how to add validation checks before changing routes, and how to check router states. We will also check how to add a typical "**PAGE NOT FOUND" (404)** error handler page and default routing page. Finally, we will learn how to use the Augury tool for checking routes in the browser for debugging and how to enable/disable routing debug trace.

What and Why Angular Routing?

As mentioned in the introduction of chapter, routing is a way of organizing web applications in a modular fashion. Consider a typical web application that contains a login page, signup page, dashboard, orders, accounts and profiles pages, and many more. The user action map will vary per user, and we would like to send a specific web page to the user's browser for his action. Such kind of action can be specified using routing. Before single-page applications like Angular, client-side routing was minimal and required lots of JavaScript coding; hence old applications relied on server-side routing to fetch new data/web pages. On the first server request, the server will send an `index.html` or default page to a browser. As a user clicks on some action to invoke another web page, then the server will send a new web page HTML code to browser for rendering and so forth. The browser will always keep visiting the server back and forth for getting web pages per request. Nowadays, with single-page applications, all web pages are sent to the browser on the first request from the server, and the browser keeps them locally. When client-side routing is invoked the SPA framework, for example, Angular captures the requests and asks the browser to render a new web page locally without going to the server. The server gets contacted for getting business data and action rather than new HTML content for rendering in the browser. Note that different SPA offers different types of routing mechanisms; for example, Angular's routing mechanism will be different than React.js or Vue.js. Still, their underlying goal is the same – server web pages locally!

Overview of Angular Routing

Before jumping to actual routing code and examples, let's try to understand Angular routing via bird's eye view. We have learned in previous chapters how to organize applications using modules and components feature-wise. We learned how to pass data between these components, whether they are in a parent-child relationship, peer-to-peer relationship using `@Input()`, `@Output()` decorators, and Angular service and events. When we organize our application in component level hierarchy, we have the static view of the application; that is, we need to manage states and visibility of component(s) based on user flow, which makes application complicated as it grows. For example, we need to mention the "selector" id of the component in the rest of the application, manage input properties and output events, and if something changes, trace the usage of component and update at all places. The Angular routing allows us creates one to one mapping with "route 🔲🔲component" which can be resolved dynamically. We can also view it as <key,value> pair where "key" is route-path, and "name" is component/module to load. This mapping is called route configuration in Angular. The routing configuration needs to be defined before the application starts and fed to the Angular routing library. As the application starts, the Angular framework loads this configuration into memory and serve different component based on the route path from the configuration. This configuration needs to be provided to the "`RouterModule`" module and import it into AppModule that is the root module. The "Router" service, which is a dependency injection ready from the Angular library, allows us to perform route change operations, events, and so on.

Since components shall be rendered at runtime, the parent component's HTML doesn't need to know the `exact` "`selector`" id of component. The parent component will hold the placeholder for rendering any component matching the route-path in the browser. Consider it as an empty canvas that can be filled with any component at runtime. This placeholder is mentioned as `<router-outlet></router-outlet>` tag in parent component's HTML. We can summaries it as simple workflow as follow:

- Create components/modules

- Define route-path for each component/module
- Provide configuration to RouterModule
- Import RouterModule to AppModule
- Specify `<router-outlet></router-outlet>` tag in parent
- Use RouterService for any route-specific operation that is changing the current route
- Start application

Building E-commerce Web Application With Routing

The Angular CLI allows us to create a new application with basic routing support. We will try to create a simple ecommerce website focusing on the main routing feature than CSS or business functionalities. Let's run *Command 10.1* to create a new project.

```
ng new ecommerce-demo
```

Command 10.1: *Create new Angular application using Angular CLI*

Angular CLI will ask if we would like to add routing to our new application to which respond "**Yes**". The output should be similar to *Figure 10.1*. If you do not see this question, then make sure your Angular CLI version is up-to-date.

```
[▶ ng new ecommerce-demo
[? Would you like to add Angular routing? Yes
 ? Which stylesheet format would you like to use? (Use arrow keys)
 > CSS
   SCSS   [ http://sass-lang.com/documentation/file.SASS_REFERENCE.html#syntax ]
   Sass   [ http://sass-lang.com/documentation/file.INDENTED_SYNTAX.html        ]
   Less   [ http://lesscss.org                                                  ]
   Stylus [ http://stylus-lang.com                                              ]
```

Figure 10.1: *Angular routing support prompt by Angular CLI*

The difference between Angular applications with routing support is that the "**app-routing.module.ts**" file will be generated with boilerplate routing code, as shown in *Code 10.1*. Let's try to understand this part of the code. AppRoutingModule is a simple NgModule class with metadata. The "**Routes**" is an array of route configuration which takes an object of "**Route**" class. Initially, it is empty, and we can put our configuration here. The "**RouterModule.forRoot(routes)**" is very interesting. It configures the route configuration and returns ModuleWithProviders; in this case, RouterModule is a NgModule with services and pipe, and so on. We will learn more about it later. The RouterModule returned by the "**forRoot()**" method is then exported back by the "**exports**" array. Hence whosoever will import

AppRoutingModule will get default import of RouterModule. As we need a global route configuration, we shall import AppRoutingModule into AppModule, which is a root module of the application.

```
import { NgModule } from '@angular/core';
import { Routes, RouterModule } from '@angular/router';


const routes: Routes = [];


@NgModule({
imports: [RouterModule.forRoot(routes)],
exports: [RouterModule]
})
export class AppRoutingModule { }
```

Code 10.1: app-routing.module.ts – boilerplate code generated by Angular CLI

The Angular CLI auto-generated AppModule class has imported the AppRoutingModule module, which contains route configuration, as shown in *Code 10.2.* Apart from that, there is no much difference in this class.

```
import { BrowserModule } from '@angular/platform-browser';
import { NgModule } from '@angular/core';


import { AppRoutingModule } from './app-routing.module';
import { AppComponent } from './app.component';


@NgModule({
declarations: [
    AppComponent
],
imports: [
    BrowserModule,
    AppRoutingModule
],
providers: [],
bootstrap: [AppComponent]
```

```
})
export class AppModule { }
```
Code 10.2: *app.module.ts – AppRoutingModule auto imported by Angular CLI*

The auto-generated AppComponent's HTML file contains one extra line at the end "`<router-outlet></router-outlet>`" as shown in *Code 10.3*. This tag is the placeholder for the component to be rendered when the route path is matched in the browser URL. Remember that if we do not have `<router-outlet>` tag, then nothing will be displayed in a browser even though route configuration is set correctly.

```
<!--The content below is only a placeholder and can be replaced.-->
<div style="text-align:center">
<h1>
    Welcome to {{ title }}!
</h1>
</div>


<router-outlet></router-outlet>
```
Code 10.3: *app.component.html – <router-outlet> tag added by Angular CLI*

Thanks to Angular CLI, with this basic setup, we are all set to create feature components and modules with route-path.

Adding Angular Material Design Library

We will add an Angular material design library in our project for basic styling. We will not go in detailed CSS for the sake of simplicity, but feel free to play around with look and feel. With the newer version of Angular CLI, adding Angular material design is effortless thanks to Angular Schematics. We can run *Command 10.2* and follow the instructions for adding Hammer.js and dependent libraries. Upon successful completion of the command, our ecommerce website will have Angular material design support.

```
ng add @angular/material
```
Command 10.2: *Add Angular material design schematic to an existing project*

We will create a separate module for importing Angular material component modules to be used in our application and use this module into our modules. This way, we will have one place where all material design-related modules are managed, and the code is not duplicated.

```
import { NgModule } from '@angular/core';
import { MatInputModule } from '@angular/material/input';
import { MatFormFieldModule } from '@angular/material/form-field';
import { MatButtonModule } from '@angular/material/button';


@NgModule({
    exports: [
        MatInputModule,
        MatFormFieldModule,
        MatButtonModule
    ]
})
export class ShareMatModule { }
```

Code 10.4: shared-mat.module.ts – Shared module for importing Angular material modules

Create Feature Modules with Routes

Let's define a simple user journey for our demo ecommerce website. We will have a login page as a default route; the user can go to sign-up page from the login page as well if he is not signed up so far. Once the user is successfully logged in, we will display a dashboard page.

Login Page with Route

Let's run the *Command 10.3* for creating the Login module and component one by one.

ng generate module login

ng generate component login

Command 10.3: Generate login module and component

The login page will have a basic username and password input field and a login button. Also, we will provide a link for the sign-up page. The HTML for login page will be similar to *Code 10.5:*

```
<h3>Login</h3>


<form>
    <div>
```

```
    <mat-form-field>
        <input matInput placeholder="Enter username">
    </mat-form-field>
</div>

<div>
    <mat-form-field>
        <input matInput type="password" placeholder="Enter
password">
    </mat-form-field>
</div>
<button mat-raised-button color="primary">Login</button>
<br>
<br>
<div>
    Not registered yet? <a href="">Register</a> free!
</div>
</form>
```

Code 10.5: *login.component.html – Login page basic structure*

As we are using material components like MatFormField, MatInput and MatButton inside Login component, we need to import SharedMatModule module into LoginModule as shown in *Code 10.6:*

```
import { NgModule } from '@angular/core';
import { CommonModule } from '@angular/common';
import { LoginComponent } from './login.component';
import { ShareMatModule } from '../shared-mat.module';


@NgModule({
declarations: [LoginComponent],
imports: [
    CommonModule,
    ShareMatModule
]
```

```
})
export class LoginModule { }
```

Code 10.6: login.module.ts– Import SharedMatModule for using material components

The last step is to create a route configuration for the Login component, as shown in *Code 10.7*. We are creating a new object of type Route and setting properties path and component. The "`path`" property specifies the route in the browser, and the "`component`" property tells the browser which component to render in `<router-outlet></router-outlet>` placeholder whenever "`path`" property is matched in browser's URL in this case "login" path will match to `LoginComponent`. Note that we have specified the "`login`" path without a forwarding slash. It is a common mistake while specifying configuration to provide forward slash.

```
import { NgModule } from '@angular/core';
import { Routes, RouterModule } from '@angular/router';
import { LoginComponent } from './login/login.component';
import { LoginModule } from './login/login.module';


const routes: Routes = [
    {
        path: 'login',
        component: LoginComponent
    }];


@NgModule({
    imports: [
        LoginModule,
        RouterModule.forRoot(routes)
    ],
    exports: [RouterModule]
})
export class AppRoutingModule { }
```

Code 10.7: app-routing.module.ts– Login component route configuration

The above configuration shows a simple example of creating a route configuration in Angular application. To verify the output, save the changes in all files and start the development server using the command "**ng serve --open**" in the terminal and let browser load application. Once the application is loaded in the browser, then change the URL to http://localhost:4200/login and observe the output. We should see our login page component displayed after the content of AppComponent's welcome text, as shown in *Figure 10.2:*

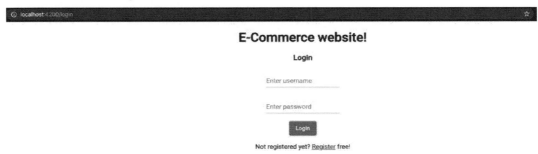

Figure 10.2: *Login component displayed by the "/login" route*

Sign-up Page with Route

We will create a sign-up page now with a similar approach to the Login page. Run the *Command 10.4* for creating a new module and component for Sign-up:

```
ng generate module sign-up
ng generate component sign-up
```

Command 10.4: *Generate sign-up module and component*

The HTML for sign-up form contains text fields for username and password and buttons. We also provide the option to navigate to the login page from the sign-up page. *Code 10.8* shows complete HTML of sign-up form.

```
<h3>Sign-up</h3>


<form>
    <div>
        <mat-form-field>
            <input matInput placeholder="Enter username">
        </mat-form-field>
    </div>


    <div>
        <mat-form-field>
            <input matInput type="password" placeholder="Enter
```

```
password">

            </mat-form-field>

        </div>

        <div>

            <mat-form-field>

                <input matInput type="password" placeholder="Confirm
password">

            </mat-form-field>

        </div>

        <button mat-raised-button color="primary">Sign-up</button>

        <br>

        <br>

        <div>

            Already have an account? <a href="">Login</a> here!

        </div>

    </form>
```

Code 10.8: sign-up.component.html – Sign-up form HTML basic structure

Similar to `LoginModule`, we will have to import `SharedMatModule` module into `SignUpModule` as shown in *Code 10.9*:

```
import { NgModule } from '@angular/core';

import { CommonModule } from '@angular/common';

import { SignUpComponent } from './sign-up.component';

import { ShareMatModule } from '../shared-mat.module';


@NgModule({

declarations: [SignUpComponent],

imports: [

    CommonModule,

    ShareMatModule

]

})

export class SignUpModule { }
```

Code 10.9: sign-up.module.ts– Import shared material design module

Finally, we will create another route configuration for sign-up page as shown in *Code 10.10:*

```
import { NgModule } from '@angular/core';
import { Routes, RouterModule } from '@angular/router';
import { LoginComponent } from './login/login.component';
import { LoginModule } from './login/login.module';
import { SignUpComponent } from './sign-up/sign-up.component';
import { SignUpModule } from './sign-up/sign-up.module';

const routes: Routes = [
    {
        path: 'login',
        component: LoginComponent
    },
    {
        path: 'sign-up',
        component: SignUpComponent
    }
];
@NgModule({
    imports: [
        LoginModule,
        SignUpModule,
        RouterModule.forRoot(routes)
    ],
    exports: [RouterModule]
})
export class AppRoutingModule { }
```

> **Code 10.10:** *app-routing.module.ts – Route configuration for Sign-up component*

We can see adding new features and routes for sign-up was pretty much similar to Login. Let's verify the output in a browser by saving all the changes and changing URL to http://localhost:4200/sign-up, and we should see output similar to *Figure 10.3*.

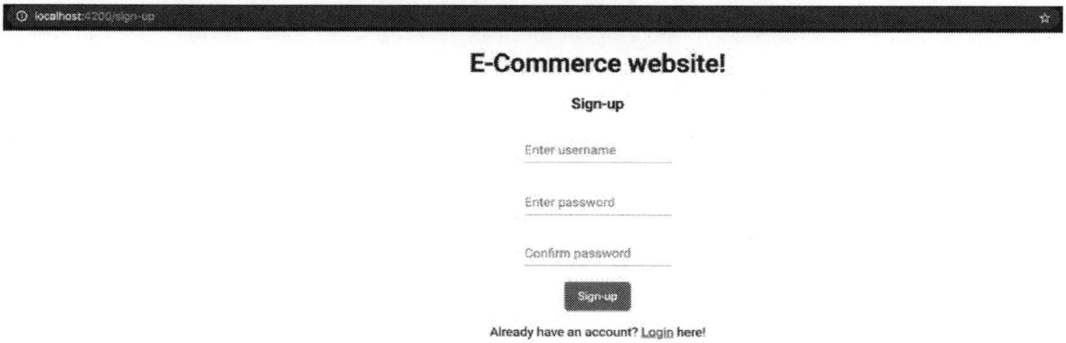

Figure 10.3: *Sign-up component rendered by "sign-up" route*

Navigating to Routes through the Link

A user can go to sign-up page from the login page and vice versa as per our user journey. We have kept a hyperlink in the Login and SignUp page for navigation purposes. A typical hyperlink tag's "href" property refers to server URL or hash-based local URL, but we would like to tell the browser change Angular specific URL. Hence we need to use Angular specific attribute in hyperlink tag -"routerLink"! A RouterLink is a directive exported by the RouterModule module from the "@ angular/router" package. Let's update hyperlink tag on the sign-up page to jump Login component as shown in *Code 10.11*:

```
    <div>
        Already have an account? <a routerLink="/login">Login</a>
here!
    </div>
```

Code 10.11: *sign-up.component.html – Using RouterLink directive to link LoginComponent route*

As mentioned `RouterLink` directive comes from `RouterModule` hence we need to import it into `SignUpModule` module as well as shown in *Code 10.12*:

```
    import { RouterModule } from '@angular/router';


@NgModule({
    declarations: [SignUpComponent],
    imports: [
```

```
        CommonModule,

        ShareMatModule,

        RouterModule

    ]

})

export class SignUpModule { }
```

Code 10.12: sign-up.module.ts– Import RouterModule module

These changes will allow the user to jump from the sign-up page to the Login component and can be verified by saving all the changes and clicking on the "login" hyperlink in the browser.

Task: Update login component for jumping to sign-up page upon clicking the "**Register**" hyperlink.

Set the Default Route of the Application

When we start our application, the default URL in the browser is set to **http://localhost:4200**. As a requirement, we would like to set our Login page as a default page whenever applications start. Angular provides a mechanism to set a specific route as a default route. To specify the default route, we need to set "path" property to empty and specify "redirectTo" property to the route-path of the default page we would like to set. It is important to note that we must prefix forward slash with the default route path here, unlike in a specific route path. The third property "pathMatch" specifies how the routes should be processed, and it goes with <base href= ""> value. For the simple case, we can mention "pathMatch" value to "full" assuming our <base href= ""> is set to empty. *Code 10.13* shows how to mark the login component as a default page. Now, if we go to the browser and change URL to **http://localhost:4200**, then it will automatically be redirected to **http://localhost:4200/login URL**.

```
    const routes: Routes = [
        {
            path: 'login',
            component: LoginComponent
        },
        {
            path: 'sign-up',
            component: SignUpComponent
```

```
    },
    {
        path: '',
        redirectTo: '/login',
        pathMatch: 'full',
    }
];


@NgModule({
    imports: [
        LoginModule,
        SignUpModule,
        RouterModule.forRoot(routes)
    ],
    exports: [RouterModule]
})
export class AppRoutingModule { }
```

Code 10.13: *app-routing.module.ts– Mark Login component as the default route*

Custom 404 Page-Not-Found page

Sometimes users can misspell the URL or route name in a browser, or the page user trying to access is not available anymore. In such scenarios, the browser displays the default page not found error page with a 404 HTTP error code. Generally, it is not a great user experience to show such a default page; hence many websites create their custom page not found a page and display it in case of a 404 error. We will create our custom page not found a page by running *Command 10.5*:

```
ng generate component custom-page-not-found --skip-import
```

Command 10.5: *Generate Custom page not found component*

For simplicity, we will keep just some text on a custom 404 page and link to go the home page that is, login page as shown in Code 10.14:

```
    <h3>Sorry! Looks like the page you are looking for not available!</
h3>
    <p>Let's go <a routerLink="/login">Home</a>!</p>
```

Code 10.14: *custom-page-not-found.component.html– Custom page not found text*

With our custom 404 pages ready, we will update the route configuration. Angular routing provides an option to specify which component should be rendered as the page-not-found page using a special wildcard for route path as ** (double asterisk).

```
import { CustomPageNotFoundComponent } from './custom-page-not-found/custom-page-not-found.component';


const routes: Routes = [
    {
        path: 'login',
        component: LoginComponent
    },
    {
        path: 'sign-up',
        component: SignUpComponent
    },

    {
        path: '',
        redirectTo: '/login',
        pathMatch: 'full',
    },
    {
        path: '**',
        component: CustomPageNotFoundComponent
    }
];


@NgModule({
    imports: [
        LoginModule,
        SignUpModule,
        RouterModule.forRoot(routes)
    ],
    exports: [RouterModule]
```

```
})
export class AppRoutingModule { }
```

Code 10.15: *app-routing.module.ts – Route config for custom page not found component*

We will verify output by saving changes in all files. In browser, type incorrect route after http://localhost:4200, for example, http://localhost:4200/wrong-url and observe the output. It should be similar to Figure 10.4 . We will allow the user to go to our login page by clicking on **"Home"** hyperlink:

Figure 10.4: *Displaying custom page not found page*

Route Configuration Ordering

The default page and page-not-found route configuration should be last entries in the Routes array because Angular tries to resolve browser URLs to route configuration from top to bottom manner. Hence if we put them on top of the array, then the incorrect route might be resolved at runtime.

Navigate to Route through Code

So far, we have created the Login page for signing in an existing user, Sign-up page for registering new user, marked Login page as a default page, and finally, we created a nice page-not-found for handling 404 error. The next user journey is to take the user to the dashboard page after successful login. So let's create a new dashboard module with the component by running Command 10.6:

```
ng generate module dashboard

ng generate component dashboard
```

Command 10.6: *Generate Dashboard module and component*

The new route configuration for dashboard can be added in `AppRoutingModule` as shown in *Code 10.16*:

```
import { DashboardModule } from './dashboard/dashboard.module';

import { DashboardComponent } from './dashboard/dashboard.
component';

const routes: Routes = [
```

```
        {
            path: 'dashboard',
            component: DashboardComponent
        }
    ];
    @NgModule({
        imports: [
            LoginModule,
            SignUpModule,
            DashboardModule,
            RouterModule.forRoot(routes)
        ],
        exports: [RouterModule]
    })
    export class AppRoutingModule { }
```

Code 10.16: app-routing.module.ts -- *Add Dashboard component route*

In the Dashboard page, we will have a simple toolbar with hyperlinks for various web pages, as shown in Code 10.17. These hyperlinks are placeholders only as we have not yet created their components and respective route configuration. Code 10.16 shows the dashboard HTML initial structure.

```
    <mat-toolbar color="primary">

        <mat-toolbar-row>

            <span class="link"> <a routerLink="/dashboard"
routerLinkActive="active">Dashboard</a> </span>

            <span class="link"> <a routerLink="/dashboard/products"
routerLinkActive="active">Products</a> </span>

            <span class="link"> <a routerLink="/dashboard/orders"
routerLinkActive="active">Orders</a> </span>

            <span class="link" class="example-spacer"></span>

            <span class="link"> <a routerLink="/dashboard/my-account"
routerLinkActive="active">My Account</a> </span>

        </mat-toolbar-row>
    </mat-toolbar>
```

Code 10.17: dashboard.component.html – *Simple toolbar with hyperlinks to other web pages*

The login page we created doesn't have any business logic. We will update login page by adding data binding for username and password and Angular form support as shown in *Code 10.18*:

```
<h3>Login</h3>


<form #loginForm="ngForm" (ngSubmit)="doLogin()">
    <div>
        <mat-form-field>
            <input name="username" [(ngModel)]="authModel.username"
required placeholder="Enter username"  matInput>
        </mat-form-field>
    </div>


    <div>
        <mat-form-field>
            <input name="password" [(ngModel)]="authModel.password"
required  type="password" placeholder="Enter password" matInput>
        </mat-form-field>
    </div>
    <button type="submit" mat-raised-button color="primary"
[disabled]="!loginForm.valid">Login</button>
    <br>
    <br>
    <div>
        Not registered yet? <a routerLink="/sign-up">Register</a>
free!
    </div>
</form>
```

Code 10.18: login.component.html – Login page with data binding

When the user clicks on the "**Login**" button, then we would like it to take him to the **Dashboard** page. To take the user to the **Sign-up** page, we have used the "routerLink" attribute in HTML, but in login case, we would like to check whether the username and password are correct and then redirect to the **Dashboard** page. The RouterModule provides a singleton service called "Router" which can be injected in the Login component. Of course, we need to import "RouterModule" into LoginModule to user Router service. The Router service has few methods for changing the current route; one of them is the "navigateByUrl()" method. We have passed "/dashboard" as an argument to this method to navigate to the Dashboard page. There is another commonly used method called "navigate()" for changing URL, we will use it in later examples. *Code 10.19* shows how to redirect from the **Login** page to the Dashboard component:

```
import { Router } from '@angular/router';
import { AuthModel } from '../auth.model';


@Component({
    selector: 'app-login',
    templateUrl: './login.component.html',
    styleUrls: ['./login.component.css']
})
export class LoginComponent implements OnInit {

    authModel: AuthModel;

    constructor(private router: Router) { }

    ngOnInit() {
        this.authModel = new AuthModel();
    }


    doLogin() {
        // TODO: check username and password
        this.router.navigateByUrl('/dashboard');
    }
}
```

Code 10.19: *login.component.ts– Login page with data binding*

We have also used the "AuthModel" class, which contains the username and password string class members. Let's verify the output by saving all the changes and go to the Login page. Enter any username and password and click on the "Login" button. The browser should load the dashboard page, and output should be similar to *Figure 10.5:*

Figure 10.5: Dashboard component loaded after login

Create Child Routes

The user journey took us from the login page to the dashboard so far. The next user can either go to the **Products** page, **Orders** page or **My Account** page. We will first create a products page and set its route as a child route of the dashboard. Run *Command 10.6* for creating Products module and component. Note that we are using the "dashboard/products" path while creating a module and component; this tells Angular CLI to create a separate folder inside the **Dashboard** and create a new module and component.

```
ng generate module dashboard/products
```

```
ng generate component dashboard/products
```

Command 10.7: Generate Products module and component inside the Dashboard

The products page will display a dummy product summary. We will use `GridList` component from Angular material design for displaying products in grid-like fashion thus make sure importing respective material modules into `SharedMatModule` module:

```
<h3>Products</h3>


<mat-grid-list cols="5" rowHeight="2:1">
    <mat-grid-tile *ngFor="let item of [1,2,3,4,5,6,7,8,9,10,11,12,
13,14,15]">
        <mat-card class="example-card">
            <mat-card-header>
                <mat-card-title> <a href="">Product {{item}}</a></
mat-card-title>
                <mat-card-subtitle>Product {{item}} subtitle</mat-
card-subtitle>
            </mat-card-header>
```

```
<mat-card-content>
    <p>
        This is a dummy product {{item}}.
    </p>
</mat-card-content>
<mat-card-actions>
    <button mat-button>Buy</button>
    <button mat-button>Cart</button>
</mat-card-actions>
</mat-card>
</mat-grid-tile>
</mat-grid-list>
```

Code 10.20: *products.component.html– Display mock product list*

The *"**Products**"* web page will be displayed inside the **Dashboard**; hence we will create a child route of the dashboard to navigate to the products page. *Code 10.21* shows how to define child routes. The *"*Route*"* class has a property called *"*children*"* which takes an array of *"*Route*"* objects. We can specify the number of child routes within this array as we have specified the 'products' route. Now products page can be rendered by URL http://localhost:4200/dashboard/products:

```
import { ProductsComponent } from './dashboard/products/products.
component';

import { ProductsModule } from './dashboard/products/products.
module';


const routes: Routes = [
    {
        path: 'dashboard',
        component: DashboardComponent,
        children: [
            {
                path: 'products',
                component: ProductsComponent
            }
        ]
```

```
    }
];


@NgModule({
    imports: [
        ProductsModule,
        RouterModule.forRoot(routes)
    ],
    exports: [RouterModule]
})
export class AppRoutingModule { }
```

Code 10.21: app-routing.module.ts – Product route added as a child route of Dashboard

The Dashboard component shall render Products page hence we need to define a placeholder for route output that is, <router-outlet></router-outlet> inside dashboard as shown in *Code 10.22*. Note that routerLink= "/dashboard/ products" attribute of **Products** hyperlink, this is how we can specify child routes for navigation in HTML.

```
<mat-toolbar color="primary">

    <mat-toolbar-row>

        <span class="link"> <a routerLink="/dashboard"
routerLinkActive="active">Dashboard</a> </span>

        <span class="link"> <a routerLink="/dashboard/products"
routerLinkActive="active">Products</a> </span>

        <span class="link"> <a routerLink="/dashboard/orders"
routerLinkActive="active">Orders</a> </span>

        <span class="link" class="example-spacer"></span>

        <span class="link"> <a routerLink="/dashboard/my-account"
routerLinkActive="active">My Account</a> </span>

    </mat-toolbar-row>

</mat-toolbar>


<h3>This is your personalised dashboard page!!</h3>


<router-outlet></router-outlet>
```

Code 10.22: dashboard.component.html – Render child route output in Dashboard

Let's save the changes in all files and follow user flow to get to the **Dashboard** page. Once on the dashboard, click on "**Products**" hyperlink in the toolbar, and we should see products being listed as shown in Figure 10.6 :

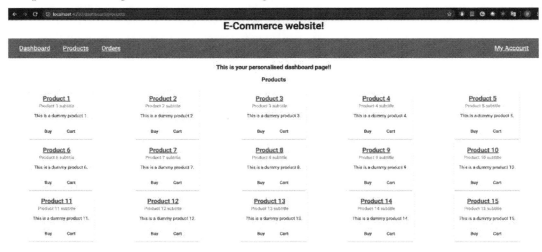

Figure 10.6: *Products page displayed as a child route*

Task: Similar to the products page, create a new module and component for the Orders page and update routing configuration to make it the child route of Dashboard.

Enable Debug Trace for Route Configuration

The ecommerce website we are building is very simple, but if we consider building something real-life product, then we will have a complex route configuration, and mistakes are bound to happen. To help analyze route configuration during development, we can enable route tracing as shown in *Code 10.23:*

```
@NgModule({
imports: [
    LoginModule,
    SignUpModule,
    DashboardModule,
    ProductsModule,
    RouterModule.forRoot(
        routes,
        { enableTracing: true }) // WARN: Disable it for
```

```
production build
      ],
      exports: [RouterModule]
})
export class AppRoutingModule { }
```

***Code 10.23**: app-routing.module.ts – Enable debug tracing of the route configuration*

Let's save the changes and reload the browser. Open the developer console of the browser and observe the logs. The default route of "/login" will get loaded in the browser, and Angular will logs route lifecycle events in a console, as shown in *Figure 10.7*. We will learn more about routing events in the next section:

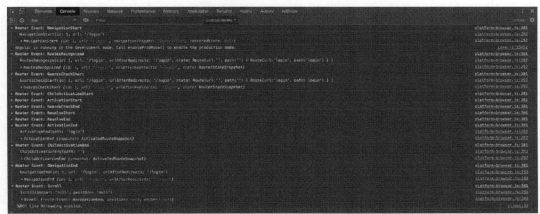

***Figure 10.7**: The /login page loading debug tracing logs*

Routing Life Cycle Events

A route change has its life cycle and during which various events are being fired by the framework. We will look into a few essential events here, but it is advised to check the complete list of events in official documentations.

- **NavigationStarts**: This event is fired when navigation start
- **RouteConfigLoadStart**: This event is fired before the route configuration of lazy load routes. We will see lazy load routes in the next section
- **RouteRecognized**: This event is fired when requested browser URL is matched with one of the entries in the route configuration
- **GuardCheckStart**: This event is fired when route guards are being evaluated.
- **ChildActivationStart**: This event is fired when a child route activation check is starting

- **ActivatationStart**: This event is fired once guard check and child activation check are passed, requested route being to activate
- **ResolveStart**: This event is fired when requested route being resolving
- **ResolveEnd**: As the name suggests, this event get fired when route resolve phase is done
- **ChildActivationEnd, ActivationEnd, NavigationEnd**: These events are fired in sequence when a respective phase is finished
- **NavigationCancel**: If route guard returns false during evaluation phase then this event is fired
- **NavigationError**: If something goes wrong during navigation, this event is fired
- **Scroll**: This is the last event of the cycle and gets fired for scrolling page

Passing Route Parameter

Our product pages show dummy product lists to the user. Our user can click on one of the items on the list and would like to see detail about the selected product. We will create a new component for displaying product details by running *Command 10.8*. We would like this new component to be part of the ProductsModule; hence we are prefixing "dashboard/products" along with a product-details component name:

```
ng generate component dashboard/products/product-details
```
Command 10.8: *Generate Products detail page*

The ProductDetails component route needs to have product-id as a route parameter so that we can display a specific product. We can define the route configuration of ProductDetails, as shown in *Code 10.24*, by specifying "product-id" after the route separated by a colon. Here "product-id" is a route parameter that will be passed to the ProductDetails component. The route parameter name can be anything, but the same name needs to be used for retrieving its value at a later stage.

```
    import { ProductDetailsComponent } from './dashboard/products/
product-details/product-details.component';


  const routes: Routes = [
    {
        path: 'dashboard',
        component: DashboardComponent,
        children: [
```

```
            {
                path: 'products',
                component: ProductsComponent
            },
            {
                path: 'products/:product-id',
                component: ProductDetailsComponent
            }
        ]
    ];


    @NgModule({})
    export class AppRoutingModule { }
```

Code 10.24*: app-routing.module.ts – Define route configuration for ProductsDetail with parameter*

The next thing is to do is update the routerLink path in the Products component. As shown in *Code 10.25*, we are building expression for routerLink as "{{ './' + item}}" – here "./" part represent the current route path that is, "products" and "item" is ngFor loop index value. So effectively it will resolve to URL like http://localhost:4200/dashboard/products/1 for product 1 and so on:

```
    <h3>Products</h3>


    <mat-grid-list cols="5" rowHeight="2:1">
        <mat-grid-tile *ngFor="let item of [1,2,3,4,5,6,7,8,9,10,11,12,
    13,14,15]">
            <mat-card class="example-card">
                <mat-card-header>
                    <mat-card-title>
                    <a routerLink="{{ './' + item}}">Product {{item}}</a>
                </mat-card-title>
                </mat-card-header>
            </mat-card>
        </mat-grid-tile>
    </mat-grid-list>
```

Code 10.25*: app-routing.module.ts – Enable debug tracing of the route configuration*

The `ActivatedRoute` is another singleton service provided by the Angular framework for extracting routing information. We will use `ActivatedRoute` to query passed product-id value from `Products` page to `ProductsDetails` page. In *Code 10.26*, we have injected `ActivatedRoute` service into the constructor. We have used the "snapshot" property of ActivatedRoute to extract the initial route parameter value by passing the parameter name. Again we should make sure that the route parameter name is the same as defined in global route configuration.

```typescript
import { Component, OnInit } from '@angular/core';
import { ActivatedRoute } from '@angular/router';


@Component({
    selector: 'app-product-details',
    templateUrl: './product-details.component.html',
    styleUrls: ['./product-details.component.css']
})
export class ProductDetailsComponent implements OnInit {

    productId: string;

    constructor(private activatedRoute: ActivatedRoute) { }

    ngOnInit() {
        this.productId = this.activatedRoute.snapshot.paramMap.get('product-id');
    }
}
```

Code 10.26: product-details.component.ts – Extract product-id route parameter value

In `ProductsDetails` HTML page we will simply display extract `product-id` with some text as shown in *Code 10.27*:

```html
<h4>Product {{this.productId}} details </h4>
<div>
    <p>This is dummy product detail here...</p>
</div>
```

Code 10.27: product-details.component.html – Display extracted product-id in HTML

To verify output, we should save changes in all the files and follow user flow from the **Login** page to the **Products** page. Once on the Products page, click on any Product header hyperlink and observe the output shown in the browser for the ProductsDetails component. It should be similar to *Figure 10.8:*

Figure 10.8: Product details are shown for the selected product by product-id

Passing Data between Routes

In the previous section, we have seen how to pass route parameter value, which is an atomic value. The situation gets different when we want to send an object to the route. Our user journey so far is like when a user enters username and password on the login page, and we simply take him to the dashboard. On the dashboard page, we would need to access logged in user details. We can pass such objects between routes using LocalStorage or Angular service. We shall pass the AuthModel object from the Login component to Dashboard via service. Let's create a new DataService by running *Command 10.9:*

```
ng generate service data
```
Command 10.8: Generate DataService for data communication

The DataService shall hold reference of AuthModel class as shown in *Code 10.28:*

```
import { Injectable } from '@angular/core';
import { AuthModel } from './auth.model';


@Injectable({
    providedIn: 'root'
})
export class DataService {

    public loggedInUser: AuthModel;
    constructor() { }
}
```
Code 10.28: data.service.ts – DataService for passing data between routes

In the Login component, we shall inject DataService service and set its loggedInUser variable, as shown in *Code 10.29*:

```
import { DataService } from '../data.service';


export class LoginComponent implements OnInit {


    constructor(private router: Router,
                private dataService: DataService) { }
    doLogin() {
        this.dataService.loggedInUser = this.authModel;
        this.router.navigate(['dashboard']);
    }
}
```

Code 10.29: login.component.ts – Setting loggedInUser property in Login component

The Dashboard component also have DataService injected and will hold reference of AuthModel class as shown in *Code 10.30:*

```
import { DataService } from '../data.service';
import { AuthModel } from '../auth.model';
export class DashboardComponent implements OnInit {


    loggedInUser: AuthModel;


    constructor(private dataService: DataService) { }


    ngOnInit() {
        this.loggedInUser = this.dataService.loggedInUser;
    }
}
```

Code 10.30: dashboard.component.ts – Reading loggedInUser property from DataService service

We shall greet user by his username in Dashboard HTML as shown in Code 10.31:

```
<mat-toolbar color="primary">
    <mat-toolbar-row>
```

```
            <span class="link"> Hi {{this.loggedInUser.username}} </
span>

        </mat-toolbar-row>

    </mat-toolbar>


    <router-outlet></router-outlet>
```

Code 10.31: *dashboard.component.html – Greet user on the dashboard*

Refresh the browser after saving all the changes and enter the username on the **Login** page and some random password and click on the **Login** button. We should see "Hi <username>" on the top left corner of **Dashboard** as shown in *Figure 10.9*:

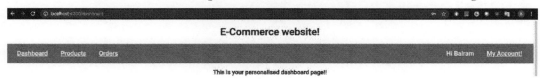

Figure 10.9: *Display greetings text with username on Dashboard*

Securing a Route Path

The routes we have so far can be changed in the browser by typing in URL, for example, /dashboard, /dashboard/products, and so on, and the respective component will be loaded. If we do not login and directly go to /dashboard URL, then we will have undefined authModel value since it is being set by the login step. *Figure 10.10* shows error logged in browser console and empty username greeting message if we skip login page step:

Figure 10.10: *undefined username if directly navigated to /dashboard route*

We need to add a check guard to make sure the user cannot directly go to the Dashboard route and must login into the system first. Angular router package provides a feature called route **"Guards"** for such requirements. As the name suggests, Guards are the checkpoint where we can add validation before navigating to the requested route. Let's create a new guard for /dashboard route by running *Command 10.9*. The Angular CLI will ask us what type of guard we want to create. We want to add check whether to activate /dashboard route or not hence we will select CanActivate and proceed further:

```
$ ng generate guard can-activate-dashboard
? Which interfaces would you like to implement? (Press <space> to
select, <a> to toggle all, <i> to invert selection)
>○ CanActivate
 ○ CanActivateChild
 ○ CanLoad
```

Command 10.9: *Generate Dashboard CanActivate route guard*

The CanActivate is an interface with single method "canActivate()". The DashboardGuard class implements CanActivate interface and must provide implementation for canActivate(). The Code 10.32 shows declaration of CanActivate interface from official documentation. As we can see canActivate() method have different types of return types:

```
export declare interface CanActivate {
    canActivate(route: ActivatedRouteSnapshot, state:
RouterStateSnapshot): Observable<boolean | UrlTree> | Promise<boolean |
UrlTree> | boolean | UrlTree;
}
```

Code 10.32: *router.d.ts – CanActivate interface documentation*

We will provide our new guard to route configuration of **Dashboard** route in "canActivate" property as shown in *Code 10.33*:

```
import { CanActivateDashboardGuard } from './dashboard.guard';


const routes: Routes = [
    {
        path: 'dashboard',
        component: DashboardComponent,
        canActivate: [CanActivateDashboardGuard],
        children: [
```

```
        {
            path: 'products',
            component: ProductsComponent
        },
        {

            path: 'products/:product-id',
            component: ProductDetailsComponent

        }
    ]
];


export class AppRoutingModule { }
```

Code 10.33: app-routing.module.ts – provide CanActivateDashboard in Dashboard Guard

The `DashboardGuard` component will check if we should continue to /dashboard route if the user is logged in. We will set a new property in DataService service to return whether the user is logged in or not, as shown in *Code 10.34*. `isLoggedIn` checks if `loggedInUser` object is not undefined:

```
@Injectable({
    providedIn: 'root'
})
export class DataService {

    public loggedInUser: AuthModel;

    // tslint:disable-next-line: variable-name
    private _isLoggedIn: boolean;

    public get isLoggedIn(): boolean {
        return this.loggedInUser ? true : false;
    }
}
```

Code 10.34: data.service.ts – check if a user is logged in or not

We will inject DataService service into DashboardGuard and use new isLoggedIn property in the canActivate() method. If the canActivate() method returns "True" then the requested new route will be navigated in browser but if it returns "False" then route navigation will be canceled. In our case, if the user is not logged in, then we will take him to /login route. Thus we need to inject Router service as well for redirection as shown in *Code 10.35*:

```typescript
import { Injectable } from '@angular/core';

import { ActivatedRouteSnapshot, RouterStateSnapshot, CanActivate,
Router } from '@angular/router';

import { DataService } from './data.service';


@Injectable({
    providedIn: 'root'
})
export class CanActivateDashboardGuard implements CanActivate {


    constructor(private dataService: DataService, private router:
Router) { }


    canActivate(route: ActivatedRouteSnapshot, state:
RouterStateSnapshot): boolean {
        if (this.dataService.isLoggedIn) {
            return true;
        }
        this.router.navigateByUrl('/login');
    }
}
```

Code 10.35: *can-activate-dashboard.guard.ts – redirect the user to /login route if not logged in*

Let's verify the output by saving all the changes and enter http://localhost:4200/dashboard URL in a browser. We should get navigated back to the Login page. On the Login page, if we enter username and password and click Login, then we should be able to be redirected to /dashboard route. In the browser console, observe the debug trace for route change when the canActivate() method returns true and false for the navigation life cycle. The CanActivateChild and CanActivateLoad are the other route guard used for route checking if the child route should be activated and route component can be loaded or not.

CanDeactivate Guard

The CanActivate makes sure whether the user can navigate into the route and its counterpart CanDeactivate makes sure whether the user can navigate out of the current route. For example, the user is on data-entry form filling up details, and by mistake, he hits the back button in the browser, then all his unsaved changes will be gone, and the user will not be happy to fill those details again. We should display a warning message to the user before he can navigate from the current route. In our ecommerce website, we will prompt the user when he tries to logout from the system to confirm his action. If the user confirms, then we will clear the authModel object removing his login status and take him to /login route. Let's add a **"Sign Out"** link in the dashboard, as shown in *Code 10.36*:

```html
<mat-toolbar color="primary">

    <mat-toolbar-row>

        <span class="link"> <a routerLink="/login"
routerLinkActive="active">Sign Out</a> </span>

    </mat-toolbar-row>

</mat-toolbar>


<h3>This is your personalised dashboard page!!</h3>


<router-outlet></router-outlet>
```

Code 10.36: dashboard.component.html – "Sign Out" link on the dashboard

Let's add "SignOut" method in DataService for removing current login details as shown in *Code 10.37*:

```typescript
import { AuthModel } from './auth.model';


@Injectable({
    providedIn: 'root'
})
export class DataService {

    public loggedInUser: AuthModel;


    signOut() {
```

```
            this.loggedInUser = null;
    }

}
```

Code 10.37: data.service.ts – remove login details

Code 10.38 shows the implementation of the CanDeactivateDashboard guard. We are injecting DataService for removing login details. The canDeactivate() method returns true to allow the current route to leave and false to stay on the current route and cancel route navigation requests.

```
import { Injectable } from '@angular/core';

import { ActivatedRouteSnapshot, RouterStateSnapshot, UrlTree,
CanDeactivate, Router } from '@angular/router';

import { DataService } from './data.service';

@Injectable({
    providedIn: 'root'
})
export class CanDeactivateDashboardGuard implements
CanDeactivate<boolean> {


    constructor(private dataService: DataService) { }


    canDeactivate(component: boolean,
                currentRoute: ActivatedRouteSnapshot,
                currentState: RouterStateSnapshot,
                nextState?: RouterStateSnapshot): boolean {
        const response = window.confirm('Are you sure to Sign Out?');
        if (response) {
            this.dataService.signOut();
            return true;
        } else {
            return false;
        }
    }
}
```

Code 10.38: can-deactivate.guard.ts – Confirm user for Sign Out action

We can update the route configuration of Dashboard route to specify CanDeactivateDashboard guard as shown in *Code 10.39*:

```
import { CanActivateDashboardGuard } from './dashboard.guard';

import { CanDeactivateDashboardGuard } from './can-deactivate-dashboard.guard';


const routes: Routes = [
    {
        path: 'dashboard',
        component: DashboardComponent,
        canActivate: [CanActivateDashboardGuard],
        canDeactivate: [CanDeactivateDashboardGuard],
        children: [
            {
                path: 'products',
                component: ProductsComponent
            },
            {
                path: 'products/:product-id',
                component: ProductDetailsComponent
            }
        ]
export class AppRoutingModule { }
```

Code 10.39: app-routing.module.ts – Specify CanDeactivateDashboardGuard in route configuration

Let's save all the changes and login to the dashboard. Click on the "**Sign Out**" link, and we should see the confirm window, as shown in *Figure 10.11*. If we select **Ok** then we will be taken to **Login** page if we click on **Cancel** then sign out action will be canceled:

Figure 10.11: Confirm "Sign Out" action

The `CanDeactivate` guard is beneficial for handling business logic before the current route is about to change. One example we saw like asking users before signing out of the website, another is canceling data entry form before submitting it.

Prefetching Product Details

The Product and `ProductDetails` components are currently displaying dummy product number text. We will create a product service that will hold mock products. Then Product and `ProductDetails` component shall use this service to display product details. Let's create ProductService by running *Command 10.10:*

```
ng generate service products
```

Command 10.10: Generate product service

The `ProductsService` file contains the `ProductModel` class for holding Product properties. *Code 10.40* shows `ProductsService` implementation. The `allProducts` is an array of `ProductModel`, and in the constructor, we are filling 15 mock `ProductModel` objects. The `getProduct()` method accepts productId as a parameter and returns matching `ProductModel` from an array:

```
import { Injectable } from '@angular/core';


export class ProductModel {
    id: number;
    title: string;
    description: string;
}


@Injectable({
    providedIn: 'root'
})
export class ProductsService {

    allProducts: Array<ProductModel>;

    constructor() {

        this.allProducts = [];
        let product = new ProductModel();
```

```
        product.id = 1;
        product.title = 'Product 1';
        product.description = 'Product 1 dummy description!';
        this.allProducts.push(product);


        product = new ProductModel();
        product.id = 15;
        product.title = 'Product 15';
        product.description = 'Product 15 dummy description!';
        this.allProducts.push(product);
    }


    getProduct(productId: number): ProductModel {
        const foundProduct = this.allProducts.findIndex(product =>
product.id === productId);
        return this.allProducts[foundProduct];
    }
}
```

Code 10.40: product.service.ts – Mock ProductsService class

The ProductsComponent component gets ProductService injected and fetches all products from service, as shown in *Code 10.41*. In ProductsComponent HTML file, we can run ngFor loop on "allProducts" and update binding to display product details:

```
    import { ProductsService, ProductModel } from 'src/app/products.
service';


    @Component({
        selector: 'app-products',
        templateUrl: './products.component.html',
        styleUrls: ['./products.component.css']
    })
    export class ProductsComponent implements OnInit {

        allProducts: Array<ProductModel>;
```

```
constructor(private productService: ProductsService) { }


ngOnInit() {
    this.allProducts = this.productService.allProducts;
}

}
```

Code 10.41: products.component.ts – Use ProductsService to fetch all products

The ProductsDetails component resolves route parameter "productId" and uses ProductsService to get ProductModel with matching productId, as shown in *Code 10.42*. The "selectedProduct" member field is used in ProductDetailsComponent HTML file displaying details:

```
import { ProductModel, ProductsService } from 'src/app/products.
service';


@Component({
    selector: 'app-product-details',
    templateUrl: './product-details.component.html',
    styleUrls: ['./product-details.component.css']
})
export class ProductDetailsComponent implements OnInit {

    selectedProduct: ProductModel;


    constructor(private activatedRoute: ActivatedRoute,
        private productService: ProductsService) { }


    ngOnInit() {
        const productId = Number.parseInt(this.activatedRoute.
snapshot.paramMap.get('product-id'));
        this.selectedProduct = this.productService.
getProduct(productId);
        console.log(this.selectedProduct);
```

```
        }
    }
```

Code 10.42: *product-details.component.ts – Use ProductsService to fetch all products*

If we run the application and follow the user journey from login to the products page. Click on any product, and we will see the selected product details.

Problem situation: Imagine a user manually enter productId in URL, which doesn't exist in `ProductsService` array, then what will happen? In such a situation, the `ProductDetails` component will display product details for a non-existing product, as shown in *Figure 10.12*. This is not good user experience. We shouldn't load `ProductDetailsComponent` in the first place if the `productId` route parameter is invalid.

Figure 10.12: *Invalid productId causes Product Details page display incorrect data*

Solution: Angular framework provide route resolver which in regular Angular service class like route guard to handle such a situation. The resolver gets invoked before the new route gets loaded and check if data required for the new route component exists or not. If data doesn't exist, then a new component doesn't need to be loaded, and routing shouldn't take place. In our example case, if the productId route parameter is invalid, then we will not load the `ProductDetails` component at all. Let's update our example with a resolver solution. Run *Command 10.14* to generate resolver:

```
ng generate service product-details-resolver
```

Command 10.11 – Generate Product

The resolver service will implement the `Resolve<T>` interface, as shown in *Code 10.43*. We will inject `ProductsService` and Router service in the constructor. The Router service will provide us route parameter "product-id" and the `ProductsService` will allow us to check if `ProductModel` instance exists with matching `productId`. If there is a match, then we will return an Observable of found `ProductModel` from `resolve()` method. But if the route parameter is carrying incorrect product-id for which no `ProductModel` exists, then we will not go to the `ProductDetails` component and will stay on `/products` route. We are using "of() and EMPTY" operators from the rxjs library. The "of()" method converts a simple object into Observable and EMPTY returns an empty Observable:

```
import { Injectable } from '@angular/core';

import { Resolve, Router, ActivatedRouteSnapshot,
RouterStateSnapshot } from '@angular/router';

import { ProductModel, ProductsService } from './products.service';

import { Observable, of, EMPTY } from 'rxjs';


@Injectable({
    providedIn: 'root'
})
export class ProductDetailsResolverService implements
Resolve<ProductModel> {

    constructor(private productService: ProductsService,
                private router: Router) { }


    resolve(route: ActivatedRouteSnapshot, state:
RouterStateSnapshot): Observable<ProductModel> | Observable<never> {
        const productId = Number.parseInt(route.paramMap.
get('product-id'), 10);


        const foundProduct = this.productService.
getProduct(productId);
        if (foundProduct) {
            return of(foundProduct);
        } else {
            this.router.navigateByUrl('/dashboard/products');
            return EMPTY;
        }
    }
}
```

Code 10.43: *product-details-resolver.service.ts – ProductDetailsResolverService resolver*

The Route object has "resolve" property, which can be set to resolver service, as shown in *Code 10.44*. The "resolve" accepts a JSON object where the key is a data object passed to ProductDetailsComponent through ActivatedRoute service:

```
import { ProductDetailsResolverService } from './product-details-
resolver.service';


    const routes: Routes = [
        {
            path: 'dashboard',
            component: DashboardComponent,
            canActivate: [CanActivateDashboardGuard],
            canDeactivate: [CanDeactivateDashboardGuard],
            children: [
                {
                    path: 'products',
                    component: ProductsComponent
                },
                {
                    path: 'products/:product-id',
                    resolve: { selectedProduct:
ProductDetailsResolverService },
                    component: ProductDetailsComponent
                }
            ]
        }
    ];
    export class AppRoutingModule { }
```

Code 10.44: app-routing.module.ts – Specify "resolve" property of Route object

In ProductDetailsComponent class, we will query "data" property of ActivatedRoute singleton service which is of type Observable<T>. The resolve() method of ProductDetailsResolverService service returns Observable<ProductModel> hence we are specifying ProductModel type name in subscribe() block. The "data.selectedProduct" will return us prefetched ProductModel based on route parameter "product-id" thus we don't need to query ProductsService from ProductDetail component anymore. The *Code 10.45* shows implementation of updated ProductDetailsComponent class:

```
import { ActivatedRoute } from '@angular/router';
import { ProductModel, ProductsService } from 'src/app/products.
```

```
service';

    export class ProductDetailsComponent implements OnInit {

        selectedProduct: ProductModel;

        constructor(private activatedRoute: ActivatedRoute,
            private productService: ProductsService) { }

        ngOnInit() {
            this.activatedRoute.data.subscribe((data: { selectedProduct:
ProductModel }) => {
                this.selectedProduct = data.selectedProduct;
            });
        }
    }
```

Code 10.45: product-details.component.ts –prefetched ProductModel object via ActivatedRoute

Save changes in all the files and follow the user journey from login to the products page. Click on any product, and we should see selected product details by the `ProductDetails` component class. Now explicitly mention incorrect "product-id" in the product route and observe the output. The browser will not load the `ProductDetails` component but will stay on the same /`products` URL; thanks to our Resolver. The resolver is very useful for managing the routing strategy and avoiding unnecessary route load and improve performance.

Asynchronous Routes

Usually, the Angular framework loads all the components and modules specified in routes when the application starts. For a small application, it is not an issue, but as the application starts to grow big with lots of feature modules and routes, then performance will get affected, and it will take time to load application. The Angular provides asynchronous routes features to solve this issue. With asynchronous routes, the modules will be loaded only when requested by the browser. This will improve application performance as fewer modules to load at the start.

We will create a new module and load it using asynchronously. Let's run *Command 10.12* to generate the `MyAccount` module. Angular CLI has a nice feature to specify the route name and parent module, and it will create a new module, component, route configuration, and link parent module. In *Command 10.12,* we are requesting to create new module MyAccount with route /my-account and base module to be AppModule:

```
$ ng generate module my-account --route my-account --module app.module
CREATE src/app/my-account/my-account-routing.module.ts (357 bytes)
CREATE src/app/my-account/my-account.module.ts (372 bytes)
CREATE src/app/my-account/my-account.component.css (0 bytes)
CREATE src/app/my-account/my-account.component.html (25 bytes)
CREATE src/app/my-account/my-account.component.spec.ts (650 bytes)
CREATE src/app/my-account/my-account.component.ts (284 bytes)
UPDATE src/app/app-routing.module.ts (2617 bytes)
```

Command 10.12: Generate MyAccount module with an asynchronous route

The *Code 10.46* shows how asynchronous routes are configured. The normal routes are specified through "path" and "component" properties but for asynchronous route "loadChildren" property is used with "import" statement to load module. Also note that "imports" array of @NgModule doesn't import MyAccountModule as it will be loaded dynamically:

```
const routes: Routes = [
    {
        path: 'my-account',
        loadChildren: () => import('./my-account/my-account.module')
            .then(m => m.MyAccountModule)
    }
{
        path: '',
        redirectTo: '/login',
        pathMatch: 'full',
    },
    {
        path: '**',
        component: CustomPageNotFoundComponent
    }
];
```

```
@NgModule({
    imports: [
        LoginModule,
        SignUpModule,
        DashboardModule,
        ProductsModule,
        RouterModule.forRoot(
            routes,
            { enableTracing: true }) // WARN: Disable it for
production build
    ],
    exports: [RouterModule]
})
export class AppRoutingModule { }
```
Code 10.46: app-routing.module.ts – MyAccount asynchronous route configuration

Code 10.47 shows the route configuration generated by Angular CLI for the MyAccount module. Note that "RouterModule.forChild(routes)" entry in import array. In AppRoutingModule, we have used "RouterModule.forRoot()" method. The Angular application can contain only one forRoot() method from RouterModule and zero or more forChild(). It is a common mistake when working with asynchronous routes to specify forRoot() for child modules.

```
import { NgModule } from '@angular/core';
import { Routes, RouterModule } from '@angular/router';


import { MyAccountComponent } from './my-account.component';


const routes: Routes = [{ path: '', component: MyAccountComponent
}];


@NgModule({
    imports: [RouterModule.forChild(routes)],
    exports: [RouterModule]
})
export class MyAccountRoutingModule { }
```
Code 10.47: my-account-routing.module.ts – MyAccount route configuration

If we go to URL http://localhost:4200/my-account, we will see the output of MyAccount component HTML.

Generating Child Asynchronous Routes through CLI

Let's create two more modules (a) Profile and (b) Invoices under MyAccount by running *Command 10.13*:

```
$ ng generate module my-account/profile --route profile --module my-
account.module
$ ng generate module my-account/invoices --route invoices --module my-
account.module
```

Command 10.13: *Generate profile and invoices sub-module of my-account*

In MyAccount HTML add router outlet to display output of child routes as shown in *Code 10.48*:

```html
<h3>My Account!</h3>
<div>
    <a routerLink="./profile">Profile</a>
</div>
<div>
    <a routerLink="./invoices">Invoices</a>
</div>


<router-outlet></router-outlet>
```

Code 10.47: *my-account-component.html– <router-outlet> added in MyAccount HTML*

The *Command 10.12* will update route configuration of MyAccount as shown in Code 10.48:

```typescript
import { NgModule } from '@angular/core';
import { Routes, RouterModule } from '@angular/router';


import { MyAccountComponent } from './my-account.component';

const routes: Routes = [
    {
```

```
        path: '',
        component: MyAccountComponent
    },
    {
        path: 'profile',
        loadChildren: () => import('./profile/profile.module')
            .then(m => m.ProfileModule)
    },
    {
        path: 'invoices',
        loadChildren: () => import('./invoices/invoices.module')
            .then(m => m.InvoicesModule)
    }
];


@NgModule({
    imports: [RouterModule.forChild(routes)],
    exports: [RouterModule]
})
export class MyAccountRoutingModule { }
```

Code 10.48: my-account-routing.module.ts– updated route configuration of MyAccount

Let's save all the changes and go to the dashboard page. Click on **MyAccount** hyperlink in the dashboard, and we should see a my-account page similar to *Figure 10.13* with two links to Profile and Invoices:

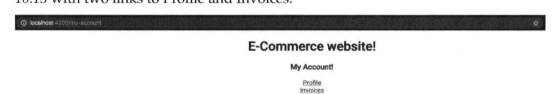

Figure 10.13: MyAccount page with profile and invoice links

This is how we can create asynchronous routes, and child routes in Angular and CLI make our life very easy. For normal routes, we have used CanActivate guard similarly for asynchronous routes; we can use CanLoad guard to check if a new lazy route should be loaded or not.

Inspect Router Tree in Augury

The Augury browser extension is handy for debugging purposes. We have seen it how to use in previous chapters. Augury helps visualize the routes configured in Angular application. *Figure 10.14* shows the Augury tool's "Router Tree" output. We can see our route configuration in a tree fashion. Note that "`my-account`", "`profile`" and "`invoices`" are suffixed by "`[lazy]`" keyword meaning they are lazily loaded by asynchronous routes. Note that when we build our application for production mode by running the command "**ng build -prod**" Augury cannot access metadata and won't display any Router Tree and other data. It works only in development mode:

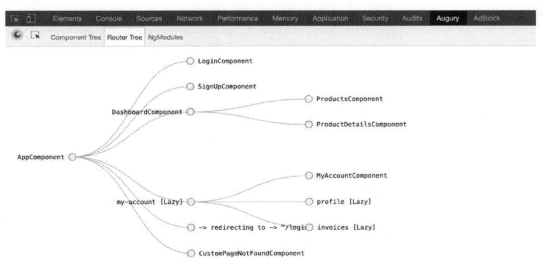

Figure 10.14*: Router Tree output of Augury tool to visualize route configuration*

Module Preloading Strategy

The asynchronous routes gradually load feature modules. But if our application requires all features modules to be prefetched, then that is also possible. The Router configuration specifies the route preloading strategy. By default, "`NoPreloading`" is set, but we can change it to "`PreloadAllModules`" for prefetch all lazy modules, as shown in *Code 10.49*. If we would like to preload feature modules based on some custom logic then we can implement "`PreloadingStrategy`" interface in service class and provide it to router configuration:

```
@NgModule({
imports: [
```

```
        RouterModule.forRoot(

            routes,

            {

                enableTracing: true, // WARN: Disable it for
production build


                // preloadingStrategy: NoPreloading

                preloadingStrategy: PreloadAllModules

            })

        ],

        exports: [RouterModule]

    })

    export class AppRoutingModule { }
```

Code 10.49: *app-routing.module.ts – Setting preload strategy to PreloadAllModules*

Conclusion

The Angular routing framework is compelling, as we have seen so far. Unlike server-side route management, Angular works with the browser to manage web pages rendering requested URL. Implementing routing can be very simple by creating a static route configuration and can become very complex by adding asynchronous routes with guards and resolvers. The best practice about routing is to use asynchronous routes when the feature module is not required to be loaded at start-up. The regular feature route can be used if we are building a simple application. The route guards should be used for adding business validation and user journey flow. Guards also help us implement an access control system. For example, if we have different user roles in our web application, we would like to restrict access to specific routes to certain user groups only. For example, the "admin" user group can visit all routes, but the "user" user group cannot and have limited access. The route resolvers are also very useful for avoiding unnecessary route visits if a new route component doesn't have meaningful data to display. It is a smart way to implement routing and achieve performance. The asynchronous routes load modules in a lazy manner, helping faster startup time and light bundle package. Such lazy modules allow managing big applications in separation, and the different teams can work on them without being blocked. The asynchronous routes also have route guards like CanLoad, which check if routes should be loaded at all or not, saving extra workload of loading module and unloading if conditions don't meet. The preload strategy for router configuration gives us a chance to tell how to load feature modules. By defaults, they are loaded in a lazy manner, but we can set preload strategy or create a custom preload strategy and provide it to configuration.

Questions

1. In our example, we are storing "isLoggedIn" value in DataService members. Store isLoggedIn status in local storage and use it in application to persist value during browser reload.

2. Create the "Orders" module and component and its child routes in / dashboard route. Display mock orders in the component.

3. Use "navigate()" function to change the current route and pass data as an array argument.

4. Extend our application by adding CanLoad guard for /my-account/profile route. Add some mock business rule which will check if a route should be loaded or not

5. Beautify application by using Bootstrap CSS or Material design

6. Create a backend server that will send data for Login, dashboard, products, orders, my-account, profiles, and invoices and consume it in our application through the HttpClient module. The server can send mock data for simplicity.

7. What will happen if we specify the forRoot() method more than once in the router configuration? Try to provide it and study the error message.

8. Create a new feature module and add its route object after default route and page not found route that is, end of the "Routes" array, and try to navigate to a new route in the browser. Observe the output and browser console.

9. Explore different ways of passing data between routes like router. paramMap, snapshot, and so on.

10. Create a new application with routing. Choose any popular website and try to create feature modules and routes with the user journey.

Deployment and Best Practices

Introduction

We have learned all the essential topics and techniques of Angular so far and built many example applications alongside. The crucial step of any web application development cycle is the Deployment process. In the old days, the Development Operations, also called DevOps, used to be the responsibility of a separate team than web application developers. Still, nowadays, an engineer should be able to build and perform all DevOps operations are the norms. In this example, we will cover various aspects of Angular application deployment and will cover best practices to follow and tools for performance analysis.

Structure

- Deployment
- ng build – Simple Deployment
- Production build
- Change dist folder path
- ng deploy command
- Different Build Configurations
- JIT and AOT compilation

- Cross-Origin Resource Sharing
- ng lint command
- Unit Testing overview
- Code Coverage report
- Performance and Optimization
- Polyfills – Older browser support
- Web workers

Objective

The objective of this chapter is to learn how to deploy Angular applications. Each web application is unique in a way, and the deployment process might vary per application based on requirement and infrastructure; thus, it is crucial to understand where and how to deploy an application. We will learn how to build application package and deploy it over servers, different built methods provided by frameworks, JIT and Ahead of Time compilation method, how to set custom environment variables, how to create different build configuration for development, gathering performance metrics, overview of unit testing and code coverage, polyfills and web workers overview.

Deployment

The deployment is a process of compiling Angular application so that it can be served by any standard web server like Apache, IIS, Azure web server, or any other web hosting providers. The compilation process goes through the entire code and tries to optimize it for deployment purposes. The term **Tree Shaking** refers to dropping any code from source code to compiled code if it is not reachable in runtime. For example, if we have created a component called TempComponent with its HTML and TypeScript code but its selector, for example, `<app-test-component></app-test-component>` is not used anywhere in rest of the application nor in routing then TempComponent will not get compiled into deployment bundle. This way, the Angular compiler makes sure dead code is left out, making the output bundle as small as possible for performance reason. The compiler has two modes, standard mode **Just-In-Time (JIT)** and another is **Ahead of Time (AOT)** compile. The AOT is a rigorous step of compilation and produces optimal build but takes a bit longer than the JIT compiler. The Ivy compiler is a new compiler introduced in the Angular 9 stable version, which uses AOT by default. We will learn more about JIT and AOT in this chapter. Another critical point is that we write an Angular application code in TypeScript. Still, the browser doesn't support TypeScript yet (hopefully new ECMA specification out to support TypeScript and will be incorporated by standard browsers in the future). Thus, Angular compiler transpiles TypeScript into efficient

JavaScript for the browser to render and execute the application. We have seen TypeScript code in the browser while debugging, but it is because of web map files and debugs metadata available. For a production-ready application, these details should be filtered out to secure business logic.

ng build – Simple Deployment

When we run **ng serve** command, then a local webserver starts to serve our application. Let's run the command **ng serve** in ecommerce application and check the logs in the terminal window, as shown in *Command 11.1*. The first modules get compiled, including imported ones like the Angular Material library. The next step is to compile the application module and to divide them into chunks. It is like Gulp/ Grunt bundling packages, which create small parts of JavaScript files so that browser doesn't have to load a big file but can load smaller in parallel and load application faster. Note that .map files work as a dictionary mapping compiled JavaScript objects to original source TypeScript objects. In the production build mode, these files will not be and should not be generated. Finally, the Angular developer server starts and loads the compiled web application on http://localhost:4200 address. The total compilation time is also shown at the end, which we give us an idea when trying to fine-tune build settings:

```
⏻ ng s
0% compiling
Compiling @angular/forms : es2015 as esm2015
Compiling @angular/cdk/platform : es2015 as esm2015
Compiling @angular/cdk/text-field : es2015 as esm2015
Compiling @angular/cdk/keycodes : es2015 as esm2015
Compiling @angular/cdk/observers : es2015 as esm2015
Compiling @angular/cdk/a11y : es2015 as esm2015
Compiling @angular/cdk/bidi : es2015 as esm2015
Compiling @angular/material/core : es2015 as esm2015
Compiling @angular/material/form-field : es2015 as esm2015
Compiling @angular/material/input : es2015 as esm2015
Compiling @angular/material/button : es2015 as esm2015
Compiling @angular/material/toolbar : es2015 as esm2015
Compiling @angular/common/http : es2015 as esm2015
Compiling @angular/material/icon : es2015 as esm2015
Compiling @angular/cdk/collections : es2015 as esm2015
```

```
Compiling @angular/cdk/scrolling : es2015 as esm2015

Compiling @angular/material/sidenav : es2015 as esm2015

Compiling @angular/material/card : es2015 as esm2015

Compiling @angular/material/divider : es2015 as esm2015

Compiling @angular/material/list : es2015 as esm2015

Compiling @angular/material/grid-list : es2015 as esm2015


chunk {invoices-invoices-module} invoices-invoices-module.js,
invoices-invoices-module.js.map (invoices-invoices-module) 7.96 kB
[rendered]

chunk {main} main.js, main.js.map (main) 89.3 kB [initial]
[rendered]

chunk {my-account-my-account-module} my-account-my-account-module.
js, my-account-my-account-module.js.map (my-account-my-account-module)
9.2 kB  [rendered]

chunk {polyfills} polyfills.js, polyfills.js.map (polyfills) 140 kB
[initial] [rendered]

chunk {profile-profile-module} profile-profile-module.js, profile-profile-
module.js.map (profile-profile-module) 7.88 kB  [rendered]

chunk {runtime} runtime.js, runtime.js.map (runtime) 9.13 kB [entry]
[rendered]

chunk {styles} styles.js, styles.js.map (styles) 179 kB [initial]
[rendered]

chunk {vendor} vendor.js, vendor.js.map (vendor) 4.7 MB [initial]
[rendered]

Date: 2020-02-15T08:02:08.015Z - Hash: 82944df64f784f9651a6 - Time:
40816ms

** Angular Live Development Server is listening on localhost:4200,
open your browser on http://localhost:4200/ **

: Compiled successfully.

Date: 2020-02-15T08:02:08.951Z - Hash: 82944df64f784f9651a6

8 unchanged chunks


Time: 585ms

: Compiled successfully.
```

Command 11.1: *ng serve command output*

Now let's try to run command **ng build**. First, stop the previous running command **ng serve** or **ng build** if any, and then run **ng build**. *Command 11.2* shows the output of ng build command. The compiler first generates ES5 bundles for imported libraries and then starts to cut down application modules into different chunks. The map files are also generated for debugging purpose:

```
⯈ ng build

Generating ES5 bundles for differential loading...

ES5 bundle generation complete.


    chunk {polyfills} polyfills-es2015.js, polyfills-es2015.js.map
(polyfills) 140 kB [initial] [rendered]

    chunk {invoices-invoices-module} invoices-invoices-module-es2015.js,
invoices-invoices-module-es2015.js.map (invoices-invoices-module) 7.97
kB  [rendered]

    chunk {invoices-invoices-module} invoices-invoices-module-es5.js,
invoices-invoices-module-es5.js.map (invoices-invoices-module) 9.69 kB
[rendered]

    chunk {my-account-my-account-module} my-account-my-account-module-
es2015.js, my-account-my-account-module-es2015.js.map (my-account-my-
account-module) 9.21 kB   [rendered]

    chunk {my-account-my-account-module} my-account-my-account-module-
es5.js, my-account-my-account-module-es5.js.map (my-account-my-account-
module) 11.1 kB   [rendered]

    chunk {runtime} runtime-es2015.js, runtime-es2015.js.map (runtime)
9.14 kB [entry] [rendered]

    chunk {runtime} runtime-es5.js, runtime-es5.js.map (runtime) 9.14 kB
[entry] [rendered]

    chunk {styles} styles-es2015.js, styles-es2015.js.map (styles) 179
kB [initial] [rendered]

    chunk {styles} styles-es5.js, styles-es5.js.map (styles) 181 kB
[initial] [rendered]

    chunk {profile-profile-module} profile-profile-module-es2015.js, profile-
profile-module-es2015.js.map (profile-profile-module) 7.88 kB   [rendered]

    chunk {profile-profile-module} profile-profile-module-es5.js, profile-
profile-module-es5.js.map (profile-profile-module) 9.59 kB   [rendered]

    chunk {main} main-es2015.js, main-es2015.js.map (main) 87.9 kB
[initial] [rendered]

    chunk {main} main-es5.js, main-es5.js.map (main) 97.3 kB [initial]
[rendered]
```

```
chunk {polyfills-es5} polyfills-es5.js, polyfills-es5.js.map (polyfills-
es5) 647 kB [initial] [rendered]
    chunk {vendor} vendor-es2015.js, vendor-es2015.js.map (vendor) 4.36
MB [initial] [rendered]
    chunk {vendor} vendor-es5.js, vendor-es5.js.map (vendor) 5.12 MB
[initial] [rendered]
    Date: 2020-02-15T08:17:17.317Z - Hash: 08278cf04424c1668abb - Time:
23481ms
```

Command 11.2: ng serve command output

The output is generated into dist/<project-name> that is, in our case, dist/
ecommerce-demo folder. The **tree** command lists the folder structure of the dist/
ecommerce-demo folder, as shown in Command 11.3. Note that tree is an external
package which needs be installed separately:

```
dist
└── ecommerce-demo
    ├── favicon.ico
    ├── index.html
    ├── invoices-invoices-module-es2015.js
    ├── invoices-invoices-module-es2015.js.map
    ├── invoices-invoices-module-es5.js
    ├── invoices-invoices-module-es5.js.map
    ├── main-es2015.js
    ├── main-es2015.js.map
    ├── main-es5.js
    ├── main-es5.js.map
    ├── my-account-my-account-module-es2015.js
    ├── my-account-my-account-module-es2015.js.map
    ├── my-account-my-account-module-es5.js
    ├── my-account-my-account-module-es5.js.map
    ├── polyfills-es2015.js
    ├── polyfills-es2015.js.map
    ├── polyfills-es5.js
    ├── polyfills-es5.js.map
    ├── profile-profile-module-es2015.js
    ├── profile-profile-module-es2015.js.map
```

```
├── profile-profile-module-es5.js
├── profile-profile-module-es5.js.map
├── runtime-es2015.js
├── runtime-es2015.js.map
├── runtime-es5.js
├── runtime-es5.js.map
├── styles-es2015.js
├── styles-es2015.js.map
├── styles-es5.js
├── styles-es5.js.map
├── vendor-es2015.js
├── vendor-es2015.js.map
├── vendor-es5.js
└── vendor-es5.js.map

1 directory, 34 files
```

Command 11.3: tree command output

The `dist` folder is ready for deployment, though not optimal. Here we will use `surge.sh` free web hosting provider for static websites. If you have a different web server, simply copy this folder into the webserver folder and follow the regular steps to deploy the website; no particular Angular configuration is required. The `dist` folder is plain HTML and JavaScript version of our Angular application and can be deployed anywhere. Let's install "surge" CLI client by running *Command 11.4*:

```
npm install --save-dev surge
```

Command 11.4: install surge client

To publish our website on the surge, change the current directory to `dist/ecommerce-demo`, and run command **surge**. The surge shall ask for username and password if it is the first time we are using a surge. Once authenticated, select directory to be deployed and name of the website. The default domain will be `.surge.sh` for free accounts. The paid subscription users can use any domain name. Please check the https://surge.sh/pricing website for pricing details. After providing all details, surge shall display a message with hosted website address as shown in *Figure 11.1* output:

Figure 11.1: *Output of surge command*

Our web application is live now for the rest of the world! Let's open a browser and navigate to *https://my-ecommerce-demo.surge.sh*. The output should be similar to *Figure 11.2*:

Figure 11.2: *The live e-commerce-demo website hosted on surge.sh*

This is the fundamental way of deployment Angular application without worrying about production mode, AOT, environments, and so on. In the next section, we will see how to improve the deployment process.

Production Build

The command **ng build** generates an application bundle without many optimizations and with debug information. Let's see the size of the output **dist/ecommerce** directory by running bash command **du**, which computes around 24Mb disk space. Note that there might be a slight difference in folder size per machine, and based on your operating system, you can choose an appropriate method to check folder size. The output of the **du** command is shown in *Figure 11.3*:

```
Chapter11/ecommerce-demo/dist  master ×
 du -h ecommerce-demo
 24M    ecommerce-demo
```

Figure 11.3: *du command output showing the size of dist/ecommerce-demo folder*

Now let's try to build an application in production mode. Simple run *Command 11.5* to build an application in production build:

```
ng build --prod
```

Command 11.5: Compile application in Production mode

The *Command 1.5* shall take more time to compile as compared to **ng build** because it tries to optimize build for production mode. Once finished, we can again check the size of **dist/ecommerce** folder and output should be similar to *Figure 11.4*:

```
Chapter11/ecommerce-demo/dist    master ×
▶ du -h ecommerce-demo
1.2M     ecommerce-demo
```

Figure 11.4: Production build output size

As can be seen, there is a vast difference in a bundled package from 24MB to 1.2MB in production mode. It is because of default AOT compile mode and dropping debug information. As an exercise, try to deploy a new bundled web application on the **surge.sh** similar to the previous example.

Change dist Folder Path

The default output folder is set to **dist/<project-name>**, but this can be changed in the **angular.json** file. Let's say for our project requirement, we want to have the output folder name as **deployment** instead of **dist**. Let's open **angular.json** file and change the value of **outputPath** key to a new path, as shown in *Code 11.1* highlighted line:

```
{
"$schema": "./node_modules/@angular/cli/lib/config/schema.json",
"version": 1,
"newProjectRoot": "projects",
"projects": {
    "ecommerce-demo": {
    "projectType": "application",
    "schematics": {},
    "root": "",
    "sourceRoot": "src",
    "prefix": "app",
    "architect": {
```

```
        "build": {
        "builder": "@angular-devkit/build-angular:browser",
        "options": {
            "outputPath": "deployment/ecommerce-demo",
            "index": "src/index.html",
            "main": "src/main.ts",
            "polyfills": "src/polyfills.ts",
        }
    },
    "defaultProject": "ecommerce-demo"
    }
```

***Code 11.1**: angular.json – Changing output folder name from "dist" to "deployment"*

Now if we run **ng build** command again we will see new folder `deployment` created with bundled output.

ng deploy Command

We have seen how to deploy web applications manually. The Angular CLI also provides a command **ng deploy** to deploy an application directly to web servers by adding their schematics through **ng add <schematic-package>.** We can deploy our application directly to Firebase, Microsft Azure, GitHub pages, and so on. Please refer to the official documentation for a complete and updated list of providers.

Different Build Configurations

The Angular application supports two types of build configuration by default (a) development and (b) production. The development mode is used while building an application and debugging. As soon as we are ready to go live, we can build an application in production mode. In many corporate organizations, there are other stages of application deployment. After development is done, the application is built for quality testing, sometimes called **Quality Assurance (QA)** build or Staging build. In development mode, we can use internal or mock server API call for fetching data; in staging mode, we would like to point to staging server API, and finally, in production, we would like to point to production server API. We will see how to manage such configurations for different build types in this section.

Let's take a use case – development, QA, and production deployment mode will have separate `access-token`, which represents a subscription ID or secret-token from the server. We will keep this token into the `environment.ts` file per configuration. *Code*

11.2 shows `environment.ts` content with dummy development access token:

```
export const environment = {
production: false,
accessToken: 'dev-access-token'
};
```

Code 11.2: environment.ts – The added development access token

We will update production environment file by adding dummy access token as shown in *Code 11.3*:

```
export const environment = {
production: true,
accessToken: 'production-access-token'
};
```

Code 11.3: environment.prod.ts – The added production access token

Finally, we will create a new TypeScript file in the `environment` folder for specifying qa environment configuration, as shown in *Code 11.4*:

```
export const environment = {
    production: true,
    accessToken: 'qa-access-token'
};
```

Code 11.4: environment.qa.ts – Added QA access token

The application logic shouldn't check which environment is currently in use. There shouldn't be any conditional business logic for environment variables like an access token. The content of the `environment/environment.ts` file gets replaced by other configuration files based on the **ng build** parameter. Hence we should always refer only "environment/environment.ts" file throughout the application and not the prod nor qa environment file. For the sake of simplicity, we shall display an alert in the browser window with current environment access token being used as shown in *Code 11.5*:

```
import { Component, OnInit } from '@angular/core';
import { environment } from 'src/environments/environment';


@Component({
    selector: 'app-root',
    templateUrl: './app.component.html',
```

```
        styleUrls: ['./app.component.css']
})
export class AppComponent implements OnInit {
    title = 'E-Commerce website';
    ngOnInit() {
        alert(`Access token: ${environment.accessToken}`);
    }
}
```

Code 11.5: app.component.ts – Display current access token in browser alert

We will update the `angular.json` file for adding our new qa build configuration, as shown in *Code 11.6*. Note that in fileReplacements, we are asking Angular to replace default `environment.ts` file with our new `environment.qa.ts` file:

```
{
    ...
        "configurations": {
            "production": { ... },
            "qa": {
                "fileReplacements": [
                    {
                        "replace": "src/environments/environment.ts",
                        "with": "src/environments/environment.qa.ts"
                    }
                ],
                "optimization": true,
                "outputHashing": "all",
                "sourceMap": false,
                "extractCss": true,
                "namedChunks": false,
                "extractLicenses": true,
                "vendorChunk": false,
                "buildOptimizer": true,
                "budgets": [
                    {
```

```
            "type": "initial",
            "maximumWarning": "2mb",
            "maximumError": "5mb"
        },
        {
            "type": "anyComponentStyle",
            "maximumWarning": "6kb",
            "maximumError": "10kb"
        }
        ]
    }
}
...
}
```

Code 11.6: *angular.json – Adding QA build configuration*

Now let's test it out. Run the command **ng serve --open** and observe the output. We should see development access token in browser alert similar to *Figure 11.5*:

Figure 11.5: *dev-access-token displayed in a browser*

Next, we will build an application for the QA environment. Since we have created a new configuration by editing angular.json, we need to tell **ng build** command exactly which configuration to pick by running *Command 11.6*:

```
ng build --configuration=qa
```

Command 11.6: *Compile application in QA mode*

Once the application is compiled and the deployment package is ready, we can run the **lite-server** command into the output directory. Note that **lite-server** is a separate package that should be installed to start a web server in any local directory. We should see QA access token, as shown in *Figure 11.6*:

Figure 11.6: *qa-access-token displayed in a browser*

Finally, we will build our application in production mode by running command **ng build --prod** and run lite-server command into the output folder. We should see production access token, as shown in *Figure 11.7*:

Figure 11.7: *production-access-token displayed in a browser*

JIT and AOT Compilation

So far, we have seen how to deploy an application without going into many details. This is very important to understand that deploying Angular application with various configuration is very easy and flexible. We have mentioned JIT, AOT, a few times so far, but now we will see what it is in detail in this section. The **Just in Time (JIT)** compiler compiles application at the runtime in a browser. Hence Angular compiler should be shipped to the browser for running applications. This increases the build size as a compiler is a bit heavy. Whereas Ahead of Time AOT compiler compiles application at build time. Thus, there is no need to include an Angular compiler into a build package at all. We have checked the build folder size in the previous section for JIT and AOT compilation while building applications, and it was a huge difference for our demo application. Imagine you are building a big ecommerce website, then with JIT compilation mode, the output will be huge, and the browser will take time to process user requests. Hence AOT is by default used for production mode with **ng build** command so that an optimal build is produced. When we run **ng serve** or **ng build** command, then the default JIT compiler is used. We can choose to use AOT mode for local development as by specifying **ng serve --aot** and **ng build --aot** commands. The official Angular documentation describes how the AOT compiler works step by step, which we will not cover here to focus on our scope.

Cross-Origin Resource Sharing (CORS)

The browser nowadays takes web security in high priority. One of the security policies is a website can access the resource from the server if they originate from the same origin. If that is not the case, then the request is rejected, and the browser logs the error message complaining about cross-origin request failed. If we are serving web applications from a backend API endpoint, then we don't need to worry about it as they share the same origin. But most of the time, Angular web application is deployed on a different web server than the backend API server. In these cases, either backend server can allow CORS requests by adding an HTTP metadata in requests telling browser it is okay to send CORS requests. Another option is Angular application creates a proxy for its backend on the same origin. We will see how to handle it in this section. Let's create a very simple Node.js and Express.js server with simple REST API to return mock users' array, as shown in *Code 11.7*:

```
const express = require('express')
const app = express()
const port = 9000


app.get('/', (req, res) => res.send('Hello World!'))


app.get('/users', (req, res) => {
    const users = [
        {
            "id": 1,
            "name": "user-1"
        },
        {
            "id": 2,
            "name": "user-2"
        },
        {
            "id": 3,
            "name": "user-3"
        }
    ]
    res.send(users)
})


app.listen(port, () => console.log(`Example app listening on port
${port}!`))
```

Code 11.7: server.js -- Node.js server returning mock data via REST API

We will call /user REST endpoint in our AppComponent and log users into console. We will import HttpClientModule into AppModule and use HttpClient service to fire GET request as shown in *Code 11.8*:

```
import { Component, OnInit } from '@angular/core';
import { environment } from 'src/environments/environment';
import { HttpClient } from '@angular/common/http';

@Component({
    selector: 'app-root',
    templateUrl: './app.component.html',
    styleUrls: ['./app.component.css']
})
export class AppComponent implements OnInit {
    title = 'E-Commerce website';

    url = '/users';
    users = [];

    constructor(private http: HttpClient) { }

    ngOnInit() {
        // alert(`Access token: ${environment.accessToken}`);
        this.http.get(this.url).subscribe((users: JSON[]) => {
            this.users = users;
            console.log(users);
        });
    }
}
```

Code 11.8: app-component.ts -- Consuming "/users" endpoints and log in console

Let's save the changes and restart the **ng serve** command. In the browser console, we should see CORS error, as shown in *Figure 11.8*:

Figure 11.8: CORS error while consuming "/users" endpoint

We can get rid of this error by creating our proxy file. We will create a `proxy.conf.json` file inside the src folder. The content of the proxy file should be similar to *Code 11.9*:

```
{
    "/users": {
        "target": "http://localhost:9000",
        "secure": false
    },
    "logLevel": "debug"
}
```

Code 11.9: proxy-conf.json -- proxy configuration file

The proxy file tells the browser how to reach the specific endpoint. In our case, we are trying to reach `/users` endpoint by targeting to **9000** port web server on localhost. We will also need to change the URL in AppComponent from http://localhost:9000/users to `/users` only.

Finally, we can pass this proxy file into `angular.json` configuration, as shown in Code 11.10:

```
{
    {...}
    "serve": {
        "builder": "@angular-devkit/build-angular:dev-server",
        "options": {
            "browserTarget": "ecommerce-demo:build",
            "proxyConfig": "src/proxy.conf.json"
        },
    {...}
}
```

Code 11.10: angular.json -- Specify a proxy configuration

Whenever we make any changes in the `angular.json` file, then we should restart **ng serve** command to new change take effect. After restart check the browser console, and we should see the mock users objects logged as shown in *Figure 11.9:*

Figure 11.9: Fetching /users data through proxy configuration

We can also pass the proxy file to **ng serve** command if we don't want to update `angular.json` file as shown in *Command 11.7:*

```
ng serve --proxyConfig=src/proxy.conf.json
```

Command 11.7: Run ng serve with a proxy configuration file

ng lint Command

As a good web application developer, we should strive for best coding practices. The Angular uses TypeScript for writing business logic and HTML for presentation. Every developer has its way of writing code, and making sure everyone follows standard practices is very important; otherwise, code will be hard to read and understand. Angular CLI provides command which checks through all application files against standard Angular best practices and reports error if there is a rule violation. The JavaScript application can check their code formatting using the `JSLint` package, and similarly, for TypeScript, there is a `TSLint` package. The linting is the process of scanning all TypeScript files for specified rules. We will try to violate a couple of rules and see if we get flagged. In the AppComponent class, we will change the `selector` prefix from the app to the test, as shown in *Code 11.11*. We will also declare one variable in `ngOnInit()` function with `let` keyword which should be declared as `const` by linter rules:

```
@Component({
  selector: 'test-root',
  templateUrl: './app.component.html',
  styleUrls: ['./app.component.css']
})
export class AppComponent implements OnInit {
  title = 'E-Commerce website';

  url = '/users';
  users = [];

  constructor(private http: HttpClient) { }

  ngOnInit() {
    let dummy = 100;
    // alert(`Access token: ${environment.accessToken}`);
    this.http.get(this.url).subscribe((users: JSON[]) => {
      this.users = users;
      console.log(users);
    });
  }
}
```

Code 11.11: angular.json -- Specify proxy configuration

The `tslint.json` file in application folder contains all the rules as shown in *Code 11.12*. One of them is `component-selector` prefix should be app:

```
{
  "extends": "tslint:recommended",
  "rules": {
    "array-type": false,
```

```
    "arrow-parens": false,
    "deprecation": {
    "severity": "warning"
    },
    "component-class-suffix": true,
    "contextual-lifecycle": true,
    {…}
    "component-selector": [
    true,
    "element",
    "app",
    "kebab-case"
    ],
    {…}
}
```

***Code 11.12**: tslint.json -- Angular Linting configuration*

We will run a linter on our application by running *Command 11.8*. For given demo application we can see one lint error is listed in output for app prefix:

```
$ ng lint

Linting "ecommerce-demo"...


    ERROR: /Users/balramchavan/Desktop/Book/Chapter11/ecommerce-demo/
src/app/app.component.ts:6:15 - The selector should be prefixed by "app"
(https://angular.io/guide/styleguide#style-02-07)
    ERROR: /Users/balramchavan/Desktop/Book/Chapter11/ecommerce-demo/
src/app/app.component.ts:19:13 - Identifier 'dummy' is never reassigned;
use 'const' instead of 'let'.
```

***Command 11.8**: Run ng lint command*

We can fix linter errors manually, or we can ask linter to fix it automatically as much it can by running command **ng lint --fix** command as shown in *Command 11.9*. As we can see, the linter can't fix all errors automatically. Thus, we need to change **test-root** selector to app-root in AppComponent decorator metadata:

```
$ ng lint --fix

Linting "ecommerce-demo"...
```

```
Fixed 2 error(s) in /Users/balramchavan/Desktop/Book/Chapter11/
ecommerce-demo/src/app/app.component.ts
```

```
ERROR: /Users/balramchavan/Desktop/Book/Chapter11/ecommerce-demo/
src/app/app.component.ts:6:15 - The selector should be prefixed by "app"
(https://angular.io/guide/styleguide#style-02-07)
```

Command 11.9: "ng lint --fix" command output

Unit Testing Overview

Unit testing is an essential part of the development cycle. As a developer, we should always write a unit test case for business logic covering normal, exceptional, boundary conditions. The **Test-Driven Development (TDD)** methodology emphasis on writing unit test case first and then business logic. Many organization is using this methodology, and it is prevalent. So far, we have not written any test cases in our journey because we would like to focus on our schedule. The official Angular documentation contains detailed steps about writing unit test cases and configuration. We will just touch base on a few points here. Whenever we create a new component, service, directive, pipe, then its related unit test case file is generated by Angular CLI. For example, we can find `app.component.spec.ts` file for `app.component.ts` component. *Code 11.13* shows the boilerplate content of AppComponent test file:

```
import { TestBed, async } from '@angular/core/testing';

import { RouterTestingModule } from '@angular/router/testing';

import { AppComponent } from './app.component';


describe('AppComponent', () => {
beforeEach(async(() => {
    TestBed.configureTestingModule({
    imports: [
        RouterTestingModule
    ],
    declarations: [
        AppComponent
    ],
    }).compileComponents();
}));
```

```
it('should create the app', () => {
    const fixture = TestBed.createComponent(AppComponent);
    const app = fixture.debugElement.componentInstance;
    expect(app).toBeTruthy();
});


it(`should have as title 'ecommerce-demo'`, () => {
    const fixture = TestBed.createComponent(AppComponent);
    const app = fixture.debugElement.componentInstance;
    expect(app.title).toEqual('ecommerce-demo');
});


it('should render title in a h1 tag', () => {
    const fixture = TestBed.createComponent(AppComponent);
    fixture.detectChanges();
    const compiled = fixture.debugElement.nativeElement;
    expect(compiled.querySelector('h1').textContent).
toContain('Welcome to ecommerce-demo!');
});
});
```

Code 11.13: app.component.spec.ts -- Unit test cases for AppComponent component

There are many JavaScript test case frameworks out there; one of them is the Jasmine test framework, which Angular CLI uses. Jasmine framework is also famous for writing **Behavior Driven Development (BDD)** which allow the developer to write use case in natural language and map them to unit test case and then to code. For running test cases, Angular CLI uses the Karma test runner. The Karma starts a browser to load an application and execute test cases. Let's try to run unit tests on our demo application by running *Command 11.10*:

```
ng test
```

Command 11.10: "ng test" running test cases

The Karma test runner will load all test cases from `.spec.ts` files and try to run them in a browser. Since we have not written or updated any of the test cases in our demo application, there shall be failed test cases, and those shall be reported in the browser, as shown in *Figure 11.10*:

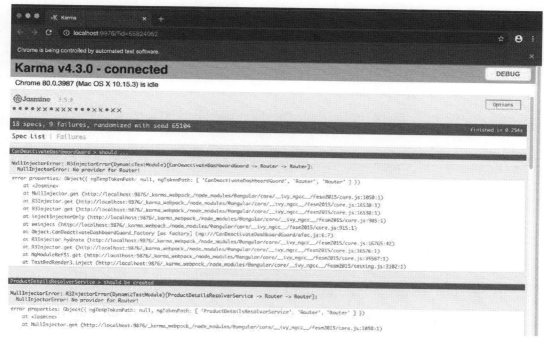

Figure 11.10: *Failed test cases output in Karma*

Let's see one of the test cases of AppComponent, as shown in *Code 11.14* for creating a new instance of AppComponent class:

```
it('should create the app', () => {
    const fixture = TestBed.createComponent(AppComponent);
    const app = fixture.debugElement.componentInstance;
    expect(app).toBeTruthy();
});
```

Code 11.14: *app.component.spec.ts -- "should create the app" unit test case*

The AppComponent constructor has an HttpClient service injected, as shown in *Code 11.15*:

```
@Component({
selector: 'app-root',
templateUrl: './app.component.html',
```

```
        styleUrls: ['./app.component.css']
})
export class AppComponent implements OnInit {
        constructor(private http: HttpClient) { }
}
```

Code 11.15: app.component.ts -- constructor with HttpClient service injected

This unit test case failed because it cannot create a new instance of AppComponent class, as shown in *Code 11.16*:

```
    Chrome 80.0.3987 (Mac OS X 10.15.3) AppComponent should render title
in a h1 tag FAILED
        NullInjectorError: R3InjectorError(DynamicTestModule)[HttpClient
-> HttpClient]:
        NullInjectorError: No provider for HttpClient!
        error properties: Object({ ngTempTokenPath: null, ngTokenPath: [
'HttpClient', 'HttpClient' ] })
            at <Jasmine>
            at NullInjector.get (http://localhost:9876/_karma_webpack_/
node_modules/@angular/core/__ivy_ngcc__/fesm2015/core.js:1050:1)
```

Code 11.16: unit test case output for AppComponent - should create the app

We can fix this unit test case by importing `HttpClientModule` into TestBed Module configuration, as shown in *Code 11.17*. A thumb rule is if we have imported any NgModules into component's module and used any service or pipes, and so on, in component then we should import those module(s) into unit test case's TestBed module configuration:

```
    import { HttpClientModule } from '@angular/common/http';


    describe('AppComponent', () => {
        beforeEach(async(() => {
            TestBed.configureTestingModule({
                imports: [
                    RouterTestingModule,
                    HttpClientModule
                ],
                declarations: [
                    AppComponent
```

```
        ],
    }).compileComponents();
}));

it('should create the app', () => {
    const fixture = TestBed.createComponent(AppComponent);
    const app = fixture.debugElement.componentInstance;
    expect(app).toBeTruthy();
});
});
```

Code 11.17: *app-component.spec.ts -- Import HttpClientModule into TestBed module*

Code Coverage Report

The Code Coverage is an analysis of source code against unit test cases written. The principle of unit testing states that all code blocks and branches should be tested via unit test cases. If we have some code block that is not covered by a unit test case, then that reduces code coverage. Angular CLI has built it code coverage tool, and it can generate reports in different format like HTML website. We will try to generate code coverage for our demo application by running *Command 1.10*:

```
ng test --no-watch --code-coverage
```

Command 1.10: *Generate code coverage report*

Once the command has finished, then a new folder shall get created called coverage in the project folder. Start a local webserver or simply open index.html file which shall display code coverage in tabular format as shown in *Figure 11.11*:

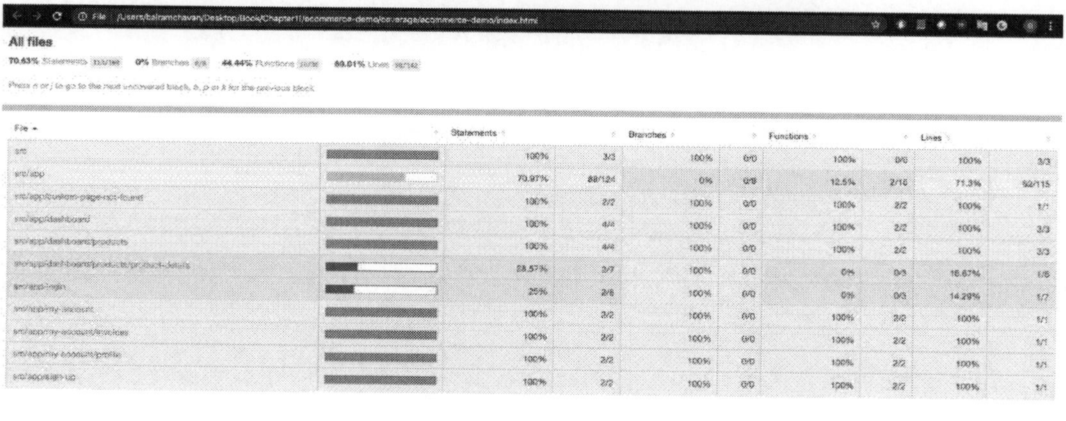

Figure 11.11: *Code coverage report generated*

Our reports good because we do not have any business logic in our demo application.

Performance and Optimization

The performance of any website is a crucial factor in its success. If our user spends time waiting for a web application to load or slow processing, we might lose them. There are various ways we can analyze application performance through tools and libraries. The most common way is to use the **Network** tab of browser; we will use the Chrome browser for demonstration, but you should be able to find such a Network tab in other browsers as well. Let's build our application in production mode by running *Command 11.11*:

```
ng build --prod
```

***Command 11.11**: Build an application for performance test*

We will start a web server in the `dist/ecommerce-demo` output folder. Open the Network tab in the Chrome browser and observe the details, especially the **Waterfall** column, as shown in *Figure 11.12*. The metrics here can give us pointer which resource took more time to load and if there was enough parallelism for loading resources:

***Figure 11.12**: Google Chrome browser's Network tab output*

Google Chrome also has another tab for website auditing called **Audits**, which runs a "lighthouse" tool internally for analyzing a website. Let's open the **Audits** tab and refresh the website. The Lighthouse tool will start to gather performance metrics and will display the result, as shown in *Figure 11.13*. This report can be exported into HTML file as well:

Figure 11.13: Google Chrome browser's Audit tab output

The report consists of different key parameters as below:

- **Performance**: The website is evaluated for different performance metrics. It checks how much time the website took for rendering useful HTML content for the user, how much time it took for becoming interactive, and so on. *Figure 11.14* shows different performance metrics in details:

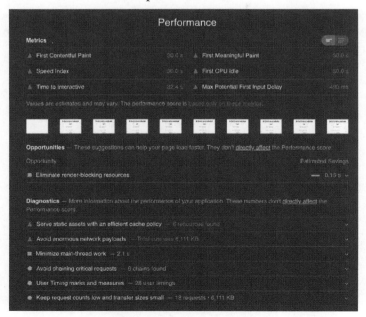

Figure 11.14: Performance metrics of the Audits tab

- **Accessibility**: The website should very easy to use for the end user. The lighthouse checks various best accessibility parameters against the website and ranks it. Few metrics are like logical tab orders, following ARIA roles, and so on, as shown in *Figure 11.15:*

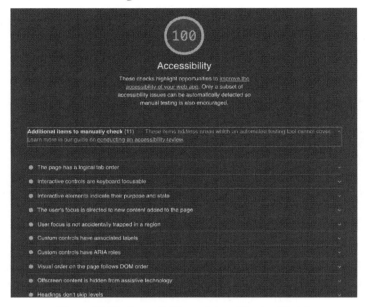

Figure 11.15: *Accessibility metrics of the Audits tab*

- **Best Practices:** The Lighthouse runs various best practices against our website and generates a rank. These include various HTTP protocols website should follow, as shown in *Figure 11.16:*

Figure 11.16: *Best Practices metrics of the Audits tab*

- **SEO**: Search Engine Optimization is a very crucial parameter of any website. If we are building a website for external users', it is essential that the website appears in the top result of internet search. There are many ways to optimize websites SEO by adding metadata and Lighthouse checks those parameters against our website and generates ranks, as shown in *Figure 11.17*:

Figure 11.17: SEO metrics of the Audits tab

- **Progressive Web App (PWA):** The PWA gives the offline capability to our websites. It is a best practice to support offline features as much as there can be for the best user experience. The PWA uses browser's LocalStorage and IndexDB for storing offline data and code to manage offline states. The

Lighthouse checks how good websites performance as offline and generates reports, as shown in *Figure 11.18:*

Figure 11.18: Progressive Web App metrics of the Audits tab

Polyfills – Older Browser Support

The website should run on all possible versions of standard browsers. Many organizations have old but stable browsers, for example, Internet Explorer 9/10, and they cannot use the latest version of browsers like Google Chrome because of company policies. The Angular is built for a standard set of browsers. Figure 11.19 shows a list of standard browsers supported by Angular 9 at the time of writing this book. It is also possible to configure an Angular application to generate output for older browsers with the help of Polyfills:

Browser	Supported versions
Chrome	latest
Firefox	latest
Edge	2 most recent major versions
IE	11, 10, 9 ("compatibility view" mode not supported)
IE Mobile	11
Safari	2 most recent major versions
iOS	2 most recent major versions
Android	X (10.0), Pie (9.0), Oreo (8.0), Nougat (7.0)

Figure 11.19: *List of supported browsers by Angular*

The Polyfills are the Javascript files which bridge the gap between older browser and newer JavaScript features. The Angular version 8 onwards has a feature called **Differential Loading,** which generates two types of JavaScript output files - ES2015 and ES5. The ES2015 is a bundle package for the latest and standard browser with new features; hence it requires no or very few Polyfills files. The ES5 is an older version of the JavaScript bundle package, and it ships a bunch of Polyfills JavaScript files to older browsers to render the website without any error. Thus ES2015 bundle output is smaller in size as compared to ES5.

The Angular CLI generates `polyfills.ts` file in a new project which contains polyfills import statements. Whenever we would like to enable any Polyfills library, then we should update this file. For example, consider we are using SVG elements for visualization in our application and would like it to run on the IE10 version. In that case, we should first install npm package for `classlist.js` by running *Command 11.12*:

```
npm install --save classlist.js
```

Command 11.12: *Install "classlist.js" npm package for Polyfills.*

Then we will uncomment import state for classlist.js as shown in *Code 11.18*. Now if we build our application with **ng build** command then the bundle package shall include `classlist.js` Polyfills and our SVG features should work on IE 10 as well:

```
/*****************************************************************
******************************

  * BROWSER POLYFILLS
  */


  /** IE10 and IE11 requires the following for NgClass support on SVG
elements */
  import 'classlist.js';  // Run `npm install --save classlist.js`.


  import 'zone.js/dist/zone';  // Included with Angular CLI.


  /*****************************************************************
******************************

  * APPLICATION IMPORTS
  */
```

Code 11.18: polyfills.ts -- import classlist.js polyfills to support IE10.

Web Workers

Sometimes we would like to do some computation in our application, which can be done in parallel. We can use web workers for offloading such tasks in a background thread and free up the main thread for other user interactions. Let's try to create a web worker for calculating the square root of a given number as a simple example. We will create a new web worker for AppComponent using Angular CLI by running *Command 11.13*:

```
ng generate web-worker app
```

Command 11.13: Generate web-worker for AppComponent

In app-worker, we will add a simple logic to calculate the square root and return a message with the answer, as shown in *Code 11.19*:

```
/// <reference lib="webworker" />
addEventListener('message', ({ data }) => {
    const sqrt = Math.sqrt(data);
    const response = `Square root of ${data} is ${sqrt}`;
    postMessage(response);
});
```

Code 11.19: app.worker.ts -- Calculate square root, in-app worker

The AppComponent class first check if the browser supports the Web Worker. If not, then we should display some message or alert to the user. If the browser has support, then we will create a new object of Worker class passing the app-worker file path and module type, as shown in *Code 11.20*. Next, we will register for a callback from the web worker's onmessage event, which will be fired whenever `postMessage()` is executed in a web worker. Finally, we will call the worker.`postMessage()` method to offload work of calculating the square root of 25 number to web worker:

```typescript
@Component({
  selector: 'app-root',
  templateUrl: './app.component.html',
  styleUrls: ['./app.component.css']
})
export class AppComponent implements OnInit {


  ngOnInit() {
      if (typeof Worker !== 'undefined') {
          // Create a new
          const worker = new Worker('./app.worker', { type:
'module' });
          worker.onmessage = ({ data }) => {
              console.log(`Result: ${data}`);
          };
          worker.postMessage(25);
      } else {
          // Web Workers are not supported in this environment.
          // You should add a fallback so that your program still
executes correctly.
      }
  }
}
```

Code 11.20: *app.component.ts -- Offload calculation to app-worker*

Conclusion

The Angular framework provides a wide range of tools and packaging support when it comes to deployment and best practices. We have seen how to deploy the application, best practices to follow, performance metrics by Lighthouse, enabling features for older browsers using Polyfills, and so on. There are different DevOps practices followed by different companies, so it is hard to generalize the process. For example, Continuous Integration and Deployment can be set up by Travis, Jenkins, Dockers, and so on. It is recommended to explore these DevOps practices and exercise them.

Questions

1. Deploy Angular application on Azure/AWS/GitHub or any other web server.

2. In our demo application, `environment.ts` file should contain a variable for storing "Version-ID," which should be updated for each build. You can write some shell/bash/python script to schedule a build with version ID.

3. Generate code coverage reports whenever there is a production build is generated.

4. Write a web-hook for GitHub to reject the commit operation if there are any **ng lint** errors.

5. Integrate Lighthouse API into your CI/CD pipeline. Set some custom metric rules, and if the rule is not successful, then build should fail.

Printed in Great Britain
by Amazon